Exceptional Children
Exceptional Art

Teaching Art to Special Needs

Exceptional Children:

Exceptional Art Teaching Art to Special Needs

David R. Henley

Davis Publications, Inc.
Worcester, Massachusetts

For Davra Elias (1961–1980)
Student-Artist-Friend

One particle of dust is raised and the earth lies therein; one flower blooms and the universe rises with it.

Zen Haiku

Printed in the United States of America

Library of Congress Catalog Card Number: 91-73179

ISBN: 0-87192-238-X

Graphic Design: Penny Darras-Maxwell

10 9 8 7 6 5 4 3

ACKNOWLEDGEMENTS

I am indebted to many individuals and institutions who have helped bring this work into being.

At Davis Publications, Managing Editor Wyatt Wade provided the foresight and guidance from the project's inception, transforming my raw experiences and ideas into something that approached a finished text. Laura Marshall, production editor, has been unfailing in her patience and enthusiasm, particularly during those periods when my energies flagged during the rewrites and my endless revisions of the case material.

My wife Dawn, artist, teacher and mother, has endured my preoccupations with this manuscript for six years and still maintains her love and good spirits. Her suggestions and feedback were crucial in insuring that the manuscript was relevant and comprehensible to the teacher in the classroom. My children, Kyle and Kimberly, have also been tolerant and encouraging throughout this project's tenure. And to my parents, R.W. and Frances Henley, who have been an indefatigable source of moral and material support, my deepest gratitude.

The institutions of the Marie Katzenbach School for the Deaf, New Jersey; The Jewish Guild School for the Blind, New York City; The Hunterdon Developmental Center, New Jersey; The Center on Deafness, Illinois and Very Special Arts: Chicago and New Jersey, have all been cooperative and supportive of my work and writings. The parents of the children and adolescents attending these institutions are applauded for their consent to allow me to publish their sons' and daughters' stories and artworks, which at times required great courage.

Colleagues and friends whose spirits and ideas have sustained me: Tim Ryan, Deborah Good, Michael Jennings, Michael Silbernagel and James Pruznick.

I am indebted to my teachers who have served as role models and influences over the years. Pearl Greenberg at Kean College of New Jersey, Laurie Wilson at New York University and Roger Cardinal at the University of Kent, Canterbury, England.

As a guide, critic and energizing force, Edith Kramer has and will always have an indelible mark upon my work.

And, finally, to all the children; without them, my life's work would not be possible.

Preface

Exceptional Children, Exceptional Art is an approach to making art with children. It views the art process as being equally accessible to all individuals regardless of their emotional, intellectual or physical capacities. In eliciting art from these children, emphasis is laid upon both the educational and therapeutic aspects of the art experience. As these two areas are pursued, equal attention is paid to the aesthetic integrity of the art they make. Thus, whether one child requires a traditional problem solving approach and another warrants consideration of emotional conflicts, the aesthetic impact of the product should not be unduly compromised.

Art education therapy is an integrative process in which the "whole" child is considered. The emphasis is on individualized attention. In this approach, it is the child who sets the agenda, meaning that each child's needs are considered, objectives are formulated and interventions are implemented which pursue the goals of education, therapy and aesthetics.

Unlike other related books in the field, *Exceptional Children, Exceptional Art* departs from the usual format of devising strategies or activities for specific populations. Thus, there will not be sections, for example, on "art activities for the mentally retarded" which indicates that only certain media, techniques or strategies are appropriate for certain students. That type of approach immediately puts unwarranted limitations upon such children, often resulting in self-fulfilling prophecies of diminished potentials.

To the contrary, this text advocates that almost every child is truly capable of creating art which has integrity and power. Only in certain situations where the circumstances demand exceptional modifications will I depart from this format and offer specific suggestions for certain problems. Otherwise, the approach is "studio-based" with an emphasis on the universal art forms of drawing, painting, design and sculpture. The reader who desires "cut and paste" projects, holiday craftwork or other "school" or "therapy" activities will be disappointed.

This book was written mainly for art educators who have sensed that their instructional strategies have reached only a portion of the child. Art therapists, too, may find this book useful, should they seek a pragmatic and concrete approach to implementing developmental and psychodynamic therapy. Practitioners in a wide range of fields, such as occupational and recreational therapists, classroom teachers, counselors and administrators, might find this approach useful in their settings.

Art education therapy is a philosophical perspective which promotes the art experience with sensitivity that appreciates the sheer wonder of the child artist. Hopefully, this book conveys the joy and satisfaction that can come from working with these children who teach us so much more than we can ever hope to learn.

David R. Henley, MA, ATR
School of the Art Institute of Chicago

Contents

Introduction

Teaching art in regular and special education classrooms over the years, I have frequently been struck by children who spontaneously depart from the format of the art activity, often producing remarkable results. The familiar images of childhood art inexplicably give way to images of a more deeply personal and intimate nature. There is something obviously more compelling than the concern for a grade or the instructor's praise that is fuelling these children's artwork. Neatly crafted and attractive images are often overshadowed by works with a strange or disturbing quality. The children often depict figures, the mainstay of most child (and adult) art, with an intensity which distorts them in the process. They explore relationships with family and peers, using memories, fantasies or current experiences as inspiration. They also handle the use of color with uncommon fervor; figures and other recognizable elements become so saturated or muddled that they are obliterated in the process. Realism often gives way to abstraction and nonobjectivism in some cases, while, in others, recognizable figures function on a metaphorical level.

These observations signify to me that children of most ages and levels of mental and physical functioning possess the capacity to use art on deeply expressive levels. Subsequent research (Henley 1987, 1989) has led me to believe that powerful images can spring from the brush of a typical child as often as that of a mentally retarded or other handicapped individual. Although normal children may possess greater technical skill and control, this often has little bearing upon whether they evoke strong and expressive images in their art.

One of my first encounters with this phenomenon involved an eight-year-old boy working in the regular classroom. His teacher had asked her students to draw a picture about an important rule. Inevitably, she received scores of pictures depicting children chewing gum in class or crossing with the traffic light. This bright and well-adjusted boy, however, drew upon material of a much deeper nature. Mike's picture entitled "Don't Kill Your Sister" enabled his unspoken fantasies over a sibling relationship to be symbolically acted upon through his artwork. His concern with technical and aesthetic control in his picture emphasizes the urgent communication of an intimate truth.

In another case, a hearing-impaired young man of seventeen was faced with imminent graduation from high school. This well-behaved and capable art student had been working with the rest of his class on figure drawings, using models culled mainly from magazines of the students' choice. During one such exercise, the boy created a fairly unremarkable figure except for the hands, which were blatantly distorted. Peter had proved continuously that he could portray hands in any range of positions, so it was not his poor drawing ability

"Don't Kill Your Sister," by an intact nine-year-old, explores the issue of sibling rivalry using dark humor and simplified yet powerful design elements. Although on relatively good terms with his sister, this boy gave form to deep-seated fantasies which probably will never be expressed verbally.

Does this drawing exhibit artistic license or a troublesome issue? Peter, an intact, hearing impaired student, drew this figure with distorted hands after being reprimanded for fighting in school.

which led to such an exaggeration. Thus, it must have been a matter of either artistic license or some other underlying issue.

Art teachers confronted with such images must make some fundamental assessment to determine their course of action. One option is to react in a traditionally neutral and academic manner by assessing the stylistic or thematic aspects of the images. While such cool detachment might be an appropriate and comfortable direction to take, it essentially ignores or dismisses the artist's intentions in these works. In both images, the artists

have created something which transcends mere technique or aesthetics; they both evoke images which explore important experiences in their lives. Thus, to respond purely to the works in terms of design elements or the laws of perspective might be insulting the fundamental integrity and truth of the artists' statements. Anything less than an empathic response to these images would amount to patronage and runs contrary to the aims of understanding and appreciating not just child art but all art.

In these simple drawings, it is the integration of technical skill, unconscious fantasy and personal idiosyncracy that charges the images and makes

10

them work on so many levels. Such an assessment, however, does not guide the art educator to an appropriate response. What *does* the art educator do when confronted with such images? Bearing in mind that the traditional mission of art education is to impart knowledge and sensibility about the world of art, are such expressions and assessments beyond our responsibilities and concerns?

It could be argued that if these images did indeed reflect deep-seated emotional fantasies that were liable to overwhelm the children and prompt them to consistently act out inappropriately, therapeutic-based responses would be beyond the art teacher's capabilities. With a consistency of maladaptive behavior or disturbed artistic expression, the proper course of action would be to refer the students for professional counseling. However, when the imagery is a result of transitory life stresses that affect the children at a particular moment without lasting effects, therapeutic intervention is more accessible and within the realm of the educational setting.

Despite the emphasis upon art educational goals in the above cases, emotional concerns did surface and were communicated via the imagery. For instance, although I knew Mike, the artist of "Don't Kill Your Sister," had a normal relationship with his sister, his art suggests that the issue of sibling conflict sometimes stirred sufficiently enough to be explored through his artwork. In Peter's "Figure and the Hand" drawing, the message was more covert. Eventually, I learned that the previous day Peter had punched another student in a rare display of anger. Surprised at this uncharacteristic behavior, I asked Peter about it. He related that he was about to graduate, which was a frightening prospect after being relatively sheltered in a special education setting. Evidently, his mother was also concerned, and took the liberty of finding a job for the boy which would be waiting for him the week after graduation. On one hand, he was thrilled with the prospect of going out into the world, on the other, he was quite overwhelmed and intimidated. Similarly, he was somewhat

pleased his mother had provided a continuation of a sheltered environment for him, yet he was resentful and upset that he would be deprived of the experience of finally choosing his own path. Subsequently, he took all these feelings out on a peer who had the bad luck of teasing him during this period of crisis.

As these cases illustrate, the child artist may be grappling with important life concerns, whose reconciliation or resolution may be directly influenced by making art (Kramer 1971, Robertson 1963, Lowenfeld 1957). In these instances, a therapeutic approach to art education can be pursued as long as teachers are prepared and informed, as well as cautious in their interventions. Empathic support and understanding can and should be integrated with aesthetic and intellectual objectives in the classroom, especially when servicing the needs of exceptional children.

Provocative images will often surface in children's artwork regardless of the art teacher's willingness to appreciate or address the child's issues. As long as the teacher's approach is not too regimented or closed-ended, the art process will stimulate the expression of unconscious material (Naumburg 1973). Except in the most unsympathetic atmospheres, the images will be there—the next question is whether the art teacher chooses to be there as well.

Evaluating the performance of the exceptional child requires both objective assessment and a subjective sensitivity and understanding of the child's capacities.

EXCEPTIONAL
CHILDREN

chapter 1

Guiding Principles

THERAPEUTIC ART EDUCATION

Lowenfeld's Art Education Therapy

Victor Lowenfeld was a theorist and practitioner who closely studied children's artwork and their involvement in the art process. Lowenfeld coined the term "art education therapy" in his discussion in the "Therapeutic Aspects of Art Education" (Chapter Twelve, in his *Creative and Mental Growth*, 1957, 3rd edition). For Lowenfeld, this theory applied to all children regardless of their handicapping condition or emotional state. The goal of his philosophy was nothing less than developing every child's creative potential by combining an academic and therapeutic approach to art education.

Lowenfeld saw the art process as possessing a power and profundity beyond the mere acquisition of skills or techniques. He considered the art process in a global context—contributing to many facets of a child's creative and mental growth. These facets include facilitating self-expression, promoting independence, encouraging flexible thinking and facilitating social interactions, as well as developing aesthetic awareness. In short, he viewed the art experience as a potential source of well-being, balancing knowledge with pleasure.

For someone who trained and influenced an entire generation of art educators, this talk of "well-being" and "pleasure," constituted (and still does)

a kind of heresy. Traditionally the educator's mission has not been concerned with fostering happiness in students—there are numerous logistical, political and professional obstacles to this end. In fact, in many contemporary art education programs, the pendulum has swung far to the right, embracing "back to basics" approaches which virtually ignore affective issues as part of the educational sphere. Lowenfeld, however vigorously asserted his concerns with characteristic simplicity and passion, exhorting the art educator to "fan the flames of the human spirit."

As a refugee from fascist Europe of the 1930's, Lowenfeld became a champion of children's freedom of expression in America, just as Franz Cizek had been in Eastern Europe. For Lowenfeld, children's right to embrace and explore their own world, in their own stylistic terms, was paramount. This position was a cornerstone of Lowenfeld's philosophy, which he tenaciously defended against those teachers who sought to impose their own prejudicial and alien forms of expression upon their students.

In 1957, when "Therapeutic Aspects of Art Education" was first published, Lowenfeld's ideas were well ahead of their time, as programs for special children were few and far between. The programs in existence considered only the highest functioning children worth educating; the rest were "put away" in institutions. Those lucky enough to

A free-spirited drawing, dated 1931, from Franz Cizek's art program in Vienna. This work embodies all that is revered in the art of children: fresh, charming, naive yet not without an innate aesthetic sensibility.

be in educational settings were consigned to vocational programs which focused on occupational training. Creativity was rarely explored. In rare instances where art programming was present at all, it took the form of craft work or other concrete art activities. After Lowenfeld's death, the chapter on therapeutic aspects was deleted altogether from the fourth edition of *Creative and Mental Growth*.

Lambert Brittain, Lowenfeld's collaborator on the later editions, never openly explained the rationale behind this historic deletion, yet we can surmise that at that time Lowenfeld had simply pushed the limits of art education too far. Given his focus on the affective lives of children with special needs, Lowenfeld essentially blurred the parameters between education and therapy. Those who were committed to practicing art education within the sole limitations of perception and cognition, found that they could not effectively orient themselves to an entirely new perspective along with new populations to serve.

Obviously, if teachers were to strike out beyond the mainstream of art education into special education or therapy, a whole new body of knowledge would have to be assimilated. Because few handicapped children were in mainstream programs at that time, it was not feasible to support such an investment. Subsequently art administrators and educators saw no reason to accommodate or pursue this alien specialization.

All this has changed. Legislation in the 1970's, known as the Education for All Children Act (PL 94-142) mandates that all children, regardless of their disability, be provided with a "thorough and efficient" education. This mainstreaming law essentially injected thousands of handicapped children into the public and private school systems. Those who languished for years in institutional dayrooms now found themselves behind desks. Children who were incarcerated for crimes, children who were committed to psychiatric wards,

Victor Lowenfeld was one of the first art educators to advocate for the creative potential of all children, regardless of their physical or mental limitations.

children who in all their lives had never left their beds due to congenital deformities, all were now to receive the same educational opportunities as any intact child.

   With this sweeping legislation came the need for teachers to adapt their materials, strategies and philosophies to accommodate the child with special needs. Much of this retraining has involved vocational, academic and behavioral approaches that are indigenous to special education settings. There has also been a resurgence in the emphasis on addressing the affective lives of special needs children through more therapeutically oriented programs. Given these developments, Lowenfeld's ideas on art education therapy have become as pertinent and refreshing as ever.

   Current considerations must go beyond the guidelines set down by legislation and public law. They must focus upon the children who need to cope with life stresses unknown by previous generations. While the plight of children who endured famine, war and other deprivations throughout his-

Edith Kramer in her painting loft. Kramer's emphasis upon the integrative aspects of the art process, has created a natural alliance between the goals of art education, aesthetics and art therapy.

tory cannot be discounted, the contemporary child must deal with the threat of global annihilation and environmental poisoning. These children face the disintegration of the family unit, as well as a culture whose values are determined by a dehumanizing technology and an obsession with material comfort. The legacy of Lowenfeld was to try and rescue the children by supporting them through an art process which breathes richness and a sense of well-being back into their lives.

Kramer's "Art as Therapy"
While Lowenfeld embodied the therapeutic-minded art educator, Edith Kramer is considered the foremost educationally oriented, art therapist. Beginning in the early 1950's, Kramer wrote about her work with culturally disadvantaged and emotionally handicapped children using an approach which has become synonymous with her name: "art as therapy." This concept implies that with proper support and intervention, there is an inherent healing quality in the art process. Like Lowenfeld, Kramer views the therapeutic aspects of the art experience as complementary to skill acquisition and aesthetic awareness.

Kramer sees the power of art as contributing to the general well-being of individuals who, in turn, enrich society through their own artistic and motivational growth. Individually, art can develop the child's personality in ways that are ego-building and gratifying as well as foster a firm sense of identity and self-esteem. In order to reap these benefits, however, art requires an "act of supreme integration" (Kramer 1971). Motor coordination, intellect, imagination and emotion must function in balanced concert so that fully formed art can be achieved. For Kramer, "formed expression" is distinct from simply manipulating materials or developing schematic representations such as stereotypes or pictographs. The goal is to elicit work which evokes emotion and serves as a symbolic equivalent for the child's experience. Kramer further states that the goal in art education and art therapy is to foster the making of artwork whose form and content is unified, work in which con-

scious and unconscious meaning complement each other and art materials are used with skill and economy (Kramer 1971).

While Kramer applies her energies to helping children in her care achieve formed expression, she acknowledges that as teachers of special populations, we will more often than not assist in processes that fail to culminate in art. Because young or handicapped children often endlessly experiment with materials, vent their anger on them or desert them before they're finished, we must expect a much lower yield of finished work than from intact children. However, Kramer foresees instances when inner conflicts and distorted perceptions become the agents of an extraordinary effort at integration which culminates in an unusually powerful artistic statement. This she terms *sublimation* (Kramer 1958, 1970, 1979).

The psychoanalytic term *sublimation* refers to the integration and release of internal or psychic tensions through normal activities. The balance and inner unity evoked in fully formed artworks suggest that both the forces of aggression and sexual instinct can be successfully harnessed during the creative act. Aggressiveness, assaultiveness, sexual promiscuity, and substance abuse can all be traced to the need to discharge tension and experience pleasure in the process. Unless redirected such behavior will put the special needs child and those around him at serious risk. Artistic activity can be a vital vehicle for both the discharge and, ideally, the transformation of primitive instincts into images or objects of aesthetic strength and beauty. Kramer views the act of sublimation as an ultimate goal in art education therapy.

In many cases, repressing the urge to act on impulses is only achieved at great cost to the individual. He or she may be able to control the anxiety that results from suppressing urges, but only by resorting to neurotic behavior. Personality disorders such as obsessive/compulsive reactions, identification with aggressors, autistic or psychotic withdrawal, and self-stimulatory behavior are especially a problem with handicapped populations. Often the disorders are a result of individuals' inabilities to cope mentally or physically with their instinctual needs. How does one, for example, explain to the mature mentally retarded individual how to relieve his sexual tension appropriately, or to the traumatic quadriplegic how to mourn the loss of her bodily functions without bitterness and anger? Appropriate avenues must be developed for these people to exercise their urges in the academic and home environment without transgressing norms of appropriate behavior. Given this background, we can appreciate the achievement of children who are able to exercise this material symbolically through the art process. Both "Don't Kill Your Sister" and "Figure with Hand" referred to fantasies based upon strong impulses. By accommodating these expressions the art teacher allowed for the safe passage of psychic issues and maybe the actual first step toward sublimation.

THE THERAPEUTIC
ART EDUCATOR

When Victor Lowenfeld originally coined the term "art education therapy," he conceived the art process as being endowed with therapeutic qualities. Although Lowenfeld was quite clear as to the scope of these therapeutic effects (such as developing self-esteem, self-concept, increased awareness, insight, etc), his use of the term *therapy* became problematic. The term *therapy* must be reserved for the practice of counseling, psychoanalysis, or other psychological services which focus upon the dynamic processes that govern the psyche. The therapist must be able to listen to clients' unconscious processes as well as their more rational communications in order to pick up verbal and behavioral clues which allow insight into the psychodynamic aspects of their behavior (Kramer 1979, pg. 138).

Kramer's definition essentially excludes the art educator from engaging in therapy despite the fact that he or she may have a thorough understanding of the therapeutic benefits of the art process. For Kramer, there is a crucial distinction between the adjective *therapeutic* and the noun *therapy*. The term *therapy* must remain within the clinical and analytical sphere, whereas, the term *therapeutic* can safely imply processes which "elevate the mind, quicken the spirit or ease the body" (Kramer, pg. 136).

Therapeutic art education, then, refers to art education which recognizes and uses the therapeutic benefits of the art process. It does not pretend to engage in psychotherapy or analysis, nor does it attempt to replace analytically-oriented support services such as counseling. This approach aspires to see children as individuals, to take their concerns seriously and respond in ways that are supportive and productive. It recognizes that the art process is an ideal medium for addressing the varied concerns of children, and strives to promote the art process as a conduit for intellectual, aesthetic, and social and psychological growth.

Historically, the integration of art education and art therapy has been seen in terms of a dichotomy. Art education has maintained a skill-acquisition approach which involves cognitive training with an emphasis on gaining competencies through problem-solving activities. In contrast, the spontaneous self-expression associated with art therapy elicits from the child a free association of images, which then leads to intuitive, emotive problem solving rather than technical mastery. In art therapy, self-expression is a means of visually processing issues of personal relevance, guiding creative energy toward obtaining emotional clarity, power and equilibrium (Seiden 1987).

The question remains whether, by drawing upon Lowenfeld's and Kramer's theories, art education and art therapy can be integrated into a curriculum that is truly conflict-free. In my view, the problem has remained unsolved due to the manner in which each discipline has been approached. I believe that art education and art therapy do not necessarily need to be seamlessly integrated. The solution may be to create a system where they are complementary through their co-existence.

In order for these two disciplines to be applied in a complementary way, the art educator must possess a thorough understanding of children from both an educational and developmental standpoint. This includes knowledge of child development and the characteristics of different populations, as well as a general familiarity with the dynamics of child behavior. This training must be accompanied by a commitment to recognize and support a child's affective concerns during the art process. When combined with the expertise gained through training in traditional art education as well as that of a practicing, mature artist, the "therapeutic art educator," as we might now designate him or her, is better positioned to pursue goals of a dual nature.

The therapeutic art educator may be an art specialist in a mainstream public school setting, a self-contained program for children with special needs, a hospital for disturbed or physically ill children, a residential group home, a prison or any number of other agencies. As a member of the interdisciplinary team, the art specialist may be required to provide input on all or some of the children who are labelled handicapped. This may include writing educational and therapeutic goals and objectives in annual individualized education plans, sitting in on team meetings, and conducting consultations with parents, teachers or administrators. The therapeutic art educator fills a crucial role in the educational setting; he or she may be the only faculty member who is considered both a teacher and a support service staff member. This dual role implies that the therapeutic art educator can provide both concrete recommendations concerning skill acquisition and other educational concerns, as well as providing a degree of insight into the affective life of the child. To effectively prepare for this dual role entails taking coursework that is mandated by state certification programs, including studies in exceptional children, and educational and child psychology. Other pertinent coursework may include personality theory, adolescent psychology and abnormal psychology, as well as introductory courses in art therapy. (While such introductory experiences will not entitle the art educator to

practice clinical art therapy, it will expand his or her knowledge and insight.)

The core studies required by most states should position the therapeutic art educator to practice both affective-based and cognitive-oriented art education. As a practicing therapeutic art educator, I see myself as integrating the affective and cognitive domains in my role as a facilitator, making myself useful, as the need arises, in ways that support the child during his or her studio experience. Hypothetically, should the child be supremely motivated, technically proficient, hardworking, critically reflective and responsible when cleaning up, I would then be doing very little during the session except perhaps staying out of the way. In future sessions I might attempt to increase the complexity of the art process, for it is only through extending challenges that we mature as artists and as people.

However, few children, intact or special needs, are so self-directed and technically proficient. Invariably, problems of motivation, techniques, media, theme, attention, social issues or emotional concerns will surface during the art process. It is at this point that the therapeutic art educator decides what goals to pursue as well as what role to fulfill. Should the problem be technical, skills clearly must be taught. If an image is consistently stereotyped, some kind of enriching motivation might be forthcoming. If behavior is disruptive, then strategies must be in place to suppress or empathize depending upon the circumstances. In short, the therapeutic art educator defines his role by the extenuating needs of the child. The emphasis of this role is to elicit expressively rich and self-gratifying artwork, tapping the full potential of each child. Should some emotion, idea, social stigma or developmental disability stand in the way, the therapeutic art educator must adapt to the circumstances, so that these issues or other handicaps do not disqualify the child from a successful art experience.

SHIFTING EMPHASIS

Therapeutic art education also recognizes the need to shift program emphasis from product to process should the circumstances warrant it. While a program's emphasis may be studio oriented, there may be times when children's personal issues interfere with their ability to do their best work (Carden 1986). Concentration, attention and productivity may all be affected by life stresses. Should a child be in the throes of some life crisis, academic expectations should be adjusted to reduce the levels of frustration and anxiety. This should not be confused, however, with allowing a child to act out inappropriately or wallow in self-pity, nor should the existence of a handicapping condition automatically dictate a suspension of expectations.

A good example of this is a congenitally paralyzed child who may be thriving in a studio art program, working on such goals as motor coordination, attention and art techniques. She might be functioning quite normally within her limitations, effectively compensating for her disability without ever thinking twice about her handicap. Indeed, she may not be able to imagine life any other way, as her handicap is ingrained in her daily life. However, this stability may be disturbed at any time. Perhaps she is awaiting an operation or she sustains a fall from her wheelchair. In these circumstances the art educator should assess the extent of the trauma, while allowing the child an increased opportunity to exercise her concerns through the art process. This increased support does not necessarily entail vast investments of time or material. It may be as simple as an extra word of encouragement or a more open-ended art process which allows for more spontaneous expression. Perhaps a seat away from abrasive peers may help or extra paper for "do-overs." The range of possible interventions should make the shift of emphasis both easy and practical in the art and special education classroom.

Art Product and Process

There is a tendency in both art education and special education programs to see the process as an incidental means to an end. The art educator is especially concerned with creating products which can then be criticized and evaluated. Special educators, also, focus on producing concrete, functional products, so that children know what they are working for and to what extent their efforts will be rewarded.

However, the art *process* is a crucial element in therapeutic art education. It allows especially young or low-functioning children an opportunity to play with materials and partake of pleasureful sensory experiences for their own sake. The kinesthetic sensations which arise from the child's bodily movements, rhythms, observations and other faculties has been seen as an act of liberation which awakens the power of the mind and facilitates creative expression (Cane 1951). Rubin (1978) discusses how the child's flow of ideas during the art process allows a kind of symbolic dialogue to take place, whereby a child can tryout ideas and feelings with minimum risk. Without undue pressures to immediately produce concrete results, a child may achieve a sense of power and mastery. Indeed, a child's productivity and the quality of the art may be enhanced.

Many theorists assert that plotting products—asking students to obediently follow a method—will result in pseudo-products that create the illusion of art (Kramer 1971). Kramer urges the therapeutic art educator to resist futile striving for a kind of preconceived perfection that guarantees impersonal and "bad" art. Both she and Lowenfeld (1977) exhort educators to restrain their critical judgments, and allow young children especially to be themselves, so that preoccupation with creating a product does not stand in the way of its achievement.

This is not to say that the product should not be effectively integrated into the process. Kramer also cautions advocates of the process not to be taken in by their own propaganda and end up believing that they really don't care what the child's work looks like. She particularly assails art therapists who confuse the aimless or contrived manipulation of art materials with true spontaneity in art expression. She believes firmly in the medium's power to stimulate the desire to give form to a product and looks dimly upon games or gambits that smother a child's initiative in this direction. Thus, Kramer considers any neglect or disrespect for the art product as depriving children both of their goals and the reward for their labors.

ASSESSMENT THROUGH FORM AND CONTENT

Another characteristic of therapeutic art education entails making informed assessments about the child's artwork. Unlike an art psychotherapy approach, therapeutic art education does not try to uncover or interpret unconscious meaning or symbolism in the artwork. Lowenfeld (1957), in particular, was very precise about reminding art educators who are untrained in analytic techniques that they are ill equipped to speculate as to the symbolic significance of the artwork.

However, the therapeutic art educator *can* be sufficiently informed and trained to see the child's image for what it is and respond to the work in terms of form and content at the level or levels which it demands. While such "seeing" does entail an element of subjectivity, it nevertheless operates on a much more obvious or overt level. It can provide the educator with some indications of how well the child is coping under stress or difficulty.

Returning to Mike's "Don't Kill Your Sister" drawing, you might begin the assessment process by noting the overt messages in the theme, content and narrative elements of the picture. At first, you might assume that the theme is of some importance to the child (because he was motivated to create it) and that it may reflect some unresolved feelings or thoughts about his relationship with his sister. In identifying the areas of concern in the piece, you would note the fantasy or theme (which connotes aggression), the guilt it produced, (as evi-

denced in the title), as well as the fear that prompts the figure to run away.

You should also note the amount of control with which this child has executed such emotionally charged material. He has instilled his picture with a sense of wit, absurdity and black humor. As a project solution, it possesses obvious depth of thinking and feeling as well as uncommon inventiveness. Aesthetically, the visual impact of the drawing is heightened by the deft handling of the figures and their expressions and actions. These sparse elements are depicted with an economy of means in which only the vital aspects of the composition are embellished. Given the integration of emotion, inventiveness and strong draftsmanship, we might consider such a work as satisfying Kramer's ideas of "formed expression" or art in the true sense of the word. This is a fairly high level of expression because it is derived from and evokes feeling and because it serves as an analogue for a broad range of human experiences (Wilson 1979, p. xxix).

Thus, we might consider this child to be coping adequately with his conflict. The extent to which he allows his concerns to be exercised through a symbolic and productive means is certainly positive (as opposed to more active forms of assault). The fact that he uses wit and humor to disarm the intensity of feeling also points to positive problem solving. Finally, the child's artistic control was never overwhelmed by destructive impulses. His emotions and fantasies were channelled effectively without the process becoming chaotic. This balance between the problem and the reconciliation points to a fairly stable situation—one which deserves a positive prognosis. Of course, the final assessment must take into account the child's behaviors, his verbal responses as well as his art productions. With these elements considered, you as an art educator are better able to make an informed referral or, if it is an isolated occurrence, deal with the child's issues in a sensitive and informed manner.

The Objective and Subjective Reaction

Lowenfeld (1957) also developed a useful concept that assists in the assessment process. Objective and subjective conditions allude to two contrasting modes of experience. The objective condition refers to the literal circumstances of a given situation, such as a diagnosis of asthma or a case of sexual abuse or an impoverished home life. The subjective condition is the individual's ideational or emotional response to the objective condition. It describes how well the individual is coping under the strain of the objective condition as it affects motivation, self-concept, anxiety levels and other areas that relate to emotional adjustments and subsequent performance in the artroom.

Lowenfeld used the discrepancy between the objective and subjective condition in assessing the extent of emotional liability as well as in formulating practical strategies which would ideally bring both situations back into relative balance. This concept can be applied in almost any situation as life is constantly providing us all with crises, while some form of individuated response is also inevitable. Lowenfeld intended that each condition should be analyzed and treated so that a reasonable balance is maintained between the two.

In the "Don't Kill Your Sister" example, the objective condition could be considered sibling rivalry. The two children might be vying for parental attention, affection and material objects. If the sister is somehow maladjusted or in some way spoiled, aggressive or otherwise abrasive to live with, this also could be considered an objective handicap. Because she was, in fact, a very well-adjusted girl who was cooperative and tolerant of her brother, the problem remained a general sibling rivalry. According to the drawing, the issue of reconciling this rivalry was not fully accomplished. There was sufficient resentment, frustration or hostility to warrant an expression of conflict. Therefore, one could state that the objective situation and the subjective reaction are in relative conflict with one another.

In the "Figure with Hand" example, the objective condition is the young man's hearing impairment, his sheltered home and school environment, as well as his being of a racial minority. The subjective response is again somewhat subject to change. The child held up well until the issue of separation from school and entering the job market precipitated high levels of apprehension and anxiety which were eventually translated into anger and a violent episode.

INTERVENING THROUGH VERBAL DISCOURSE AND MOTIVATION

Another distinguishing characteristic of therapeutic art education is that, in the educational setting, a child's objective and subjective concerns are rarely explored through verbal psychotherapeutic interventions. Because the educator lacks the extensive training necessary to engage in verbal analysis, he or she should not and could not address a child's free associations or underlying feelings via extensive verbal discussion. Apart from his or her lack of proper training, there is neither the time nor opportunity for such intimate and in-depth engagement in the classroom.

However, perceptive and personal discussion is an important component of any intervention. Lowenfeld (1957) developed a particularly effective means of intervening through verbal dialogue so that issues can be articulated and explored by the child during the art process. Lowenfeld's verbal dialogue, focuses the child's attention on particular sensory impressions associated with his artwork. By questioning the child as to the "How" and "Why" of his pictures, the child is assisted in making corrections in his images that might have previously escaped his attention.

For instance, in the case of "Don't Kill Your Sister," the art educator might intervene by first communicating his or her acceptance of this image using fairly neutral terms. He or she might say that the picture is interesting or intense, or that it was bold, sensitive or humorous. These terms convey support and praise without sending mixed messages or stimulating the child to stir up the issue even further. It would be irresponsible in the art education sphere to attempt to interpret the symbols to the child or to go into detail about their overt or covert meaning. Commentary or questions should remain open-ended so that the child's responses are not prejudiced or imposed upon by one's own projections (Rubin 1978, pg. 61). Finally, a child should never be coerced into talking about his work. The right to let an artwork speak for itself should be honored whether created by a child or adult artist.

It is important not to overstimulate the child whose images are emotionally loaded. Questions should be designed to assist in exploring the relationship between the art and the artist. With this relationship in place, the child is in a better position to elaborate, embellish and otherwise process ideas or feelings through more dynamic imagery. One might have asked the artist of "Don't Kill Your Sister," "Where is the boy running for support or comfort?" In this way the art educator acknowledges that something horrible has symbolically taken place, while also providing the child with a scenario which is not totally hopeless. By articulating where he is running to, the child may alleviate some of the burden of fear or panic—if indeed those feelings accompany the picture—and gain an opportunity to seek emotional shelter. In subsequent sessions, if this theme is still an issue, the child might be encouraged to explore the positive aspects of his relationship with his sister, such as their habit of baseball card trading or soccer playing. It is sometimes helpful to increase a child's awareness of those positive and productive aspects of a relationship. These positive aspects often color a child's perceptions to the extent that future attitudes and experiences echo this optimism. However, the educator must again take care not to interject his or her own material into the story or coerce the child into remaking sanitized versions of his or her theme.

INTERVENING THROUGH THE ARTWORK

While verbal interaction and intervention are a vital part of therapeutic art education, an equally effective means of promoting positive change is through intervention in the art process itself. Kramer (1986) developed such a technique, which she refers to as the "Third Hand." This is an approach in which the therapeutic art educator suggests modifications in the style, content or media of a child's artwork. The circumstances which prompt these interventions are not limited exclusively to aesthetic concerns. They may involve deep-seated issues which the therapeutic art educator attempts to engage, and perhaps resolve to some degree, during the modification process. Kramer is careful to point out, however, that such interventions must not be intrusive, distort original meaning, or impose pictorial ideas or preferences which are incomprehensible to the child. Third Hand interventions attempt to promote the art process with the recognition that style, content and media can function metaphorically for a child's personal issues. Interventions that use the power of metaphor as a vehicle for personal change do not, however, neglect the educational or aesthetic elements of the art experience.

The case of Peter, the hearing-impaired young man who drew the figure with distorted hands, offers an example of a Third Hand intervention. The separation trauma Peter was experiencing had raised his anxiety level, which in turn had led to a temporary loss of impulse control. After discussing his anger and the treatment of the hands in his drawing, I suggested to Peter that hands seemed to be important to him right now and that continuing with them in his artwork might be worthwhile. I first suggested working with quick contour sketches in which the hands were fluid, loose and abbreviated—not far removed from his first distorted image. In this stylistic suggestion I attempted to convey that abstracting or emphasizing a part of a figure was perfectly acceptable so long as one could maintain control over the image.

After being encouraged to do some studies of hands, Peter depicted a mirrored glass ornament being gripped with great intensity.

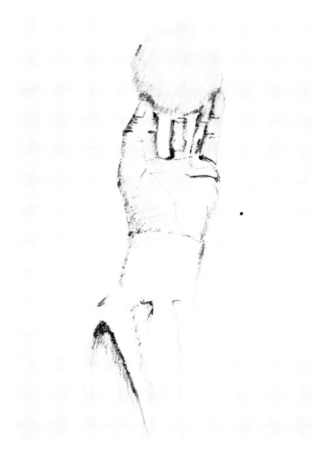

Peter's second hand study shows that hand control can be firm without becoming destructive. The mirrored surface is now held with great care, suggesting that the art process has furthered the student's capacity for reflection and insight.

Next we looked at how other artists treat the hands: Escher's irony, the gritty realism of da Vinci, the childlike simplicity of Picasso. Using these visual aids, Peter was able to see how the figure could be manipulated to express a mood as well as to portray reality. I then encouraged him to choose a style to emulate. At first he worked in Picasso's thick simplified style, eventually moving on to Escher's realistic yet playful manner of working. He began to draw his own hand while it held a glass reflective ball.

Working carefully and intently, he drew as realistically as possible. He became frustrated with several problematic areas such as the nails and the architecture of the palms at which time I saw fit to intervene. Drawing next to him on separate paper, I showed him how to use shading to convey depth and contour instead of relying on line. This assistance pleased him and he requested that I continue drawing so that he could refer to my work when

needed. Eventually he finished two pieces to his great satisfaction and appreciation.

Several interventions transpired in this process. The first drawing exercises conveyed that lightly and quickly sketched forms are acceptable. Second, the use of positive role models, such as Picasso and Escher, afforded examples which were within his capability to emulate. Third, a drawing partner, who worked in a style which was reminiscent of his own realistic capabilities, provided motivation to continue and develop his own work.

In the first drawing, the artist's hand is depicted tightly gripping the glass ball suggesting that at any minute it may be crushed in his grasp. The rendering is much more developed than the earlier tentative figure with misshapen hands. It convincingly holds and controls the object with obvious strength. However, because the pose lacks a sense of delicacy or control, one continues to sense that there is a great tension in the hands, as if the object is tightly gripped so as not to let loose this tension upon some other object—such as a class peer.

I asked Peter if such a grip might be adjusted in order to handle an object of such delicacy. He responded with the second, more sensitive drawing in which the glass ball is accorded care and balance. Fingertips now control yet preserve the object, suggesting that the issue of "hand equals strength equals control" has been worked out thoroughly. The draftsmanship is more solid, the grip convincingly in control while the hand seems responsive to the object's fragility. There is no image cast in the reflection on the ball, which might suggest Peter has some continuing sensitivity over his own self-image. Yet, the issues are being courageously explored while maintaining the artwork's formal aesthetic quality.

While not every case is explored and resolved with such poignancy as in Peter's case, the art process remains a powerful tool for encouraging a child to reflect his or her feelings while remaining engaged in what is essentially an art education process.

THE INCLUSION OF THE ART EXPERIENCE THROUGH CAMOUFLAGING

A last yet equally major principle of therapeutic art education refers to the inclusion of the art process in the special needs or mainstream setting through a procedure I have termed *camouflaging*. Camouflaging recognizes that children with special needs should have the opportunity to create artworks whose aesthetic integrity and visual richness is on par with their mainstream peers. Although it is unreasonable to expect every child to create with the same technical skill and conceptual

sophistication, this should not discount the possibilities for creating genuinely expressive work. I assume that artwork is not solely dependent upon technical proficiency, but can also prosper with the freshness of vision and eccentricity of approach which many children with severe deficits possess in abundance.

In order to set the stage for parity and integrity of the artwork, the therapeutic art educator must not condescend to or patronize the special child. Children with special needs should be prompted to solve problems, work with real tools and extend their limits just as any other art student. To insure a healthy challenge, the art process must encourage independent functioning with materials, techniques and themes that are age and socially appropriate.

The art experience should contribute to both personal integration and social inclusion. By inclusion I don't mean that we should deny or discount a child's exceptionality, but that we should not make an unwarranted issue of it. Particularly in mainstream settings, social inclusion becomes a key to integrating a child with special needs into the studio. Motivation, participation, and self-esteem all depend on whether children feel able to express themselves confidently without inhibition.

It becomes vital, then, that the art teacher choose and adopt media and themes which put children on equal footing. The art process should not accentuate a child's deficits or broadcast to others the extent or nature of a disability. By sensitively and strategically modifying the different facets of the art experience, a teacher can essentially *camouflage* a child's weaknesses and exploit whatever strengths he or she possesses. Projects should be chosen that can be scaled to different levels of complexity without sacrificing the integrity of the process or product. Some techniques, media or artistic styles are more suitable for this purpose than others. The teacher must learn to choose those projects that possess a universal, unprejudiced quality.

**CHILD DEVELOPMENT:
ATTACHMENTS, SEPARATION
AND INDIVIDUATION**

To effectively practice therapeutic art education one should understand the processes that children undergo as they develop and mature. The stages that children invariably pass through as they develop an awareness of self and establish relationships—particularly with parents—have a direct bearing upon their artmaking. The process of bonding and forming attachments to "significant others," impacts upon nearly all aspects of a child's life.

The psychological need for maternal nurturance is vital to an infant's emotional well-being. The Harlows (1953) demonstrated this in experiments with infant monkeys. Those infants who were deprived of maternal warmth and affection developed emotional disturbances similar to autism, including self-injurious behavior. Similarly abused or ignored infant children also have been found to suffer severe psychopathologies in childhood (Bettelheim 1950). Margaret Mahler (1968), along with other child analysts (Bergman, Pine 1968, Spitz 1955, Winnicott 1965), developed theories that placed vital importance upon the successful making of attachments or bonds between a "mothering agent" and the infant. Mahler outlined the first stage as normal autism, in which the child exists in a blissful twilight state. This begins while the fetus is carried within the mother and continues for a time after delivery. Mahler refers to the subsequent bonding stage as *symbiosis,* during which the infant develops such enmeshed bonds with the mother that it cannot conceive of itself as a separate entity. Once this secure symbiotic tie is established, the child begins to develop a dim awareness of self. After five months the child has developed sufficient self-awareness and differentiation so that a primitive body-ego emerges. Mahler saw this "*hatching stage*" as the psychological birth of the child, the period during which alertness and curiosity about self and mother expands. It is soon after this stage that the child begins to

practice separation from the mother through crawling and games such as "peek-a-boo." To support the process of even brief separation, the child often resorts to a phenomenon called the *transitional object*. Described by Winnicott (1965), the transitional object is usually an inanimate object which symbolizes or takes the place of the mother. Most infants prefer objects, such as blankets or toys, which are lasting, pliable, warm and possess the mother's smell. This developmental milestone indicates the period in which the infant is defusing the tension and anxiety which occurs when mother and infant separate.

In normal development, children will continue to explore their world and tolerate separation with less anxiety or tension as their confidence grows. However, Mahler found that this new-found freedom reaches a stage of ambivalence because the child is pleased with his ability to be free of mother, yet his needs for maternal symbiosis are also still strong. Subsequently, the child enters the rapprochement phase, as the ambivalence between separation and unity creates the temper tantrums common in "terrible" two-year-olds. During this time of conflict, the child may harbor intense feelings of both love and hate for the mother, as she oscillates between her role as a needs satisfier for the child and her own needs. Mahler's term for the phase during which the child works through rapprochement is *individuation*. During individuation, the child demonstrates the capacity to separate and function without the mother, despite pangs of separation anxiety. Mahler's final stage is *object constancy* when reality-testing, tolerance for frustration, and a mutual give-and-take relationship has been reached between the three-year-old and his primary love object. Unless arrested at any of the earlier stages of development, one can expect children to continue to develop their self-identity and relationships with others through latency and adolescence. The quality of these relationships is known as *object relations*. In psychoanalytic terms the word "object" refers to the self, people or things that are significant to the child (Brenner 1974).

The quality of a child's object relations affects behavior throughout the school years. For instance, it is a familiar sight to see five-year-olds being traumatized by their first separation from their mothers upon entering kindergarten. Such separation anxiety is normal, unless it persists to the extent that it inhibits a child's ability to meet normal educational expectations. The forming of attachments in school also influences a child's classroom performance. The process of making friends, developing role models in teachers or coaches directly affects a child's motivation, concentration and independence in the artroom.

As a child develops self-confidence and positive self-esteem, relating is facilitated, even between the child and his or her artwork. The relationship between one's artwork and one's self is seen by Lowenfeld as reflecting the quality of self-identification and investment that a child brings to his or her art (1951). Lachman-Chapin (1987) also points to this as a relationship that mirrors a child's self-concept and self-empowerment. Problems in this area may be observed in children whose self-image is tenuous; their art often stagnates and relies heavily upon stereotypes. Such problems can be found in every art school, as students struggle to develop their own individual visions while trying also to satisfy the expectations of peers, tutors and the artworld in general. This situation often gives rise to conflicts and ambivalent feelings, both on the part of the art student and teacher. Often, rapprochement is rekindled, as the emerging artist asserts his or her individuation, yet still remains dependant upon the guidance, wisdom and role-modeling that teachers provide.

Teachers often respond with frustration and defensiveness, as they try to reassert their influence and control over the rebelling student. Whether this relationship can be reconciled effectively, depends upon a myriad of dynamics, beginning with how effectively the child negotiated these developmental stages during infancy, how much resilience and fortitude the child innately possesses, as well as how much support and guidance is provided by adults during these trying times. When this process breaks down there is a tendency to split the authority figure into good and bad objects. Most parents of teenagers have had the experience of being played off against each other, as the child manipulates the lenient or "good" parent against the disciplinarian or "bad" parent. Such splitting can be considered a normal part of adolescence so long as it is transient in nature or constitutes an occasional defense that is resorted to only during times of great stress. Splitting during adulthood is considered a serious psychopathology (Brenner 1974).

Separation and individuation problems are often observed in children by therapists and teachers who have established close bonds with their students. A child will transfer emotions from an earlier maternal experience to this significant person, much to the consternation of the teacher who is usually not prepared for such intense relating. Such close attachments can provide guidance and role modeling for the child, yet a professional distance must be maintained. Robbins (1987) summarizes the message that must be communicated thus: "I am with you, will help you and teach you, but I am also separate and must promote in you, regardless of the displeasure or pain, your own independence and autonomy." Facilitating the forming of attachments, and creating separation as well, is a basic activity for anyone who works closely with students. We are forever promoting positive self-identity for our students, helping out with social skills, separating fact from fiction, fantasy from reality, dilemma from solution (Rubin 1978). In this respect, the teacher acts as an auxiliary-ego, lending maturity, insight and empathy to children. The art activity itself can play a crucial part in facilitating this process by acting as a transitional object—one that bolsters self-relating and empowerment and provides a bridge between the student-artist and others who have a significant impact upon his or her creative and mental growth.

chapter 2

Structuring the Art Process

LEAST RESTRICTIVE ENVIRONMENT

The guiding principle in structuring the art process for special needs children is based upon maintaining the "least restrictive environment." This term was coined as part of PL94-142. It refers to creating an atmosphere which is as normalized and as barrier free as possible (Federal Register 1977). In the artroom, least restrictive environment means that the structure should minimize special education adaptations in media, technique, theme and work setting if they are not warranted. It also implies that the structure of the art process not be overly directive, controlled or otherwise stifling for the children. Regardless of how tightly structured a project is, it should remain sufficiently open-ended to allow for individual responses. The finished product should then reflect not just the skills and objectives taught by the teacher, but also the child's cultural, physical and emotional temperament.

It is important to keep in mind that different children require different amounts of structure in order to maintain their freedom of expression. Depending upon individual needs, the structure must be resilient enough to tighten or loosen as the need arises.

Most theories of art education counsel the teacher that structure should always begin on the tight side. Once the children display the capacity to handle freedom, the teacher can then ease control and become more spontaneous. There is truth to this theory particularly when dealing with children with high distractibility or other behavior deficits. The popularity of this theory, however, is based more on teachers' need to maintain behavioral control than on creating optimum learning circumstances. If structure is not to be unreasonably rigid or arbitrary, its rationale must stem from the needs of the students. Just as the individual needs of the child can define whether the emphasis should be on skill acquisition or dealing with issues, the needs of the children should also influence the kind of structure required.

For instance, faced for the first time with a spastic cerebral palsied child in a mainstreamed class, chances are, that an inexperienced art teacher would lower his or her expectations regarding all aspects of the child's performance. This is an unreasonable supposition and does a disservice to the child. Perhaps all that's needed is a thicker paintbrush or precut collage materials. Spasticity has little bearing on a child's depth of imagination or vitality. Implementing unnecessary adaptations, such as dictating a theme or planning a composition, will only repress the child's potential and, in the long run, will make the child more dependent. Ultimately, it may socially stigmatize the child also and cause a loss of self-esteem and confidence.

Exceptional children require different degrees of direction and structure. Caught in a motivational lull, this child required an intervention that presented options and an opportunity for decision making within a sheltered framework.

On the other hand, a severely learning disabled or mentally retarded child may not be able to walk in the door unless given clear, concise directions. The child may need assistance in finding a seat, accepting art materials, sequencing the steps of the art process, using the medium appropriately or following the simplest clean-up regime. In this case, the most directed, orchestrated structure would still constitute a least restrictive environment, because the child has demonstrated that these interventions are necessary in order to function successfully. This child may also have the capacity to create fascinating images or ideas. Every effort should be made to stimulate this creativity through the structure of the art process. Only then will the structure be truly non-restrictive in theory and practice.

In the clinical art therapy or special education setting, where groups of one or eight are most common, the prospects for maintaining a least restrictive structure are optimum. Here, medium and technique can be finely tuned to the immediate and changing needs of each child. Concern over disparate working paces, emotional volatility and physical adaptation can be handled without diffi-

culties in logistics or teacher/student ratios. However, in the mainstream art education setting, the ratios loom to fifteen to thirty students. In this setting, it may be difficult or impossible to have each child working on different materials and techniques, as is the routine in the art therapy setting. Therefore, the teacher must modify the structure so that the aims of therapeutic education are not compromised.

One solution is the use of a project approach in which everyone in the group will be working at least on the same media and, possibly, the same technique in different variations. By using a project method, the teacher can minimize the time devoted to different verbal presentations and, instead, concentrate on giving individual attention. Motivational strategies can be directed to common goals, while materials and tools can be organized and distributed more effectively. Students who are engaged in similar projects have the opportunity to learn from each other and derive stimulation from the groups' cumulative creative energies.

Adapting or shifting between instructional or therapeutic emphases can still be accomplished in this format. By remaining open-ended, and inviting children to use the medium as a vehicle for their own purposes, the opportunity for variation, to interpret a problem, extend the use of materials and improvise a technique is built into the structure. In this way, adaptations that accommodate children with special needs become only one of many improvisations during the art process.

In addition to adopting a project approach, another important step toward creating a least restrictive environment is the grouping of children according to their individual needs. Grouping takes one of three forms: the individual, one-on-one setting; the self-contained group and the mainstream setting.

The Individual Setting
Individualized art education calls for an intensive involvement with the child, increased adaptation of the art activity and closer monitoring of the child's responses and behaviors. It allows for an in-depth, more therapeutically-based relationship with the child.

Individual sessions are usually the result of a recommendation or referral by a multidisciplinary team which has identified a particular problem as requiring intensive intervention. Usually the child is having great difficulty in functioning the entire day within a group. This type of child might be overly aggressive or reckless, psychotic and out of touch with reality, or withdrawn and depressed. In some instances, a child will be referred to the art teacher or art therapist because he is non-verbal and cannot benefit from verbal counseling. For others, the issue at hand, such as sexual abuse, demands a private session.

Individual settings may be seen as overly restrictive and limiting, as they do not allow for peer interaction and group stimulation. For this reason individual sessions should be approached with the goal of moving the child into a less restrictive environment if and when the problem is resolved. In the therapeutic art education setting, the least restrictive environment would be a studio which services small groups of children.

During the individual session, the child is faced with confronting the teacher on a more intimate basis. Such intimacy may be uncomfortable or stressful. Therefore, I often set the child up with materials, motivation or a technical demonstration, before deciding whether to leave the child alone with the art project. By leaving the child while I wash brushes, erase the board or get more paint, I communicate that I am interested in the child's work and available for support should he or she falter. Yet, I also communicate that I am not going to sit with a fixed stare upon the child while he or she tries to work. In this way, I attempt to maintain a neutral, casual, non-confrontational approach to the individual setting which approximates the routines of a normal studio.

Although I may appear to be busy cleaning the erasers, I am monitoring the child's progress closely. Should he or she have a problem with the materials, be stuck for a theme or become discouraged, I will intervene as needed. As the work progresses, I will often make comments while taking care not to distract the child. Upon its completion, I will mount the work upon the temporary gallery board to discuss its meaning and its aesthetics.

Although the atmosphere of the individual session should be kept as natural and relaxed as possible, it may become more charged and intense than a group setting. This is particularly the case if the child's issues become urgent and the intimacy factor intensifies interactions. Children often respond in this situation by creating work which is also more intense, explicit and personal.

Despite the severity of their handicapping conditions or the extent of their emotional disturbance, children often adjust and use the individual setting to their advantage. An emotionally disturbed child once came to me both as a member of a group of emotionally disturbed students in an art education setting and on an individual basis. Despite her handicaps, she was able to sense the differences between the two settings. In the group, her artwork was more guarded, stereotyped, attractive and pleasant with an age appropriateness in terms of theme and style. In the individual sessions, her work was charged and intimate. She allowed her emotions more free reign and exorcised them through the artwork. The results were spontaneous and direct expressions explicitly representative of her emotional problems.

No one ever explained to this child the different expectations of group and individual settings. It is doubtful whether she could have comprehended them. Yet, she was able to effectively use both formats to suit her needs; she could be more social and student-like in the group; while in the individual setting, she was more in touch with her true feelings and, thus, more amenable to change.

Although created by a student with severe emotional problems, this drawing is relatively neutral in content and style, perhaps because it was created during a group session.

In another one-on-one session, this child's preoccupation with dogs takes on a more ominous and nightmarish tone when stripped of any environmental context or personal reference.

In a one-on-one setting, the same emotionally disturbed child depicted more disturbing ideas in her drawing, such as the dog shown here relieving itself in the school yard.

Self-Contained Groups

The self-contained group serves children whose difficulties are not so severe that they require an individual session, but who continue to need an environment more sheltered and accommodating than the mainstream classroom. Here children are usually grouped by the nature of their disability or the extent of their symptoms. Thus cerebral palsy children would be grouped together so that the facility could respond to their specialized physical needs. Emotionally disturbed children would be similarly grouped so that the behavioral expectations and program strategies can remain consistent and more effective. For the mentally retarded child, the pace can be slowed and emphasis placed upon life-skill development and vocational training. Even the gifted child can gain from such a setting, in which independent study work can be more conducive to accelerated learning.

While self-contained groups are effective from many standpoints, there are both philosophical and practical difficulties. First, the self-contained program does not allow for the "normalized" art experience called for in a least restrictive environment. It remains an artificial arrangement where the child is not exposed to varied life experiences. Second, because this setting consists of individuals with a common pathology, there is little opportunity for these children to assimilate the behaviors of their intact peers. Thus, an autistic child may never actually observe children who effortlessly and bravely interact, because he or she is always surrounded by their emotionally disturbed peers, or a hearing-impaired child may eventually have difficulty joining the hearing world because he or she has never been forced to read lips, write messages and use his or her voice.

The issue becomes whether it is worth the stress and, in some cases, trauma, of placing a child in a more mainstream environment. This is a decision for the multidisciplinary team who can weight the different factors, then recommend the best setting. In any case, the self-contained classroom is usually the least stressful environment for special needs children with severe emotional or physical problems. For better or for worse, the retarded child can simply be retarded without fear of ridicule. The deaf child can learn to identify and act in accordance with deaf culture. The cerebral palsied child can work and learn in a facility that is designed and constructed for absolute accessibility.

Within the self-contained setting, children can be exposed to the mainstream world in a cautious manner. Both academic and behavioral expectations can accommodate the child's current needs and develop at the proper pace. As the child demonstrates the capacity to endure a less-sheltered atmosphere, modifications can be made in the self-contained setting. Often, children with special needs experience the artroom as their first foray into the mainstream. Given the subjective and pleasureful nature of the art program, this is often a reasonable strategy to take. However, such a first experience will often place the art teacher in a challenging position.

The Inclusion Setting

The practice of placing mildly or moderately handicapped children into classes comprised of normal student populations has been a controversial issue that continues to elicit highly emotional reactions from teaching specialists. The idea behind mainstreaming centers on giving the special child an opportunity to broaden social and learning experiences, while deemphasizing the physical or mental deficits. It discourages the educator from lapsing into the belief that the handicapped cannot be challenged by a more normalized educational environment. By dispelling the stigmas and stereotypes that characterize the disabled as being unreachable or uncontrollable we, as educators, can advocate the achievement of the child's full social and academic potential.

The inclusion of special needs children is of particular concern to the art education specialist who practices in a large public school system. In many cases, the environment in which the art teacher is expected to function is not conducive to the creation of fully realized works of art. Logistics such as immense size and rapid turnover of classes, unsuitable studio space or cleanup facilities, and shortages of materials all may combine to lessen the effectiveness of the art program. The placement of a handicapped child or children creates an additional burden upon the teacher's resources by disrupting the pace and more sophisticated level of instruction that is geared for normal students.

Any deviation from the mental or physical capability of intact classmates will necessitate specialized attention from the teacher in the form of physical or technical assistance (such as in cutting, fabricating, or cleanup procedures) or a further simplification of verbal instruction. Special needs students who have behavior control problems can also adversely affect the productivity of the entire class with their distracting or disruptive behavior. The art teacher is then forced to suppress such disruptions by resorting to disciplinary measures which then interfere with the relaxed casual atmosphere that is needed to encourage a creative environment.

As unsettling as all this may be for the art teacher, it may be even more unsettling for the mainstreamed disabled child. Removed from the sheltered environment of the special class, the child enters a potentially threatening, anxiety provoking situation. Normal children can possess a perversely aggressive attitude toward another child who is physically or mentally different. This form of aggression can pervade even the most mild-mannered child. The resultant harassment or ridicule often affects the conduct of other children. Once again, it is the therapeutic art teacher who must bear the responsibility of fostering positive peer interactions.

In large, diversely populated classrooms, how to acknowledge the presence of the handicapped child is usually the first problem to be faced. The issue of who this child is, why he or she is here and how he or she can be helped must be addressed by both the teacher and the student body. One possible approach is to prepare the students before the child is placed or at a time when he or she is not present. While it may be somewhat distasteful to speak behind the child's back, it is nevertheless an opportunity to frankly address the issue in a straightforward manner. It allows the

students to voice their reactions or concerns and attempt to reconcile these feelings before the situation becomes complicated further. By appealing to the students' sense of compassion and civic mindedness, the teacher can encourage mature, supportive behavior in a group effort. Using this approach does not imply that the handicapped child should be overtly singled out by other students. Given proper guidance, the normal student can gain a degree of positive self-regard by explaining an unclear concept or by briefly assisting the handicapped child with some physically demanding procedure. In this respect the student body contributes to the handicapped child's prospects for social adjustment and success.

Any teacher who prepares projects for a large mainstreamed class must develop a highly organized procedure for material preparation and distribution. Otherwise, the already brief forty-minute period will be unduly consumed by setting up the media, issuing instructions and cleanup. The degree of organization during these procedures will determine the depth and breadth of involvement enjoyed by the students while they create their own work. When working with mainstreamed special needs students the project organization must further reflect the different working pace and styles of both the mainstream population and the special students.

The art program should emphasize the creation of individual artworks, yet this seemingly obvious concept cannot be taken for granted with the problems of student discipline, rigid curriculums, safety concerns and pressures from administration. Teachers must keep up their vigilance and resist distractions that attempt to dilute their energies or divert attention from the real task at hand. Every effort should be made to spend quality time with every art student. With the logistical difficulties faced by teachers, it becomes all the more imperative that we set our priorities in the direction of meeting the needs of the children. Allowing the mainstreamed, special needs child the opportunity to discover art and then seeing the results as expansive creative growth, can be one of the teacher's most satisfying experiences.

32

A strategy used by many art educators in mainstreaming special needs students involves the creation of individualized work centers. For instance, Pine (1979) adopts a painting activity by furnishing each child with a lunch tray which can hold materials for the project, including pigments, mixing cups, brushes, paper, cleanup sponge and wastewater can. This way, children can work within their own self-contained units without violating the space or materials of their neighbors. The turned-up edges of the tray serve to confine spills or other messiness, while furnishing children with a definable boundary within which to operate. In this way the children can exercise complete control over the manner and pace of their working. There is less commotion than when sharing the muddied colors, avoiding the splattering paint or taking responsibility for cleaning a group mess. As the art productions are completed and lined up to dry, the trays wiped and brushes washed, the children are automatically setting up for the next group of children. Thus, the teacher is less burdened with directing every detail of the cleanup/setup process: every child, regardless of handicap, knows his or her job and responsibilities.

Adapting to the slower, more irregular pace of the handicapped child is another challenge faced by the art specialist. While the self-contained material tray will encourage individual responsibility and territorial boundaries, the rhythm in which the children work can be additionally manipulated. Each project, whether it be painting, cutting and pasting, printmaking, etc., can be analyzed to identify areas that are not essential to the creative process.

By eliminating extraneous procedures which are difficult for the special needs child and only contribute minimally to the learning process, the teacher can simplify the concept without sacrificing the problem of working through the technique. The child can then devote all of his or her energies toward the creation of art, without requiring radically special treatment. This is, of course, contrary to least restrictive thinking, yet the circumstances dictate compromise, particularly if the teacher is working without the assistance of an aide.

For example, if the project is potato printmaking, the normal children could be expected to peel the potato and prepare the printing surface. For handicapped children, this may only be an unnecessary additional operation that would tax their attention span and manual dexterity. The child might become increasingly frustrated and eventually bored as well as fall behind the rest of the group. The art teacher can effectively compensate for this by cutting the material so that the handicapped child can focus upon incising the design almost immediately.

LOWERING THE RATIOS IN THE PUBLIC SCHOOL SETTING

Therapeutic art education is conceived as an individualized approach to working with children. Ratios of twelve-to-one are ideal for either intact or special needs children placed within the mainstream setting. Such a ratio is certainly possible in most private schools where the average class size is fifteen. In special education classes, ratios are usually dictated by the state: roughly twelve-to-one for moderately handicapped children, and six-to-one or even three-to-one or one-to-one for the profoundly retarded, autistic, cerebral palsied or those with other severe handicaps. In the mainstream public school setting, however, thirty-to-one is a common ratio. Spending quality time with each student in a class this size is almost impossible. Ratios this high allow for only mass education with diminished opportunities for meaningful interactions with both staff and peers. This is especially crucial should one or more special needs children be placed in this size grouping.

Although there is a movement afoot to reduce ratios in the classroom on a nationwide basis, it is unlikely that administrations will soon accomplish this crucial task. It is especially unlikely to expect ratios to fall in the artroom when academic classes remain taxed and over-crowded. I have always expressed to the administration, however, that ratios could fall if we used a vital resource that often remains untapped: people. Parents, college students,

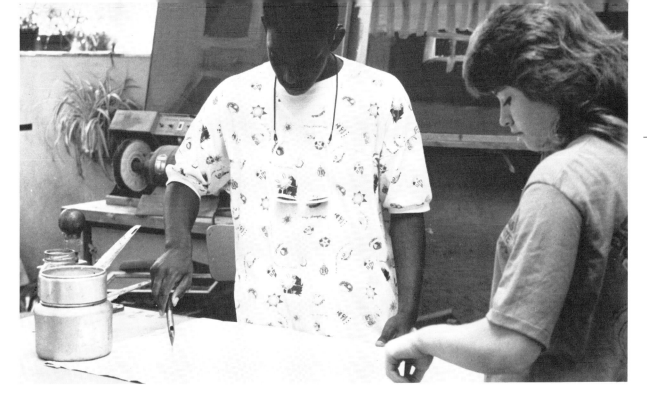

unemployed artists, the financially secure, and retired people all have one common feature: they have the time and, hopefully, the civic-mindedness to pitch in and spend time in the artroom.

How does one arouse these people's interest and mobilize them to volunteer? With the cooperation of my supervisors, I have set up presentations for these groups, instituting workshops, lectures and demonstrations that communicate the goals and mission of my programs. During these presentations I explain my philosophy, benefits to the children and the satisfactions of facilitating art expression in children. I present case histories, tell funny anecdotes and display a range of intriguing artwork which often arouses enthusiasm. After four presentations at the beginning and mid-term of the school year, I recruit usually a dozen individuals. Most volunteers are concerned parents and college students who donate a morning or afternoon per week to assist me in my program.

Once a pool of assistants is recruited, what do they do? Here again, prior preparation is crucial. I first focus all volunteers on the children and my objectives. I then assign them *specific* duties which leave little room for improvisation. It defeats the aides' usefulness if I must take time during the sessions to offer lengthy explanations or instruct them. Instead, I give them responsibilities such as cutting collage materials, pouring glue into

One means of cutting ratios while promoting greater self-initiative and social responsibility is by creating cooperative learning situations. This entails the strategic grouping of students who can mutually enhance one another's learning styles.

cups, washing paintbrushes or examining ceramic sculptures for strength and durability. They often take up duties at the sink at the end of a session or monitor trips to the bathroom. In situations where I wish them to work directly with a child, their interventions remain carefully defined and specific. I might direct them to support a spastic child's elbow or lessen the pressure of the drawing instrument upon the paper. Or, their task might be to keep a child's palette unspoiled by over-mixing.

There are numerous advantages in using volunteers. If used effectively, they free up the teacher to get on with the real task at hand: working with and guiding the children's art experience.

REFLECTION AND CRITICISM

My approach to the art process is decidedly studio-oriented with an emphasis upon learning through the process of creating. However, verbal reflection is a vital part of reinforcing both skills

34 and the act of image making. Musing over how a work may have come into being, what techniques were involved, what the historical influences were, and what significance the images hold for the child are all important topics to explore. Some children may not possess sufficient intellect, language capacity or emotional stability to offer coherent art criticism of their own or a peer's work. However, if an attempt is made—even if it is the teacher who does all the talking—to narrate back to the child what he or she has done, the possibility exists that the child may progress in his language development, cognition and affective stability.

The term *reflection* can have several different connotations. The first vestiges of reflection emerge as the child begins to be aware that he or she has produced something which is a product of his or her own hand and mind. As object awareness is developed, the child may begin to deliberate over aesthetic issues such as what color to use or the kind of line that is most effective in a given situation. Reflection may eventually involve a child's emotions, such as self-esteem, self-concept or emotional conflict. By confronting the finished art product, a child may develop an awareness of his or her affective state of mind and subsequently begin to work through issues that are projected through the artwork.

Reflection can also remain a predominately intellectual function whereby children develop the capacity to critically explore their artwork. This implies that children develop a vocabulary that articulates the visual elements in their work as well as their ideas, intentions and the influences which brought the work into being. Whether it be by verbal, sign or written means, such articulation of the language of art is a crucial part of the reflection process.

Reflection is also a cross-referencing process. Exposure to and discussion of works of art from history, from the Paleolithic to contemporary art, can help students in motivational, technical and critical areas. Because many children naturally work in styles that can be influenced by artists working throughout history, exposure to this material should be integrated into the curriculum.

Promoting Reflection

Looking and talking about art increases the academic and therapeutic worth of the art experience. In a secure, non-judgmental atmosphere, such a critique can help a child address issues that might ordinarily remain incomprehensibly remote, while enhancing the aesthetic aspects of his or her art. All children can approach some phase of reflection and benefit from its cognitive, aesthetic and emotional insight, depending upon their functioning levels and degrees of sensory capabilities. However, many lower functioning or emotionally resistant children may balk at being interfered with during or after the art process. How then does one promote critical awareness and personal insight in such children?

In one such case a multiply handicapped boy had not developed the capacity to reflect over his artistic efforts, but was instead obsessively consumed by them. This presented quite a problem because he vehemently resisted any interruption of his working. Patience, and determination paid off, however, as this child eventually began to pause during the art process. The first opportunities to encourage reflection were during his protracted stays at the pencil sharpener, when he would mercilessly grind his Prisma-colors down to nubs. During these periods, I took up his work in progress and simply held it before his eyes. After a while, I interrupted him between works to point out with great enthusiasm the figures and other forms in his composition. I named or labeled things, discussed the setting or context and offered praise and encouragement.

Eventually, this child began to endure these interruptions without becoming agitated and frustrated. As he displayed a readiness to stop, look and listen (to my verbal and sign language), the stage was set for me to venture a few simple questions about his art. I interspersed these rudimentary dialogues with examples of other artists' work, such as that of Miró, which was in sync with his own style and aesthetic sensibility. At this point, he engaged in limited dialogue over his works. His pace is now less frantic and a modicum of reflection has been firmly established as a routine and integral part of his art process.

It is important that during or after the art activity each child has the opportunity to process what has occurred. This may take the form of an individual quiet time, when the child silently views his or her work against a backdrop, preferably mounted on a temporary or permanent mat. Presentation of the piece can change the appreciative nature of a work drastically. It is therefore crucial that the work be viewed away from the clutter and chaos of the work space and, instead, against a clean, white background suggestive of a gallery.

After individual viewing and reflection, the teacher may include verbal discussion if the children are capable of verbal responses. If not, then the teacher can compensate by offering some commentary. Often, administrators or other visitors in my classroom have been startled to witness me holding forth with a group of severely disabled children, discussing their pictures as though I were lecturing at the Louvre. Regardless of whether every child comprehends every word or concept, maintaining such dialogues without condescending or patronizing my students is part of the studio routine and atmosphere. After consistent and comprehensible use of terms and language, students with severely limited speech have referred to this or that "element" in their "piece," often astounding onlookers.

TASK ANALYSIS

In adapting the art processes to particularly young physically handicapped or lower functioning children, the concept of a "task analysis format" can be used. This method analyzes the art project so that each operation is broken down into a series of sequential steps. Depending upon the functioning level of the child, a project can be scaled so that virtually nothing is taken for granted. A lesson can be mapped out, succinctly describing each step needed to perform the task. As children master each step, they can then move through the sequence to more complex techniques.

For example, in assuming that painting a picture involves simply the act of brushing paint onto paper, it is taken for granted that the child can seat him- or herself at the worktable, make eye contact with the materials, grasp the brush securely and sequence it properly to water, paint and paper. With some developmentally disabled children, these tasks cannot be taken for granted; it may take months of consistent training for them to master each of these steps. By breaking the project down into these discrete operations, the teacher can identify the point of departure the child needs in order to progress through the art process.

Analyzing a task forces the teacher to become thoroughly familiar with a given process. By possessing a clear understanding of what a process entails, the teacher can better anticipate at what step children might begin the process or when they might encounter problems. This format will be particularly useful for inexperienced practitioners who may have to retrain their thinking about techniques so as to better assess what processes will be appropriate for each population.

By noting where a child is in the progression, the teacher maintains a detailed account of skill development status. Progression, stagnation and regression can all be pinpointed with accuracy, which assists the teacher in ascertaining a child's developmental growth. This may be crucial with children whose work and behavior seems not to change until the notations on task analysis are consulted. Only over a long period of time, in these cases, can the child's progress be plotted.

Thinking in terms of task analysis also assists the teacher in maintaining a least restrictive environment. For instance, if a child can pick up a brush without having to be directed, giving directions would be a restrictive intervention. Should a child be unable to seat him- or herself at the worktable without creating a disturbance, assistance in the form of a verbal reminder, extra practice or even punishment may not be overly restrictive because it constitutes the appropriate intervention which supports the child's independent and normal functioning.

chapter 3

A Review of Exceptional Children

None of us who work with special needs children are enthusiastic about labeling or categorizing according to some outstanding handicap. Such a taxonomy can undeservedly stigmatize the child. Especially to be avoided are labels which infer that the creative potential of the individual is somehow diminished. The labels I use in this text are intended only as necessary clarifiers which benignly refer to the child's condition. Referring to the etiology of a handicapping condition does not infer a pejorative connotation as to a child's potential in art education. In addition to referring to specific etiologies, I will also refer to children more generally as being intact or deprived, or as functioning at certain cognitive, emotional or aesthetic levels. These terms cut across specific disabling conditions and allude to those aspects of the individual child which affect the way he or she makes art.

In reviewing the special needs populations an art teacher may expect to work with, I use a "presenting problem" format. This means that I will focus upon those salient characteristics which the art educator might encounter in the art setting, in either behavioral or performance terms. By using this focused approach, I hope to spare the reader the detailed clinical information which is not directly relevant to the task of teaching art. The reader is encouraged to regard my review here as an introduction which can be expanded if a particular population is of particular interest or is encountered in the educator's practice.

THE INTACT OR TYPICAL CHILD

By definition exceptional or special needs children are those who deviate mentally or physically from the norm to the extent of requiring special modifications in the classes (Kirk and Gallagher 1989). Most children who do not meet the definition of exceptionality must make do with a system which relies upon mass education. Unless deficits in performance or problems with behavior draw attention to these children, they make their way noiselessly through systems which are not sufficiently sensitized, caring or capable to acknowledge the subtle exceptionalities of each child. The logistical and financial problems facing public schools today prohibit the possibility of attending to children who only deviate from the norm slightly or infrequently. Despite this, educators continue to advocate mental health services and empathic-oriented teaching as being a sound investment for preparing children to meet the vocational challenges of adulthood by supporting them toward emotional well-being and social adjustment (Moustakas 1966, pp. v–vi).

We might conceive of the presenting problem of the intact child in most general terms: Typically, children deal with life circumstances in a range of varied degrees of resiliency and effectiveness (Shaffer 1956). How a child adapts will depend upon his or her constitutional predisposition as well as the quality of environmental support and

Children with handicaps can often work with independence and minimal adaptations. Despite this child's multiple impairments, she demonstrates a quiet determination and intensity in her work.

nurturing. As Lowenfeld theorized in his discussion of objective and subjective responses to stimuli, children will respond and adapt differently to identical situations (1957). A common example of this in the intact population is the case of the brother and sister whose parents have divorced. One child endures the trauma adaptively, while the other's devastation drives him or her to depression, substance abuse or any number of other maladaptive responses.

There are uncountable scenarios of personal crisis that can beset the intact child in contemporary Western culture. Divorce occurs in three out of four families; it splits parents, grandparents and children apart emotionally, financially and geographically. Substance abuse and codependency occur with frightening regularity, while sexual, physical and emotional abuse are also rising in frequency. Parents are often absentee custodians, with both mothers and fathers working longer and harder to meet the requisite standards of living. Often the children themselves are prematurely pressured into preparing for their adult lives, with child precocity being one of the most revered values of the middle class.

There is also an ever-widening gap between material wealth and impoverishment in contemporary society. Never before have so many increased their standard of living while so many others languish in poverty. The discrepancies between family support, health care and education are severe, despite years of government funding and social reforms. Children raised in these dangerous and depressing environments turn to gangs, crime, drugs, sex and other destructive forms of social and self-abuse. For those educators working within our inner cities, these chronic problems have become the norm. Children who would ordinarily be considered educable mentally retarded, conduct disordered, or substance abusive may make up a major segment of the school population; thus numbing and overwhelming those educators responsible for their care.

The influx of foreign children into this country's school systems may also necessitate profound adjustments for all children. In several states (California, New York, Texas) former minorities—Latinos and blacks—are now in the majority (Schwartz 1989). The tensions which arise from cultural diversity and discrepancy have forced educators to address this problem on a group basis with minimal emphasis upon the fate of the individual (American Folk Life Center, Library of Congress 1989).

The world is in a state of change unequalled in history. Technology has affected everything and has overtaken our capacity to adjust our values and morals to cope with such sweeping changes. The fabric of the family unit, the workplace, our forms of recreation and socialization have been completely upended, causing confusion and anxiety in both adults and children. The world is now incomprehensibly dangerous, with the nuclear threat, worldwide environmental poisoning and population explosions posing problems of greater enormity than children in any other period of history have had to face. Unfortunately, spiritual support has been supplanted by an emphasis upon short-term gains in material objects. Children may have little recourse but to become increasingly greedy and to crave material comforts to ward off the stresses of the modern world (Kramer 1971). Other reactions often take the form of boredom, cynicism, apathy and nihilism. These feelings often reflect an overwhelming sense of powerlessness and hopelessness.

The intact child should be supported with an empathic atmosphere which places value upon individual expression. In a time of mass production, mass agriculture, mass housing and mass education, the art studio can become a bastion of individuality. There children can exercise an element of mastery over their lives and discover a sense of beauty. Individualized attention to both educational and therapeutic needs of intact children forms the basis and starting point for therapeutic art education.

THE ARTISTICALLY TALENTED

Artistically talented individuals possess a specific aptitude, such as precocious ability in drawing skills, visual perception, or creative problem-solving (Henley 1986). They should not be confused with the intellectually gifted, who process facts, ideas and relationships with rapidity and thoroughness that is above the norm. There is a demonstrated relationship between artistic precosity and high intelligence, however, and it is not unusual for a child to be both artistically and intellectually gifted (Barron 1963).

The most common identifying trait of the artistically talented is an aptitude in drawing which is manifested at an early age and is characterized by a well-developed representational style. Often these children's drawings are richly elaborated with details, themes and other embellishments which enliven and personalize the work. Guilford (1967) considers "divergent thinking" to be central to these characteristics. She sites the fluency or quantity of ideas, the flexibility, breadth or originality of responses as correlating to superior performance. Torrence (1976) drew upon these criteria in developing a test for creative thinking which has been adapted by art educators for the purposes of identifying creative potential (Silver 1978). Kramer (1971) takes a more psychodynamic view of the artistically talented, describing them as children whose powers of sublimation are particularly well developed. This infers that an innate predisposition for art is coupled with intense libidinal energy which is invested with an emotional charge, an economy of means and a capacity for expansiveness with regard to visual and creative problem solving.

In any event, the criteria for identifying artistic talent reflects upon the nature of their presenting problem in generally two ways: The first supposes that the child is well adjusted within his or her talent; while the second infers that the giftedness has been somehow frustrated or thwarted resulting in an "underachieving talented child" (Kirk and Gallagher 1989). Although they share the distinction of being talented, these two groups have disparate program needs. The former group will require programs which address their need for enrichment, while the latter require modifications which address the antagonisms which have rendered them maladjusted. The presenting problems of these children may mirror those of the learning disabled or emotionally handicapped.

The cognitive and creative needs of the well-adjusted, talented child call for more advanced and stimulating problem-solving activities. These may include exploratory and experimental projects which incorporate both traditional media and unusual materials which challenge divergent abilities. Individual study projects will allow the talented child to research and experiment at his or her own pace, while also creating an atmosphere which promotes originality. It is often a project, a theme or a technique's unique qualities that motivates the talented child, as opposed to simply accelerating a task (Kirk and Gallagher 1962). While advanced studio work may be integral to challenging the talented child, promoting a child's curiosity, intuition and thirst for learning are more often the key to maintaining a high level of motivation.

Managing the precocious child can sometimes be a challenge in itself for the art educator. Talented children, whose spirits have not been crushed or dulled by their home or school experiences, are often given to candor, contentiousness and rule-breaking. They rarely accept a teacher's unsubstantiated claim or tenet. On the contrary, they are more likely to rebel, reject or ignore anything which smacks of the status quo. Teachers who present material in a dogmatic, rote or unimaginative manner are likely to be challenged by the talented child. Strategies predicated upon rigid procedure or standardized solutions may be similarly challenged or rejected by these individuals.

The artistically talented require greater challenges which may take the form of advanced techniques, sophisticated media and individualized instruction. This high school freshman is an accomplished and published cartoonist.

Unlike the oppositional behavior of the normal child, the provocative behavior of the gifted may contain an aspect of precocious reason and deep insight. In their ability to associate, interrelate and evaluate a number of ideas, these children are able to reach entirely new lines of thinking and perceiving. This power of synthesizing fresh solutions to timeworn problems is often one of the hallmarks of the truly gifted and talented child.

It is the task of the art educator to create an atmosphere free of restrictions that promotes the flourishing of skills, originality and productivity. In the role of facilitator, the art educator can assist the talented child by structuring and guiding the art experience so that talent does not flounder in disorganization or a theoretical vacuum. These children function remarkably well in an inspirational or intuitive mode, yet will often need assistance in grounding their ideas. This is often the root of the difficulty in dealing with the underachieving talented child. Kirk points out that a lack of clarity and definition of ideas often coexists with technical or creative precosity, resulting in a lack of practical implementation which often leads in turn to creative blockage. A balance be-

tween inspiration and firm decision-making and other functions of the ego must be maintained by these children so that ideas, regardless of how fantastic they are, can be implemented in concrete terms (Winner 1982). Only then will their art serve as self-expression *and* as a means of communication (Kramer 1971).

Motivational problems with the talented are also often rooted in the pressures that come with being seen as "brilliant." Insecurity, lack of confidence and chronic dissatisfaction over results are some maladaptive subjective responses to the high expectations of others. These children are also sometimes insecure in their breaking of social taboos and will keep low profiles so as to not attract the attentions of their often punitive peers and teachers. Some children actively withdraw and become isolated socially, with only their art being a saving grace. Unless these children are guided supportively, their productivity and motivation may diminish and they may lapse into the secure and anonymous confines of an "average" performance.

It is a commonly held perception that the artistically talented are, as a group, unorthodox individuals. The contentious, yet highly sensitive and delicate nature of these children is often a liability in itself, especially when their appearance or actions do not endear them to their peers or teachers. In some cases such acting out is naive in its purpose; art students have traditionally been free-spirited and are encouraged to stretch the limits of appearance, visual vocabularies, and social customs. In other cases, anti-authoritarianism is more pronounced, with the child attempting to gain attention through outlandish, obscene or other controversial art. This behavior becomes problematic when the antisocial aspects of the activity begin to overshadow the aesthetic/creative attributes of the work. Historically, the line between raw provocation and aesthetic expression is ambiguous at best. Deciphering, managing and supporting the artistically talented student who is exploring this line is the responsibility of the art instructor; he or she must promote experimentation in a responsible way.

LEARNING DISABILITIES

Learning disabilities now affect almost 50% of the student population (Kirk and Gallagher 1989). The term is a catchall label which includes the dyslexic, the perceptionally impaired, those with attention deficit disorders, the neurologically impaired and the hyperactive. All of these groups may vary widely in presentation and degrees of severity. In the milder forms, the learning disabled is associated with erratic or underachieving academic performance despite the fact that the child possesses average or even superior intellectual ability. Although the intellect is considered to be intact, the etiology of the learning impairment is seen to be organically based, with central neurological dysfunction being the central cause of the diverse symptoms. (Federal Register 1977). However, this contention has been challenged by researchers who insist an organic cause has never been actually proven.

The list of presenting problems that may emerge in this population are lengthy and varied. They include hyperactivity, perceptual–motor impairment, emotional lability, attention deficits, impulsivity, memory–recall problems, discrete learning problems (which may be specific to a particular cognate area such as reading comprehension or math skills), as well as a range of other neurological "soft" signs: (Bryan and Bryan 1986).

Learning Disabilities
The learning disabled child's performance in the artroom may appear erratic and it may be difficult to assess or pinpoint the areas of difficulty. I have observed children who have trouble following verbal instructions or a sequence of steps in a project. Calculating measurements with a ruler might be difficult for one child, while copying a design off the board might give another child problems. Some children may do adequate or even excellent work, yet require extra time to complete a project. In other children, the deficits will not affect the learn-

ing process as much as their behavior. They may lack concentration or fail to follow social protocols or safety procedures. In the mildly learning disabled, the presenting problem is often the dramatic peaks and valleys in their performance. I have seen children who could draw with great facility, but could not tie their shoes with any dexterity at all. Or children who could not follow a compound verbal direction, yet when given a demonstration, out-produced every other child in the class. These discrepancies in performance or "soft" neurological signs are often overlooked by the teacher because they are inconsistently presented and difficult to detect unless comprehensive testing is undertaken. If properly identified, these signs alert the educator to modify his or her expectations and to offer increased tolerance and patience, as well as to modify the program to address the specific or general deficits.

It is important that the deficits be addressed in a low-keyed, non issue-oriented manner. Given their high level of functioning and acute social awareness, these children may be extrasensitive to their problems. The child who is not managing his or her problem adequately may easily give way to frustration, apathy, defeatism, anger or even rage.

In keeping with a least restrictive philosophy, deficits need to be unobtrusively accommodated with a great deal of camouflaging. These accommodations should facilitate the child's functioning in the class, using whatever modifications are called for to meet the specific needs without calling undue attention to the child or the handicap.

Attention Deficit Disorder with Hyperactivity (ADHD)

Approximately 20% of those with learning disabilities also present with attention deficits and hyperactivity (Silver 1990). In most of these ADHD cases, problems with academic underachievement are overshadowed by attention deficits and behavioral disorders. These often take the form of hyperactive, hyperdistractive and impulsive behaviors which preclude the application of the child's intellectual powers. Thus the ADHD child may

have difficulties staying situated, focusing on a task for any length of time, blocking out extraneous sights and sounds, or processing verbal directions or demonstrations. The impulsivity displayed by these children can constitute a danger to themselves and others, especially when dangerous tools are used. Social and work relations with peers are often strained and a general atmosphere of chaos and disruption seems to follow these children whenever they may be working (Gonnick-Barris 1976).

The chief concern in working with this population is providing proper structure. Those with ADHD often require a highly controlled and directed program in which every facet of the art activity and studio procedure must be painstakingly spelled out. Verbal instructions should use short, decipherable, concrete terms and include a visual demonstration. Constant cuing will probably be required to increase the child's awareness of his or her conduct. This is especially crucial when the student has little control over body movements or lacks the ability to monitor social interactions, otherwise these students may inadvertently create enormous conflict in the artroom (especially when finished artworks are at stake). (Insights 1987).

Children with ADHD are often treated with medications, such as ritalin, which decrease hyperactivity in often dramatic terms. (Lerner 1981). To support the effects of medication, a behavioral modification program can provide the child with constant feedback as to his or her progress or regression during the art session. When the problem is distractibility rather than acting out behavior the teacher must adapt the environment to the child's needs, such as using study carrels, to assist concentration and ability to focus. Such a program might be considered restricted or contradictory to the least restrictive policy, yet this is one situation where if we are to preserve order in the artroom, both for the staff and peers, we must resort to these extreme measures.

VISUAL IMPAIRMENTS

Blindness occurs in degrees. Complete blindness, particularly the congenital type (from birth), is the most severe form, followed by adventitious complete blindness (which occurs during one's lifetime), with partial (legal) blindness followed by the milder forms of visual defects (where one wears corrective glasses) (B. Lowenfeld 1955). The term "partially sighted" means seriously defective vision with less than 20/200 acuity in the better eye after correction, or in the case of tunnel vision, peripheral vision which subtends an angle less than twenty degrees (Kirk and Gallagher 1989). The prevalence of mild defects requiring correction is the highest form of physical anomaly, with approximately twenty percent of school children wearing corrective lenses (Dalton 1963). Because of the range of visual defects, the presenting problems naturally differ depending upon severity.

The Completely Blind
Completely blind children must cope in a world which is profoundly lacking or distorted in stimulation. Beginning with infancy, these children must learn to relate to a mother they cannot see and an environment that must seem unfathomable. Only through persistent, yet gentle attempts at stimulating the blind child's residual senses can he or she develop a sense of self, of belonging and other forms of orientation that assist in developing firm object relations. This profound developmental arrest often takes the form of autistic-like object relations which constitute the presenting problem in this population (Fraiburg 1977).

Fraiburg found decidedly autistic behavior with particular hypersensitivity and resistance to environmental conditions among blind children who have not had the benefit of compensatory stimulation (including maternal nurturing). It is common for the blind child to be aversive to activities which expect participation in the form of tactile involvement or body movement. Many of these non-stimulated children will respond by a flight or fight reaction, either escaping from the activity physi-

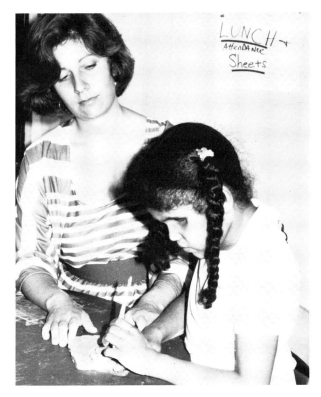

Young blind children require extra guidance and stimulation if they are to actively explore media and develop an awareness of the art product. This child reached a stage of security and independence after two years of patient guidance.

cally or emotionally, or resisting through aggression (Tinbergen 1983).

It is imperative then that visually impaired children receive attention as early in life as possible. Because sensory stimulation activities are well within the art sphere, the therapeutic art teacher is an ideal interventionist for this purpose. Activities may include working with textures, manipulating different materials—such as water or sand—and experiencing other design elements through residual senses. The purpose is to allow the child to feel sufficiently secure and oriented so as to arouse his or her curiosity about the environment without the usual accompanying anxiety.

The art educator should be aware of the perceptual modes through which the blind child will function. Lowenfeld (1957) discussed a theory involving the visual and haptic modes of experiencing the environment. Despite total blindness, the child operating in the visual mode organizes stimuli in a manner reminiscent of visual discrimination. To accomplish this seemingly impossible task implies that the child's sense of space—how it is organized, its scale, its workings—is well-developed. Children of this type are often obsessed by assertively exploring their environments so that an overall image is somehow developed in their mind's eye. Often they will ask for the art educator to describe scenes or objects, feeding their thirst for visual stimuli—despite the fact that they have never experienced sight in their lives.

Lowenfeld's other perceptual type is the child who experiences in the haptic mode (through the sense of touch). These children are much less assertive in exploring their environment and do not have an advanced sense of object constancy or permanence. Similarly, their overall object relations are impaired, because the self is perceived in a much more primitive manner. However, the haptic mode can serve a strong adaptive function particularly when the blindness is complicated by mental retardation or autism. Often the caution these children exhibit acts as a regulatory mechanism which feeds the child stimulation in tactile doses he or she can comprehend and assimilate. In this sense, however, haptic perception constitutes a less adaptive defense mechanism than the extroverted and stimulatory visual mode.

The Partially Sighted or Legally Blind
The partially sighted child has the advantage of being able to process at least a portion of the visual stimuli in the environment. This crucial element aligns this handicap more with other physical handicaps, such as deafness. These children often possess adequate object relations and are able to manage visual stimulation without the anxiety or resistance often evidenced by the blind child. Most researchers have concluded that the general

health, psychological adjustment and intelligence of partially sighted children are on par or slightly below average when compared with their intact peers (Myers 1976). This infers that, given modifications in materials, techniques and the studio environment, partially sighted children should perform similarly to their intact peers. However, there is a subgroup of the partially sighted who have sustained multiple impairments due to congenital problems, such as prenatal rubella, which change this prognosis considerably. Among the multiply handicapped, partially sighted, the presenting problem often echoes or imitates mental retardation, autism or complete blindness. Developmental arrest, retarded intellect and disturbed affect are all manifest in differing degrees of severity. In these cases, there must be a shifting of focus to those impairments which constitute the primary, most debilitating handicapping condition.

This partially sighted student relies upon her residual vision, as opposed to her haptic sensations.

THE HEARING IMPAIRED

There are three hearing impaired groups: children who are pre-lingually deaf (deaf from birth), the post-lingually deaf (became deaf after language had developed), and the hard of hearing. All three populations are characterized by a significant hearing loss which deprives them from using sounds in the environment on a functional basis (Streng et al. 1958). Hearing impairment may be due to conductive loss (which inhibits vibrations from reaching the auditory nerve) such as wax blockage or a broken ear drum, sensory–neural loss (in which the auditory nerve that transmits the impulse to the brain is damaged) or central deafness due to injury in the central nervous system. Regardless of the etiology, children who have sustained a hearing loss of over sixty decibels are considered to be educationally deaf—meaning that specialized programs are required (Kirk 1989). This means that an alternative means of communication must be practiced in the classroom so that sensory stimulation and information can be provided. The current philosophy is "total communication"—every means of communication is pursued, including sign language, amplification (hearing aids), speech, lip reading and writing, as well as developing a visual vocabulary through art. With these avenues available to the deaf child, he or she can then begin to compensate for the missing vital auditory input.

In working with congenitally deaf children, the presenting problems do not focus as much on their hearing impairments as on the grave difficulties they have in conceiving, developing and functionally using language. For the pre-lingually deaf child in particular, language acquisition is a most arduous skill; for those who cannot hear what they must learn, it is a task of immense proportions (Moores 1978).

Language is crucial for developing concept formation. This means that unless the deaf child understands that symbols stand for concepts, there will be difficulties in comprehension and thinking skills. This is especially the case when we try to teach a deaf child intangible concepts which go beyond concrete objects. In the art setting much of our material involves the abstract concepts of aesthetics and the subjective areas of emotion and nuance. Without sufficient language, the deaf child may have difficulty articulating his ideas through art, regardless of how rich his life experiences or fantasy life may be.

For instance, a hearing impaired child working on a life drawing may have sign language to describe the figure and its features, as well as some effective signs for such concepts as happy, sad, excited, bored, etc. However, the child's language capability may not keep pace with his or her capacity for expressivity. The child may have no signs for more subtle shades of emotion. Thus the "sad" face may not be sad at all, but more introspective, peaceful or pensive. The child who has only one generic term (or sign) for a variety of facial expressions cannot hope to explore the nuances of theme with the same sensitivity or insight as if he or she had a greater range of expressive words (or concepts) at his or her disposal.

This impaired process of abstraction has historically posed problems for deaf children in the visual arts. For years, the purported concreteness of deaf children was used as a rationale for not including them in programs which emphasized abstract concepts and subject matter. Only survival subjects such as speech, language and vocational training were deemed appropriate for these children's needs. The child who has suffered under this system and has not had the benefit of arts programs may offer initial resistance to dealing with concepts and activities which have little immediate survival value and focus purely upon elaborating an idea. It is a certainty, however, that the capacity for reflection, for processing ideas and feelings as well as expressing them through visual art is within the potential of deaf children. Art specialists who have developed successful programs such as Silver (1978) have disproven the myth that deaf children cannot benefit from the arts. Given sufficient support and some compensatory modifications in the teaching strategies, deaf children can progress on an even par with the intact hearing child (Myklebust 1960).

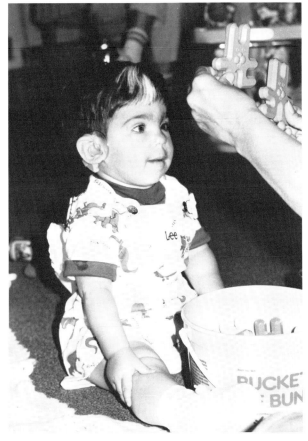

Young hearing impaired children also require extra stimulation to compensate for gaps in sensory information, so that art expression becomes a natural extension of their communication.

Even when paralyzed, cerebral palsied children can often work with minimal adaptations. They are often quite independent minded and resent unneeded assistance.

There is a disturbing footnote to all of this. The deaf population is currently in a state of change, with many more multiply handicapped children with hearing impairments now supplanting the "normal" deaf child (Schlesinger and Meadow 1972, Carden 1986). Increasing numbers of socially and economically disadvantaged, minority, emotionally handicapped and multiply physically handicapped children are entering the system. This means that the teacher will in the future encounter increasing numbers of deaf children who have secondary deficits which in some cases prompts a shift in the presenting problem away from the sensory deficit toward issues pertaining to behavior control, learning remediation and cultural assimilation (Henley 1987). With the unfortunate rise in secondary handicaps comes the need to develop programs which can address the total emotional and cognitive needs of the contemporary deaf child. It will be recognized that art programs have that capacity to engage the deaf child on all these fronts.

ORTHOPEDIC IMPAIRMENTS

Cerebral Palsy
Cerebral palsy is a crippling impairment in which parts of the brain are injured (either prior, during or after birth) resulting in motor coordination handicaps. The extent of motor involvement can be as slight as a limp or it may be as profound as paralysis, spasticity or speech problems, as well as associated disorders of learning problems, sensory deficits, convulsive and behavioral disturbances of organic origin. Cerebral palsy is differentiated by four major types: Spastic paralysis involves damage to the cerebral cortex where impulses, contractions or stimulations are controlled and suppressed. Athetosis infers a lesion in the fore- or mid-brain, in which motor activities such as walking are affected, resulting in lurching, writhing or

Cerebral palsied children are not always profoundly debilitated. This student is ambulatory and can, with extra effort, accomplish craftwork requiring fine motor control despite her spasticity and weakness.

stumbling kinds of gaits. Ataxia is due to lesions in the cerebellum and also affects one's gait, with unsteady movements and stumbling being the major features. Although Kirk and Gallagher (1989) separately differentiate these types, they can occur in combinations with varying degrees of severity.

The task for the teacher of palsied children is two-fold: making necessary adaptations in the artroom to insure a least restrictive environment and maintaining the child's positive, well integrated self-image. The first concern is rather straightforward: devising adaptive devices which allow the child to participate fully (such as a paintbrush holder which compensates for rigid, immobile hands). Promoting a positive self-concept, however, may be more difficult, since it involves confronting the deformities and limitations these chil-

dren experience. It is disconcerting enough for these children to be in such a physical state; yet to possess an intact (or nearly so) intellect and maintain a healthy disposition about the body can be doubly difficult.

These children may remain aware of social situations with regard to peers, family and community relationships. When the capacity to handle these relationships becomes strained, often the result of such frustration is immature behavior, shyness, verbal aggression or withdrawal into fantasy (Anderson 1978). A more adaptive response is overcompensation, in which the child may engage in schoolwork or social relationships with almost frightening intensity and energy, which often results in the child becoming overextended or physically depleted. The effects of such overachieving should be monitored so that a balance can be struck which recognizes the need to achieve while also developing recognition and insight as to one's limitations. The art process can play a crucial role in developing a positive sense of self, as well as allowing the cerebral palsied child to vent frustrations, explore feelings and communicate ideas which may not be possible through verbal means.

Art experiences must be devised to exploit any strength or ability which the cerebral palsied child possesses. Emphasis should be placed upon developing themes and techniques which compensate for motor deficits in ways that are socially normal and age appropriate. A positive self-concept can be developed in these children, given sensitively administered modifications that maximize challenge yet are not overly frustrating. When cerebral palsied children are treated as normal, well-adjusted art students, one is often surprised at how eventually inhibitions, shame, fear and frustration diminish.

Congenital, Traumatic and Infectious Paralysis

Children who are paralyzed from birth often suffer from spina bifida, a congenital defect which results in spinal membranes protruding through a cleft in the vertebral column (Lindsay 1972). Spina bifida victims are usually paraplegic, meaning they are paralyzed from the waist down and do not have sensation or bladder control. Most often these children are confined to wheelchairs, although recent developments in surgical interventions have allowed increasing numbers of spina bifida victims to walk with support.

Victims of traumatic paralysis have experienced an accident in which the spinal cord has been pinched, severed or otherwise damaged. The severity of paralysis is dependent upon what part of the spine has been injured; vertebra injured in the neck result in quadriplegia, while injuries to the back result in paraplegia. As with spina bifida, sensation, bladder, bowel and sexual functions can be incapacitated with traumatic paralysis. Victims may also experience respiratory problems and other medical complications, particularly with upper vertebra damage.

Infectious paralysis includes conditions such as poliomyelitis, muscular dystrophy, arthritis and Guillain-Barré syndrome. Each of these diseases varies in severity and each requires intensive medical and rehabilitation intervention in order for art education to resume.

In all three types of paralysis, the child's physical condition inevitably affects his or her capacity for personal and social adjustment. Cruikshank (1955) has found that these individuals may have difficulty facing social situations and building self-esteem and confidence, particularly if the paralysis is traumatic or infectious. Presenting problems often include depression or lack of motivation, high frustration, anger, guilt, regression to more infantile behavior, substance abuse, and over-compensation which lead the child to overwork the body attempting to reclaim its normal functioning. It is crucial that these individuals be provided with a challenging yet supportive environment, in which the drive to succeed and surmount the handicap is balanced by an acceptance of limitations and compromised expectations in art, school and life.

MILDLY MENTALLY RETARDED

The mildly mentally retarded child often appears to be normal, particularly in early childhood, but later begins to exhibit developmental delays and severe learning problems. Unlike those with severe or profound retardation, educable children have usually not sustained brain damage nor is their handicap traceable to other organic etiologies. Because there is no clear-cut or prevalent cause of the retardation, this is one of the more ambiguous disorders identifiable mainly by its symptoms or characteristics. Kirk and Gallagher (1989) refer to a higher incidence of vision, hearing and motor deficits in this group than is the norm—also, low performance on verbal and non-verbal intelligence tests (I.Q. between 50 and 80), slowness of overall maturation, short attention span, low frustration tolerance and poor impulse control. Kirk points

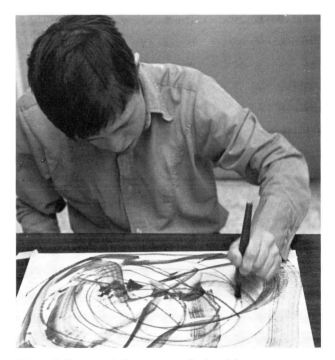

The mildly retarded are typically healthy appearing children who cannot achieve at the same rate or complexity as their intact peers.

out, as do other writers (Ingram 1960), that the educable child is often brought up in a substandard socioeconomic environment. Recent studies have found a prevalence of minority children who have been raised under conditions of poor nutrition, poor pre- and postnatal medical care and in hostile environments that lack adequate stimulation (Hewett 1974). Thus, it is conceivable that an educable child may not have any appreciable physical anomalies, but suffers retardation purely on the basis of environmental deprivation.

The thrust of much educational programming for these children focuses upon teaching vocational skills, social relations, leisure time activities and emotional stability. Art has been used with this population as a means of addressing *all* of these goals, using manipulative and problem-solving activities to reinforce vocational skills while also emphasizing possible avocational applications. Thus, one often sees the educable mentally retarded involved in projects such as weaving, assemblage, woodworking and other applied arts (Anderson 1978).

While a highly directive and applied approach to art instruction is certainly a viable strategy for this population, one should not discount these childrens' capacities for expressive work as well. Although educable mentally retarded children have traditionally been considered concrete in their thinking processes, they have been shown to be capable of spontaneous creativity (Kenny 1979). Indeed, given this population's propensity for loose object relations and reality testing, their art is often pervaded by the impossible and even the dreamlike. Although pathological in nature, this feature can be used by the art educator as a point of departure for activities that allow for expressions of the fantastic while developing the child's ability to discriminate between fantasy and reality.

The presenting problem for this population essentially defies generalization. The characteristics of the mild mentally retarded child are extremely diverse. One may find a child's social skills immature; behavior may be impulsive; learning can be painfully slow; self-concept may be impoverished; thinking processes disturbed. Art can play a vital therapeutic role for these children given the absence of academic pressure and emphasis upon "correct" responses. The mildly retarded child can find self-worth, confidence and mastery of skills in the artroom, when in other areas his deficits are more obvious.

THE PROFOUNDLY RETARDED

This population has only recently been introduced to the art education setting, following the implementation of the 1977 mainstreaming law. These children were traditionally perceived as being incapable of benefiting from educational or therapeutic experiences. The etiology of the profoundly retarded is usually rooted in pre-, peri-, or postnatal brain damage which results in an extremely low I.Q. (between 10 and 25), often bizarre behavior, gross physical anomaly, and a profound incapacity to manage in classroom settings. Prior to PL94–142, these children often languished in residential institutions which offered little more than custodial care. Programs were later developed which addressed such issues as developing self-help skills and other basic activities of daily living. While self-help is certainly an appropriate program emphasis for these children, it has been demonstrated that they can participate and derive benefits from art activities (Henley 1991).

The presenting problems indigenous to this population are many, but they stem from one source. The lack of impulse control which characterizes the profoundly retarded pervades their functioning in various maladaptive ways, such as pica (ingesting inedible objects), bingeing, ruminating, self-stimulating, masturbation and so on. Needless to say, these behaviors are indicative of the most primitive psychological functioning, which explains the predominance of autistic-like behavior found in this population (Baumiester 1973). Partic-

ularly when placed in stressful, high expectation settings such as the classroom, behavioral problems often escalate. Tantrums, assaultiveness and self-injurious behavior sometimes occur because more adaptive responses are beyond the repertoire of behavioral responses of these children. The task for the teacher is to guide the profoundly retarded child to hold his or her instinctual needs in abeyance and to channel them through more adaptive experiences such as the art process. The goal is to assist and support the child through the developmental milestones of object relations (Wilson 1977).

Although the congenital basis of profound retardation makes it particularly intractable and the prognosis for progress is poor, this can be a most rewarding population with which to work. The teacher who can adjust to the behaviors of these children and reassess his or her own expectations

The profoundly retarded often require one-on-one supervision and adapted equipment in order to participate in the art activity. This child often ate the clay medium, hence the clay is made of salt dough. The teacher monitors the child's movements closely while the chair and table arrangement secures the child in place.

of what constitutes progress often can effect wondrous changes in both behavior and artistic productivity. An essential aspect of this process is to find some positive aspect of the child which can be exploited. Because minimizing academic pressures to perform is naturally stimulating for the senses, the art activity is an ideal vehicle for developing the sensory, cognitive, affective and manual capabilities in these children.

Severely retarded students often need hand-over-hand interventions to assist them. This student has already drawn an interesting head type shape. The art teacher then interceded by assisting the student in placing the facial features.

THE SEVERELY RETARDED CHILD

Trainable or severely retarded children have usually sustained some form of genetic, infectious, or traumatic brain damage which limits their functioning to an extremely low cognitive and developmental level. Their subnormal I.Q. (between 25 and 50) and arrested motivation and behavioral symptoms usually require a self-contained, highly individualized program. Unlike profoundly retarded children, these children do have the capacity to learn self-help skills, adjust to social protocols and function adaptively in academic and sheltered vocational programs (Kirk 1989). In addition, moderate children also have the capacity to be creative and productive participants in art activities, provided that instructional strategies and therapeutic interventions are geared to their needs.

In studying the art of the retarded, most researchers draw upon the work of moderate mentally retarded children particularly those with Down syndrome, since they are functioning high enough to produce representational imagery yet low enough to clearly exhibit indications of intellectual and developmental deficits. The abstract, primitivistic quality of their figurative imagery often is reminiscent of African or even modern art. The children's developmental immaturity translates into simplified yet bizarre forms which are often endearing to the informed viewer. The fact that their impoverished object relations coexist with sufficient intellect, often allows these children to create interesting images. This productive paradox may also indicate the presence of pathologies which require art education and therapeutic attention. Much of the art of this population emerges from the defenses the child employs to ward off the anxiety and stress that come with instinctual pressures. Thus, the presenting problems of the severely retarded include rigidity, self-stimulatory behavior, obsessive/compulsive reactions, tantrums, and disassociative or disturbed thinking processes. It is the teacher's task to support the child in developing less stultifying defenses so that more flexible behaviors can be achieved (Kramer 1971).

While sufficient ego strength for sublimation is rare among the severely retarded, stereotyped and otherwise neurotic behaviors can be relaxed and expanded so that both adaptive functioning and art experience are enhanced (Henley 1986, Wilson 1979). Art instruction and therapeutic programs for the trainable or severely retarded must maintain a delicate balance between structure, direction and open-endedness. The trainable child can respond to basic techniques and materials given a careful task analysis of what's involved in manipulating, sequencing and improvising within the medium. These children often have the capacity to create wholly unexpected solutions which combine the naive charm of young children and the deceptive sophistication of primitive styles of imagery. This paradox makes this population a most rewarding and challenging one with which to work.

EMOTIONAL HANDICAPS

Emotional handicaps include a wide range of classifications which include emotional disturbances, behavior disorders, conduct disorders or social maladjustment. Although these terms vary depending upon the severity of the problem, they all point to extreme deviations of behavior which are chronic and intense, and in conflict with social or cultural norms. The Federal Register definition outlined in PL94-142 defines these as "children who demonstrate inability to build or maintain interpersonal relationships, display inappropriate behavior, pervasive mood disturbances and phobic reactions." Kirk (1989) also identifies children who translate fears into psychosomatic symptoms (accident-proneness, malingering), regress to immature or primitive behaviors (impulsivity, low frustration tolerance, egocentricity), exhibit unbridled aggression and hostility, as well as withdrawal and inhibited behaviors. With the more severe forms of emotional disturbance, such as in schizophrenia and autism, the characteristic symptoms may include delusions, hallucinations, catatonia, autistic withdrawal, and obsessive/compulsive disorders.

With the enormous breadth of characteristics presented, I will focus first upon those children whom teachers will encounter in mainstream settings, then describe the more severe forms found in self-contained classrooms and finally, those found in special education settings or hospitals.

Behavioral and Conduct Disorders

In the mainstream setting, where the art teacher may be working with twenty to thirty students at a time, the inclusion of a child who is disobedient, hostile to authority, destructive, boisterous or otherwise acting out can be overwhelming. Children such as these are not sufficiently disturbed to warrant a self-contained setting, since they can often function in the mainstream with the proper modifications. However, their impulsivity often has the effect of creating intense conflict and chaos in the class. Often the educational experience of the intact children is compromised by the disruptive influences of these children.

The etiology of behavior or conduct disorders is complex and diverse. Depending upon the theoretical perspective, one may cite biological causes such as minimal brain dysfunction (which may equally result in learning disability) or metabolic imbalances (such as bi-polar mania/depression). A psychodynamic practitioner on the other hand may analyze the dynamics of early childhood interactions with the family and environment in concert with the underlying or unconscious pressures of instinctual or drive processes. In this view, early rejection, abuse or other traumatic experiences may be carried through and reflect later behaviors in the school situation. Learning theorists such as Skinner (1965) would view negativistic behaviors from a stimulus-response perspective. The child has learned through experience that acting out will bring about favorable consequences. For instance the child acting out in class may have learned that this will bring about the attention of peers or teacher. The fact that this attention may be punitive or unpleasant in nature is evidently worth the trouble to the child who craves it.

Needless to say, the complexity and depth of these dynamics make for presenting problems which may be well beyond the scope of the art teacher's capabilities. One is often left to deal solely with the manifest symptoms of aggression, disruptiveness and disobedience without being able to address the underlying causes of the behavior. Given this difficult state of affairs, how does the art teacher contribute through the art program? In least restrictive terms, children should be able to interact with peers, participate in projects and generally function freely as members of the group until they demonstrate that more structure may be needed for support. Support in this context might involve verbal cues, modified seating and projects or behavioral programs which involve modification techniques. I am generally not in favor of behavioral modification; however, as a last resort some children may have to be offered material compensation in return for increased self-control. This is not to say that such an approach cannot be implemented in a humanistic and empathic manner. The hard-won rapport and sense of trust which is built between child and teacher are often the difference between an effective and ineffective behavioral program.

In working with this most difficult population, it is crucial that the art teacher retain a sense of perspective. We cannot hope to heal wounds which were traumatically sustained over the course of years. We can only work with the children in an empathic yet firm manner, demonstrating to the child that we care, that we are concerned and determined to stand beside him or her as much as our position allows. However, our expectations with regard to a return on our investment of kindness and understanding must be minimal. We must appreciate that what the child gives back may be the best he or she can do under the circumstances. As we strive to remain consistent and dependable, we must watch for the opportunity for making a positive connection. Given enough time and luck, positive gains might outnumber demoralizing regressions. Success then becomes a matter of small victories, which may or may not add up enough to sustain the child during his or her life at school.

Aggressive Behavior Disorders

Sociopathic children are usually characterized by the lack of anxiety or guilt accompanying their severely aggressive behavior (Kirk 1989). Recent thinking in the area recognizes that socialized aggression may be a cultural phenomenon of the urban environment, where it is considered a survival trait (Bronfenbrenner 1979). Family and social values in this setting are seen to breed destructive role models. Children identify with family members or older peers on the street which in turn reinforces aggressive and often guilt-free behavior (Bandura 1977).

Given the severity of the aggression, which may include assaultive, delinquent and other violent behaviors, these children require a highly structured, strictly supervised program. To some extent, the severely disturbed, aggressive child who is in a hospital or self-contained program may be easier to work with than the mainstreamed behaviorally disturbed. Although the behaviors will be more noxious and difficult to handle, the severity of the condition will insure that the self-contained program has addressed these contingencies. Behavioral modification programs will be already instituted and monitored by specialists in this field. Expectations with regard to academic and behavioral achievement will be adjusted to bring them more in line with the childrens' capabilities. Generally, there will be more emphasis upon treating the underlying dynamics of the child's disturbance than in the mainstream setting, with greater emphasis upon therapeutic support in a multidisciplinary context.

Autism and Child Psychosis

Autistic children are emotionally and behaviorally handicapped children who may possess an intact intellect, yet suffer speech or language deficits. They are often intensely ritualistic and self-stimulatory, profoundly shy or avoidant of interpersonal relationships (including sometimes the family), as well as bizarre in their play or daily behavior (Kanner 1972). Although there is a small percentage of individuals who completely fulfill Kanner's criteria for classic autism, there are far more children who exhibit autistic-like behaviors (such as the mentally retarded child who is echolalic or the blind child who self-stimulates). The autistic are among the most demanding children to work with.

Often they are exceedingly sensitive to changes in routine, particularly as they relate to smells, sounds, objects or people in the environment. Their capacity to modulate incoming stimuli is often hyper- or hypo-sensitive. They may overact to some stimulation (such as screaming whenever they hear a car horn on the street) while in other situations they may be psycho-genetically deaf (such as when someone crashes a cymbal close to their ears, they do not even flinch). Needless to say, autistic children are emotionally primitive and have failed to develop any sense of ego or object relatedness. Their sense of self is so tentative that any threat to themselves (in the form of a changed routine or unfamiliar food for example) can precipitate extremely violent episodes as well as withdrawals which are equally severe. Those autistic children who have progressed in their capacity to participate in art activities often do so because the role of the teacher can be minimized. In this respect, the art materials act as a buffering agent, softening both the confrontary aspects of interaction, as well as serving as a link between child and staff.

Often, autistic children have accepted me more as the giver of art materials than for my nurturing qualities. The fact that this is often the first crucial step in establishing a relationship bears out the effectiveness of art programming as usually the first setting where mainstreaming is tried. While autistic individuals rarely achieve academically or emotionally normal relationships, they are capable of becoming productive artists producing images of astounding expressivity and uniqueness (Rimland 1978, Selfe 1977).

The symbiotic psychotic individual is one who has progressed through the stage of autistic isolation and avoidance and becomes fixed at a stage which is symbiotic with the mother figure. These children develop an extremely distorted, dependent relationship with the mother (Cameron 1963). While this condition too is rare in the classical sense, the art teacher may encounter children whose inability to separate from the mother precipitates panic or anxiety attacks similar to those of autistic children. Separation anxiety often surfaces in the art of these children.

The child schizophrenic may possess characteristics of both the autistic and symbiotic psychotic individual, but usually displays more advanced personality characteristics. The rudiments of ego functioning are established to the extent that the child usually can care for basic needs, attend school, etc. However, the onset of schizophrenia is marked by progressive intrusion of primary process material in the form of bizarre fantasies, delusions or hallucinations. Such thought or sensory disturbances can be terrifying for the child, as they can prompt severe regressions which potentially continue back to an autistic state (Cameron 1963). Like most forms of schizophrenia, the child form is usually treated with medication which is effective in minimizing delusions or hallucinations while also stabilizing anxiety levels and mood swings. Art educational programming for these children echoes that of other developmentally based disorders which focus upon building ego strength, and enhancing reality testing while minimizing stress in the learning environment.

chapter 4

Devising a Studio Space

The art-making environment influences every aspect of the child's performance. Work habits, behavior patterns and social exchanges will all be affected by the atmosphere of the art studio. As we address these aspects of performance it is important to realize how malleable our environment is—that the art teacher can, in most cases, create an environment which suits the temperament of staff and child alike, as well as positively affecting the quantity and quality of the art that is elicited. The immediate goal is to provide a minimally restrictive, lively environment which promotes intensive physical and mental concentration, as well as liberating the creative fervor which is latent in all children.

Often the art studio is the teacher's most telling statement about how he or she perceives or feels about art, its making and the part children play in this process.

It is an unavoidable reality that all programs are not equally endowed with the resources to create the "ideal" studio. Most art teachers I have known who have created successful environments have done so without large budgets (and in some cases without budgets at all). Aside from the requisites of being given a space—hopefully one which is well lit and with running water—these art teachers and art therapists most often rely upon their own resources and ingenuity to create a stimulating, personable and functional space, They solicit donations of such materials as motivational props, paper products, scraps of wood, metals and dry goods from museums, cafeterias, papermills, and building suppliers. They search through school basements for cast-off tables, chairs, rugs, partitions or other equipment which can be adapted improvised, and salvaged.

Resourcefulness, aesthetic sensibility and a commitment to arousing and guiding creative fervor are the art teacher's greatest and most important attributes. The studio which one creates will reflect these attributes and this forms the single most crucial element in facilitating the art process so that it is accessible to all children.

THE SELF-CONTAINED STUDIO

Whether a studio is spacious, airy and bathed in light, or cramped and dark, it is vital that the space be planned to offer optimum working conditions. This means that the space should be an effective teaching environment for the art teacher, as well as a good place for children to create and learn. In some instances, for example, this will mean media and tools will be invitingly laid out for self-initiated use, while in other instances materials will be kept from sight and issued in increments. Careful organization of the art environment will ultimately enhance the children's art experi-

Creating an atmosphere that is conducive to the moods and rhythms of the creative process is central to devising an effective studio space.

ences and allow for greater quality time to be spent on the individual child. The extra time devoted to this preparation will be repaid by the atmosphere of psychological safety it provides for the child.

To create an effective studio, consider partitioning the space in a flexible way, allowing for the adjusting and readjusting of the environment depending upon immediate need. Partitioning involves the placement of furniture, work tables, shop equipment and room dividers so as to organize and differentiate the work stations. The floor plan should harmoniously accommodate both the interior furnishings and inhabitants. Children should be allowed to move in a variety of ways: walking, wheelchairing, sitting, reaching and stretching. Furnishings must be arranged to provide barrier-free pathways. Traffic patterns should facilitate movement and avoid congestion or conflict. The floor plan should also allow for efficient material distribution, cleanup and room maintenance, and for the safe operation of shop equipment. The room must also be laid out to allow for efficient monitoring and supervision of children.

ZONING AND ACTIVITY CENTERS

Given sufficient space, I have always zoned the artroom into activity centers to provide an organized means of individualizing the art instruction so that both therapeutic and educational objectives can be better accomplished. Activity centers, differentiated by the media or technique, can serve as mini-studios where students can engage in divergent art activities while remaining in close proximity to the instructor for supervision and instruction.

One of the advantages of partitioning the studio by media or technique is that incompatible materials can be segregated from one another. For instance, the dust and mess produced in the clay or sculpture area can be controlled without contaminating the relatively clean life-drawing area. In a similar vein, the noise and sawdust emanating from the band saw in the wood center will not infringe upon students working on academics in the research area.

Some activity centers reflect the adaptations needed to address specific problems brought about by a child's emotional or learning disability. For instance, an emotionally disturbed or hyperkinetic child might need a localized, self-contained environment that can be effectively monitored and structured to encourage self-control. Children who are perceptionally impaired or learning disabled may become overstimulated by the audiovisual stimuli present in the normal art environment. In this case, such a child's work space might be a partitioned area devoid of all extraneous sights and sounds, with only a limited selection of materials available in order to encourage concentration on the art activity.

The artroom should reflect the needs and goals of the children, regardless of the resources available. I have instituted partitioning and zoning in basement classrooms, old servants' quarters and storefronts as well as in luxurious, custom-built art studios. What is needed is a sense of vision which sees the environment as an adaptable entity which can be shaped according to immediate need.

Depending upon the facility, and the needs of the populations served, the art teacher is at liberty to devise a number of activity centers. Zoning can be approached in several ways: by medium and techniques; by the group context, which recognizes the size of the class, the need for individual work stations, etc.; and by the degree of stimulation that is desired based on the capacity of the class or individuals to handle environmental stimuli. Activity centers may include a motivational center, a research or reading area, an exhibition or gallery space, technical centers (i.e., ceramics, woodworking, etc.) and a behavioral control area.

MOTIVATION

Many children with special needs have difficulty drawing upon their own internal resources (i.e., imagination, memory recall, etc.) to generate subject matter for their art. In many cases a child's impoverished home life may offer little stimula-

tion; in others, a physical disability involving the senses (such as sight or smell) might prevent a child from developing the urge to create. Whatever the case, a motivational area or simply a collection of motivational props may compensate for a lack of creative energy and ideation.

Sensory Stimulation

Many children with sensory deficits—the visually impaired, the autistic, the mentally retarded or the multiply handicapped—may initially not be able to work with regular art media. This is particularly true with very young students. They may find the material's texture or smell unpleasant, or they may ingest the medium as a means of exploring its properties. Many of these children are simply resistant to experiencing anything that is new or unfamiliar, making it almost impossible to expect normal participation and progress in the usual studio setting.

A sensory stimulation or motivation area can expose the resistant or immature child to a wide variety of tactile, visual and kinesthetic experiences in a secure and sheltered environment. Contained within the sensory stimulation area are different props and materials that engage the child in one or more sensory modes in a non-threatening, passive way. The child may begin participating by merely gazing into an aquarium or watching a movie screen for brief periods of time. He or she may be encouraged to follow the beam of a flashlight or to visually track a column of water being poured from a pitcher. As the child becomes oriented to the room and its objects, some basic play activities, such as interacting with a puppet, may be introduced. Once the child can tolerate touching and feeling different textures and consistencies, he or she is encouraged to explore and manipulate as many different kinds of objects as possible. The final goal is to reach a stage of self-initiation and interaction with the environment, where objects such as blocks are routinely observed, manipulated and eventually constructed into new forms and configurations. Once the child has reached this stage, the teacher can begin introducing basic

For children who are resistant to physical stimulation, puppets are often effective. Here the art therapist engages a hearing child of deaf parents. The child responded to this form of activity as a prelude to directly manipulating materials.

Sand and water play are important activities which set the stage for later art techniques of sculpture, painting and other art forms.

art techniques and mediums in the different activity centers of the art studio.

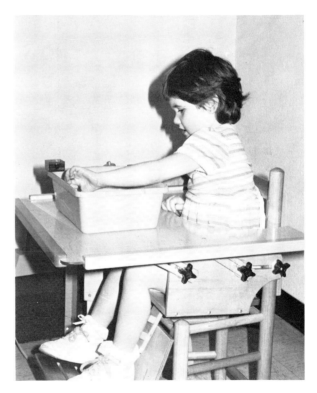

The most common introductory art activity is the water play table, where a child can touch, splash and play in warm soapy water. Even the most defensive child may tolerate this activity since its sensations will be as familiar and comforting as a bubble bath. From there the child can increase his or her active participation by pouring through sieves, cups, and other toys. Eventually a readiness to splash a brush appropriately in a water bowl will serve as a prelude to the painting process.

The sand table is an excellent counterpart to water play, as it demands somewhat more tactile tolerance and physically demanding manipulation. Wet sand offers the child an excellent medium for pouring, straining, impressing and casting as an introductory ceramic activity.

Props such as bones, skulls, rocks, art objects and curios can all compensate for a lagging imagination.

Other useful props in this area may include a full-length mirror which can foster the child's body awareness and self-concept while also acting as an introductory drawing activity. Basic gymnastic equipment can be used to explore the body's movement possibilities. Bending, twisting, swinging and sliding exercises are excellent for animating rigid, withdrawn children.

Light sources such as Tensor lamps, overhead projectors, slide and movie projectors, and black lights can be manipulated for a variety of visual effects.

Motivational props can be seen as one compensatory strategy that may effectively counteract the effects of sensory loss and cultural deprivation. Many handicapped children lead sheltered, protected lives and have limited contact with much of

their natural environment. Children who are handicapped or brought up in the lower social and economic classes may be additionally deprived. Even children who are materially well off sometimes rely upon commercialized media and products to stimulate their imaginations. In this context, props provide concrete models for experimentation, as well as promoting aesthetic sensitivity by allowing both unusual and common objects to be appreciated in new ways.

Motivational Materials

Most of the resources used for motivation which I have used were not bought or requisitioned but simply collected. For instance, I received a donation of several plastic anatomical models of human fetuses at various stages of growth, a full-size human skeleton and several ancient stuffed and mounted ducks, squirrels and other small animals. These proved to be excellent models for life drawing, as well as teaching tools which incorporate science and other disciplines into the artroom. Weekly class field outings have yielded a lively assortment of rocks, driftwood, polished glass and shells of all sizes which lend diversity to the collection.

Often objects made in class and donated to the studio are incorporated as motivational props. Ceramic sculptures, origami birds, mobiles and junk sculptures are all welcome additions which inspire future generations of art students.

Donated pets have also found a place in the motivational collection. Terrariums with turtles, gerbils and land crabs make fascinating subjects as well as lending an air of earthiness and liveliness to the studio. In close proximity to these is a recycled mobile science center replete with donated microscope and magnifying glasses for studying specimens. In another corner, a group of anatomical castings of hands, faces and torsos are grouped into a life-drawing area with two outlandishly dressed mannequins salvaged from the sewing department. Old televisions, clocks and other equipment are partially dismantled, their components used for student sculptures, wind chimes and wall reliefs.

The diversity and richness of these objects is the basis for a multisensory, interdisciplinary approach to motivating and inspiring the art student. Divisions between the art object, art activity and art environment have been de-emphasized. The interplay between these objects and the imagination of the children insures that very few children will be at a loss for a design or theme.

Stimulation is essential for motivating students to create. Here, a collection of plants, wood and an aquarium with various creatures in it assists in yielding ideas and themes.

Collections of photographs of different themes, objects or techniques can be a valuable resource for the child who is in need of a model upon which to expand or improvise.

RESEARCH CENTER

The research center may be a self-contained area or simply a separate table which is used for preliminary planning, inspiration or academic research. Research can be conducted in art history, art appreciation or any area that gains the child's interest. It is a relatively quiet and clean area that encourages the students to collect information, solve problems or be aesthetically stimulated by a range of printed materials.

Bulletin or blackboards are useful in this center for creating assemblages and montages of all kinds of visual images. I encourage students to contribute newspaper cuttings, poster or magazine cutouts, thumbnail sketches, old greeting cards— anything that creates a colorful and interesting resource display. This collection of random images may serve to explain a new idea, communicate an event, or simply exhibit interesting images.

Filing cabinets can be recycled to house a collection of visual images, which can be retrieved according to theme, artist or technique. If a child needs a realistic photograph of an animal or house or landscape, he or she can go to this file and pull the appropriate folder. Stylizations or abstractions taken from realistic subjects are also available from which to adapt designs for metal, jewelry or other craft projects. An adaptive art collection can be created for special needs children who have difficulties in getting started with their projects. Starter pictures, for example, are sheets of drawing paper with fragments of magazine illustrations glued to them (Anderson 1978). For instance, one page may depict an arm holding a ball, or another, a sunset over a mountain peak. The child can then select an image that invites him or her to continue the design, elaborate upon it, or change its context completely until an original image is arrived at.

Completing the research area in my classroom is a collection of books and periodicals on subjects such as science, history, geography and art. Old *National Geographic*, *Audubon* and *Arizona Highway* magazines contain images that can spark a child's imagination. Complementing the art library is a collection of handmade books, containing drawings, cutouts and short narratives about feelings, facts and concerns. These books were created and donated by previous student artists. Children of all levels delight in perusing these chronicles, especially when they are reviewing material that they themselves created years before.

The equipment needs of the research area can be as elaborate or as sparse as budgets permit. Typewriters, personal computers, slide projectors and videotape recorders can all further the possibilities of this work station.

Resources can also be filed away until a child requests a certain image to research or from which to improvise and expand in his or her own style.

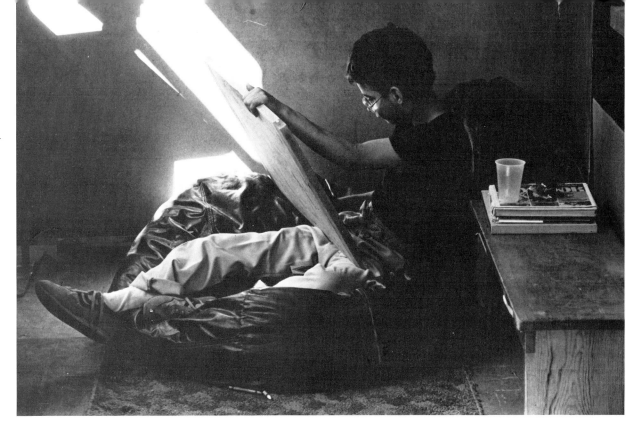

BEHAVIORAL CONTROL AREAS

Until calm and collected, this child will work in this secure and relaxed area of the studio where his behavior will not affect the other students.

While some children with special needs require an overabundance of sensory stimulation in order to generate creative ideas, others need an environment in which sights, sounds and other extraneous stimuli are minimized. Just as the motivational area attempts to arouse and excite, so should there be an area devoted to calmness, relaxation and reflection.

In my dealings with special needs children who demonstrate hyperactivity, attention deficits, impulse control problems or aggressive behavior, I have devised two zones in the artroom which address the need to decrease stimulation: the relaxation area and the time-out area.

The relaxation area is a minimally stimulating environment to which a child who is experiencing frustration, giddiness, talkativeness, impulsivity, etc., can retreat, yet still be allowed to create art. The space itself can be a partitioned area or corner that allows for minimum interaction with peers and other stimulation. It is an alcove where a child can find a measure of peace until ready to rejoin his or her peers and return to the activity.

The relaxation area can be furnished with furniture and other items that are comforting and soothing. A soft chair, rocker or stack of pillows can encourage a child who is tense and irritable to relax. The area can perhaps face a window so that the child can gaze outside toward a bird feeder or set of wind chimes, in a kind of purposeful daydreaming. For students who are in need of a longer-term respite, basic art materials can be on hand to displace some of the anger or anxiety.

The time-out area is a similar facility—often made of recycled partitions (bolted to the floor to absorb belligerent behavior) or a room (sometimes padded)—that also allows for minimum stimulation and interaction. However, in contrast to the relaxation area, the time-out area has a more punitive feeling to it. It lacks comforting appointments or the opportunity to do even limited art making. Upon being seated in the time-out area, a child immediately is deprived of stimulation and is forced to confront the consequences of his or her behavior. Both the relaxation area and the time-out area function best when used for brief intervals. Children can go and compose themselves, reflect on their actions, and then reintegrate sufficiently so that they can rejoin the class for the remainder of the session.

GALLERY SPACE

Once the art process is completed, it may be difficult for the students to appreciate their efforts unless a suitable area in which to exhibit their artwork is provided. Although the artwork may be finished, it is usually surrounded by dirty water, paper scraps and other debris and may still seem to be part of the chaos left by the art process. Upon completion it is vital that the teacher remove the piece to a clean, white backdrop where the children can appreciate and constructively criticize their freshly created pieces.

The final stages of the art process can be a most crucial time for the student artist. Both regular and special needs children are susceptible to abandoning, aborting or destroying their work as it approaches completion. Having to call a piece finished means that the child must confront aspects of the picture that he or she perceives as being unresolved, immature or just plain lousy. This can be a painful experience unless the art educator supports the child through this stage with extra attention and intervention. Pieces may need repair or cleaning; some areas may need to be resolved; sometimes pieces must be retrieved from the trash and restored. The next stage is to mount the artwork on an illustration board, under Plexiglas or on white paper, so that a sense of order and cleanliness can be achieved. Once mounted in a space specifically designed for artwork exhibition, pieces take on a new life. Even the most chaotic scribbles or random brushworks of the retarded child can begin to command respect and become worthy of study once the work is matted, mounted on a base, given a "gift" box or exhibited in a show.

Exhibition space can be made from an unused room divider, foam core panels, bulletin boards or unused blackboards that have been painted white

Gallery space can be temporary and mobile. Shown here is hinged cork board used for "quick crits."

An impromptu "crit" between peers need not include the instructor.

64

The proper storage and organization of artwork greatly affect the value students place on their work.

and adapted to hanging artwork. These exhibition boards can be mobile or stationary. They can be arranged as a single exhibit area or grouped together in a configuration that creates a self-enclosed gallery space. Gallery spaces can be used for different purposes. Works in progress or just-completed projects can be tacked up for quick criticisms, while previously mounted works can be exhibited as an ongoing show in a more formal setting. Lighting such as track lights or clamp-on floodlights can add an extra dimension when displaying and appreciating student works.

STORAGE FACILITIES

Artwork created by children deserves respect and should be accorded value equal to that of the established, mature artist. Student artists invest considerable energy and emotion in their artwork, waging the same creative struggles during the art process. It is vital that the teacher follow through with the art process by providing the child with an orderly, secure and protective facility for storing artwork.

The educational and therapeutic implications of this issue are evident in the countless cases where the success of the art activity was negated because of the eventual soiling, creasing or breaking of the artwork in storage. This happens especially frequently when working with children with special needs. A marred or damaged piece may be the deciding factor between savoring the art experience or abandoning the work altogether. The long-term effects may include a further increase in resistance, depressed motivation, or even future conduct disorders.

The child with behavioral problems is particularly at risk, since damaged work may result in tantrums or even violent episodes. This is most often seen in the ceramics studio, where the unfired work is very fragile. In one case, extra time on the potter's wheel was being effectively used as therapeutic experience for an emotionally disturbed child. A classmate, innocently making room in the damp closet, broke the lip of one of the child's bowls. The result was a violent episode in which all the pots in the closet were destroyed, including those pieces created by the child himself. Episodes such as this may easily occur, unless the art teacher takes the necessary steps to store artworks securely.

Two-dimensional artworks should be stored clean, dry and unwrinkled in an accessible and easily operated facility that encourages the children to be responsible for the condition of their work. In many instances, it is the artist who damages the artwork by leaving it unattended or by handling it carelessly. Flat files, cabinet shelving or tote tray units are excellent, not only for secure storage but for separating and organizing the artwork by individual artists.

With certain special need populations, such as the autistic or the visually impaired, surrendering their artwork to an uncertain fate can arouse deep concerns. Because of their incomplete or distorted perceptions, once the work is given over to forces beyond their control, they assume anything can happen. One visually impaired, yet highly gifted art student constantly reflected this fear in his hurried, agitated working manner at the close of the art session. He would insist that he complete his highly detailed drawings in one sitting. This limited the scale and scope of the artwork he attempted, while also adversely affecting the therapeutic benefits of the art process. Assigning the child an individually labelled drawer remedied this situation. This gesture provided a sense of security and consistency so that giving up his painstaking artwork was less traumatic and more a matter of course.

THE ITINERANT ENVIRONMENT

Certain programs require that the art teacher work on an itinerant basis—meaning that an art studio either cannot be used or is not available for art programming. In some situations, the childrens' educational and therapeutic needs will dictate that they not be disturbed or uprooted from their resource rooms. In other settings, such as residential institutions, hospitals, correctional facilities or separate campus buildings, itinerant programming may be a necessity.

I have pedaled a bicycle weighted down with saddle-bags of material, driven by car, as well as pushed a cart to different facilities or rooms in order to provide services in circumstances like these. To accomplish itinerant programming, the logistical problems of carrying material such as various media, tools, props, audiovisual aids, etc., must be efficiently organized. Usually the problems of working off a cart are compounded by minimal planning time and wasted traveling time between sessions, making the art teacher's task all the more demanding.

In most situations I will attempt to share the burden of hauling material by relying upon the classroom setting to supply clean-up products and exhibition space. I also rely on the school or institution to have established contingency areas for behavior problems. Should this not be the case, however, I will not hesitate to consult with the classroom teacher to rearrange a room so that I can manage children who present behavior problems.

Because less equipment and materials can be used, the itinerant art teacher must often adapt the art experience. Motivational props, research materials, media and tools, all must be minimized and the projects streamlined. After one develops experience in anticipating what will be needed and what can be improvised, a productive rhythm can be established. Art can endure under such conditions, although being a guest in a setting in which the classroom teacher may be unfamiliar with the sounds, smells and messes which accompany the making of art will undoubtedly put stress upon even the most conscientious and organized art specialist. It is vital that itinerants establish clear lines of communication and a sense of trust with those whose environments they invade and that they attempt to minimize the friction which often results. The positive side to this dilemma is that the classroom teacher can experience firsthand the creative fervor, productivity and lively spirits which children often bring to their art—in contrast with the deficient performances that often occur in the academic setting.

CAMOUFLAGING IN THE STUDIO

In mainstream classes the art teacher must foster an atmosphere of equality and mutual respect in order for students to accept and adapt to each other. To develop such an atmosphere, the children with special needs must be individually accommodated, yet integrated into a normal group environment.

To the casual observer, the students in a typical mainstream art setting are distributed among the different activity centers in small groups, presenting an individualized, yet otherwise unremarkable class arrangement. For instance, on any given day, five children, including one in a wheelchair, may be throwing pots on the potter's wheel. Beside the fact that the wheelchair-bound child is working at an adapted wheel, nothing seems preferential or unusual in the class arrangement. At the research center three children may be working on a design problem, such as creating a cartoon strip. Again, nothing seems out of the ordinary unless the observer knows that one of the participants is learning disabled and cannot read. Yet the learning-disabled child is successfully contributing to the project by researching images, drawing and providing input about the style and content of the piece. As well as concentrating upon the imagery, this student can collaborate with peers in composing the cartoon's narrative.

The casual, normal atmosphere in the artroom suggests that curriculum considerations alone guided the students' placement at their respective activity centers. Whether a group contains a child confined to a wheelchair or another who is working by a sense of touch, there should be nothing to suggest that students have been located, grouped

or given art activities that reflect their handicapped condition.

The apparent ease with which these children are absorbed within the artroom, however, is no accident. The students are well integrated due to the astute observations, assessments and planning made by the art educator or art therapist prior to their placements. Each child is assessed as to his or her emotional, cognitive and aesthetic needs and each is accommodated in an environment where strengths and weakness are camouflaged so as not to make an issue of the disability. The students' social needs are also analyzed so that children can be paired who may have positive effects upon each other's behavior and productivity. Finally, the art teacher provides the needed orientation, adaptive equipment and environmental arrangements that will assist the special needs child in performing the art activity successfully.

SPECIFIC ADAPTATIONS

The following describes environmental arrangements only for those disabilities that require specific adaptations. For other disabilities a mainstream set-up will be adequate, with only individual cases requiring intervention.

The Orthopedically Handicapped
The physically handicapped child usually requires the most elaborate adaptations in order to function in the mainstream artroom. Simple functions such as sitting up or holding a pencil cannot be taken for granted when integrating an orthopedically handicapped student. Because so many of these severely disabled children possess otherwise healthy, normal intellects, it is vital that we provide every opportunity for them to learn and grow in a normal learning atmosphere.

Movement is essential for effective interaction within the environment and is a primary learning channel for many young children. Therefore, plenty of opportunity for independent movement should be provided in the artroom. For many orthopedically handicapped children, the wheelchair is the most common means of gaining freedom of movement. This implies that sinks, storage facilities and equipment should all be made accessible to a child confined to a wheelchair. Tables, in particular, require 27″ of clearance to accept a wheelchair. Staff should become familiar with the wheelchair itself: how to disassemble it, lock it, or adjust it to an individual's need.

While the wheelchair is a most vital tool, staff must also be reminded that it is intended as a means of transportation and not a place where the child must remain indefinitely. Too often wheelchair-bound children languish in this device for entire school days, despite the fact that they are quite capable of sitting in armchairs, laying on mats, or standing up in adaptive devices. Maintaining a least restrictive environment means providing the opportunity for normal movement as part of the classroom routine. Activities that require sitting on the floor, kneeling or standing should all be available to the orthopedic child if he or she is physically able, despite the fact that this may draw more attention to the child's disability.

For children who must remain in their wheelchairs, work spaces can be built around them using trays and slant boards. Different arrangements might be made to bring the activity center to the child in the form of extended easels and other work spaces.

It is imperative that the art educator or art therapist find ways for the student to draw, paint or sculpt independently. Unfortunately, orthopedic students usually have grave difficulties in manipulating drawing implements that demand a degree of fine motor control. For students who cannot hold a drawing implement or cannot coordinate their movements, several adaptations can be devised. Alternative equipment may also be employed, such as ink stamps, sprayers and paint rollers for those children who cannot control a pencil. For children who are paralyzed in their hands but retain some gross arm movements, commercially

prepared splints and cuffs that clamp the drawing implement into a stationary position can allow the arm and shoulder to compensate for this weakness. Students who only have the use of their head and neck muscles can use a helmet stylus, which can be fitted with everything from pencils to sculpture loop tools.

It is useful for the art teacher to obtain assistance from physical and occupational therapists or rehabilitation engineers in acquiring or fabricating adaptive equipment that will allow for comfortable and independent functioning. Basic to the selection of equipment for the handicapped child is a thorough understanding of his or her developmental level. Equipment is needed that will assist the child in his or her particular developmental stage. All adaptive equipment is not useful for all children, even if their disabilities are identical. With proper adaptive devices, the art teacher/therapist should find that the student's ability to perform effectively within the mainstream setting is enhanced.

For the physically disabled child to manage the artroom environment with a minimum of stress, it is important that the art teacher empathize with the child's predicament. To be paralyzed, weakened or speechless can cause tremendous feelings of helplessness. Objects in the environment that we ordinarily take for granted as relatively harmless can represent a formidable threat to a child who is virtually defenseless. Considerable emphasis has been placed upon filling the studio with a wide range of natural and humanmade objects that serve to arouse the student's creativity. Yet, from the perspective of a child who cannot protect him- or herself, the bite of a otherwise harmless hamster can represent a dire threat. The power and torque of the drill press can be extremely frightening. Even a stack of clay boxes has the potential of falling over and injuring the child who cannot run away or raise an arm in self-protection. Therefore, the art teacher should take the time and effort to acclimate each orthopedic child to the environment. Allow them to analyze the room for potentially dangerous situations and ask them to provide input as to how to make the artroom a safe and enjoyable place to be creative.

The Neurologically Impaired

Because of the wide range of brain injuries, the environment should be adapted to reflect the severity and kind of disability on an individual basis. For example, a severely cerebral palsied child who is paralyzed and without speech may require different environmental accommodations than the child who is hyperactive. Despite the differences in their characteristics, however, both brain injured children are likely to share disturbances in visual perception and behavioral disorders that limit or delay normal development. An environment that encourages behavioral self-control and intensive concentration on the task may best serve both their needs.

Throughout these discussions, emphasis has been placed upon compensating for sensory deprivation by employing a range of highly stimulating objects, sights and sounds as part of the art environment. In addressing the needs of some brain injured children, a complete reversal of strategy is in order. Children with problems such as spatial distortion, distractibility and hyperactivity require an environment devoid of extraneous stimuli. Should the resources be available, this can be accomplished by devising a minimal-stimulation activity center. For instance, carrels or partitioned spaces can serve to create a self-contained art studio for the distractable or hyperactive student. The walls of such an area should be bare and painted a monotone, muted grey. Furnishings should be sparse, with tables, chairs, floor coverings and props being plain, uncluttered and painted the same quiet grey. Materials should be stored out of sight and be introduced in increments as the child displays the ability to handle or process them. Dangerous tools or equipment should be similarly beyond the child's reach and out of view until employed in the task. Outside distractions can be minimized by employing shades to discourage window-gazing. The activity center should be located so as to minimize auditory distraction, using soundproof walls and thick carpet as sound mufflers.

The Visually Impaired

As the sighted child interacts within the environment, vast amounts of information are obtained visually. The visually impaired child must develop alternate modes of deriving stimulation, orientation and information from his or her environment. To gain a unified impression or visualization of the space, the blind student will use haptic perceptions to touch and feel everything from the perimeters of the artroom walls to the tools and media of the art activity.

The art teacher can begin to acclimate the visually impaired child by maintaining a consistent, clearly discernable traffic pattern throughout the studio. Unattached furnishings such as chairs, easels and sculpture stands should be tucked away after use to minimize the obstacles in the aisles. The blind child should be taught to negotiate the floor plan every time it is changed or readjusted, pausing to identify the major features and landmarks of the room. Trailing a hand along the walls and furnishings, the child should be allowed to explore each object and space, with the teacher taking the time to describe their distinguishing characteristics. A review of the sounds common to the art studio can also supply much needed environmental clues. Sounds created by electric tools, potter's wheels and even the sink faucet can be sources of agitation and confusion unless the art teacher takes the time to familiarize the child to the noise. A mobility map may assist in giving the visually impaired child a greater sense of the room as a whole. A bas-relief map-making activity may be a creative way of incorporating the mobility training into a productive studio project that all the children may enjoy.

The art techniques available to the blind child should not be limited to purely tactile or three-dimensional media. In keeping with the principle of the least restrictive environment, visually impaired children should be allowed to freely use paint, crayon and other two-dimensional media along with the rest of the class.

The activity centers used by the visually impaired student should be adapted for optimum recognition and independent participation. Storage components such as stacking crates or tote trays can separate and define paper supplies, while differently shaped containers can indicate the contents of paint or other media. A consistent layout of tools and materials will encourage the blind child to be self-reliant and assertive during the art sessions. A child who can freely and confidently go to the sink or find the needed tool will almost certainly benefit by the enhanced self-esteem that comes with increased responsibility and independence.

Many visually impaired children are light-sensitive, and may require lighting adjustments whenever they are working in the studio. Children with thick, corrective lenses may "light-gaze" as one of their self-stimulatory mannerisms. This type of child may require subdued lighting to reduce the glare or reflections that encourage staring into light sources. Window shades or draperies may counteract the effects of sunlight filtering through the windows. Some visually impaired children require highly specific light sources, such as flashlights or floodlights, to illuminate the areas of the art activity that require their attention. A beam of light may also assist in teaching the child how to follow or track a moving object.

Hypersensitivity to light and sound may affect the visually impaired child's productivity and emotional adjustment to the art program. One autistic-like, visually impaired child was virtually uncontrollable in my classroom if even one light was in use. I eventually found that it was not the presence of light itself that the child found unendurable, but the subtle blinking and hum of the fluorescent fixtures. By switching to pure sunlight or incandescent track lighting, this child was able to successfully make the adjustment to the mainstream art class.

chapter 5

Motivation

ESTABLISHING RAPPORT AND ATTACHMENTS

Fostering motivation in children, regardless of their functioning level or emotional state, demands a range of responses and strategies. Common to all motivational techniques is the importance of establishing a rapport with even the most difficult child. Much rapport is gained by being straight with children. Honesty, firmness, sensitivity, confidence, and concern are the qualities necessary for gaining students' confidence. The therapeutic art teacher must also demonstrate empathy toward his or her students. Empathy is not so much an attitude as a discipline that demands training. As mature, practicing artists who have experienced artistic struggles firsthand, art teachers can empathize with most children's creative processes. However, developing empathy for children with physical handicaps or emotional disorders may require workshops and training exercises.

Relating to children does not require a certain kind of personality. Some successful teachers are exuberant, high energy individuals who motivate children through the sheer force of their optimism. Teachers of this kind are fascinating to watch. They are able to cheerlead even the most jaded child through a session by generating a "can-do" atmosphere where learning is exciting and fun despite the most depressing circumstances. My own approach is low-keyed and understated, relying not so much on exuberance, as on projecting a sense of kindredness to the children. I understand these children and am confident in my ability to work with them. Thus, in my case, professional experience, determination and empathy serve as the building blocks of rapport.

Essentially, rapport is an individualized process that depends upon the exceptionality of each child. It may involve months or even years of patient relating or it may occur spontaneously after an exceptional incident or breakthrough. For instance, I worked with one very angry, hearing-impaired child who remained suspicious and distant for months until I passed a test of courage. One day as he was confronted by a more powerful and delinquent classmate, I managed to bail him out in such a way that enabled us all to save face. This incident served as proof to him of my caring attitude. (Henley 1987)

In the case of autistic children, it may take long periods of time in order for them to not only cooperate, but to endure sharing the same studio space or possibly the same field of vision. I saw one autistic child individually and in small groups for five years. During this time, I worked in parallel to this boy, without overtly confronting or demanding his attention, allowing him instead to concentrate upon his artwork. After years of maintaining a consistently secure environment, our relationship

The process of self-identification with ones culture, experiences, fantasies and emotions sustains motivation during the art process. The vibrant treatment of a West African Dogon Dancer reflects this child's connection with his African-American heritage.

eventually reached a point where he began to tolerate simple interventions. However, we never reached what one would consider real rapport, but only a timid coexistence.

In working with the mentally retarded, the route to establishing rapport often lies through establishing a secure, predictable environment. The retarded tend to require routines or rituals in their behavior. One group of Down syndrome boys responded to listening to music while they were setting up materials. After several months they had narrowed the records down to one particular song which they played without variation. It became a motivational trigger that launched them into the art activity. Rapport in this case had little to do with my personality, but rather with how I anticipated their interests and allowed for stimulation on their level.

Rapport can also emerge from the most unexpected circumstances. I once had to prove myself to a group of preadolescent, hearing-impaired boys who had resisted art class for weeks, judging it to be effeminate and infantile. It wasn't until I appeared as coach of the wrestling team and proctor in the weight room that they saw me in a different light. At this point they began to appreciate that activities such as throwing large pieces on the potter's wheel or welding hunks of steel together were anything but effeminate.

The capacity to establish a bond of trust and

sense of rapport may be rooted in the child's earliest mother/child relationship experiences. Children who have difficulties relating to the art teacher or peers might not have had adequate nurturance during their first few years of life. This may be seen as a lack of empathy—an inability to identify with another person due to an unawareness of one's own feelings and thus the feelings of others (Brothers 1989). Brothers reviews the different factors for developing empathy which include biological/neurological factors, as well as environmental factors such as maternal or familial nurturance. Social communication is present from very early infancy (Meltzoff 1977), although it requires a complex interaction of social, physical and intrapsychic elements for it to fully develop (Brothers 1989). For instance, the failure to make attachments during the symbiotic stage may not result in autistic behavior since there may be no biological basis for such extreme pathology. Although a mother might be indifferent, cold, inattentive or even rejecting, children are resilient creatures and usually a child will compensate by bonding to other family members or even objects such as stuffed toys. However, such compensation is usually imperfect and may be reflected in symptoms later in the child's life—such as aloofness, flatness of affect or lack of empathy. Any of these symptoms may affect a child's capacity to relate personably with the art teacher. Paradoxically, children who have endured a smothering, overindulging mother may later behave in a clinging manner, with a constant need for attention and physical contact. This failure to resolve the mother/child symbiosis may also hinder rapport, since the child's insatiable needs for maternal nurturing cannot be met in the art studio.

The reapproachment phase of development is also a crucial period for developing trust. It is at this stage that the toddler begins to separate from the mother by cautiously crawling away to explore its environment. Such a separation is based upon a bond of trust, since the child depends upon the mother to remain accessible and supportive during these forays. Should there be consistent inatten-

tion or abandonment, the child may realize that the mother cannot be trusted. This may later translate into a generalized distrust of nurturing figures, including art teachers.

Rapport can be a difficult, perplexing process, one that is painstakingly established, falters, stages a comeback and becomes solidified, only to be tested once more. It is a crucial aspect of this process that the teacher become sensitized to these dynamics and recognize the underlying developmental forces which shape behavior. This does not infer that we gratify a child's unmet needs for mothering, however, for this would be dangerously inappropriate. As Robbins (1987) points out, growth can only occur when we allow the pain of early trauma to run its course in a safe, supportive environment for the child. Robbins states this as the paradox of rapport: "I am with you, but separate; I understand your needs, but I cannot take away your pain."

CREATING A LEARNING ATMOSPHERE

Once rapport has been established and a working alliance is operating between the teacher and the students, attention should turn to the learning atmosphere. The teacher is responsible for creating an atmosphere in the art studio which directly affects the motivation of the students. Performance expectations, criticism, praise—any sort of intervention—affects the child's urge to create. An atmosphere should be created in which experimentation and creative risk-taking take precedence over evaluating results. Too much emphasis on evaluation and judgement can lead to a fear of failure in children, and once a child's confidence is shaken and he or she becomes fearful of making a mistake, true learning begins to stall.

Children with special needs see failure as a result of the deficiencies associated with their disability. They routinely fail to measure up to normal levels of performance and are frequently subjected to criticism, despite their teachers' and parents' best intentions. Under such pressures, they are not about to encourage further humiliation by taking unnecessary risks. These children must learn that in the artroom a smeared pastel or lost piece on the wheel is not an error, but rather an experience. Experimentation and trial-and-error thinking must be seen as a constructive way of building skills and self-expression.

To counteract the effects of a child's fear of failure, the teacher must know how to respond when the child begins to struggle. Often, inexperienced teachers emphasize how easy a given technique is to master. Many times children are counseled to "Try it, it's easy"? Unfortunately, this seemingly innocent comment will backfire and aggravate a child's sense of humiliation. The child may reason that even if he works his hardest and succeeds, he'll only prove that he can accomplish something easy. And should the child fail, it becomes painfully obvious that he can't do even the easiest task. The child is set up in a no-win predicament and subsequently becomes even more reluctant to try.

A successful technique in this situation might be to emphasize how difficult a given task is and how you will be there for support should the child need it. Another strategy is to emphasize to the child the art *process* as opposed to the finished art *product*. By encouraging the pleasureful manipulation and exploration of the paint or clay, the teacher helps the child avoid feelings of pressure or inadequacy. Many children need the art activity as a source of stimulation. They need to relax and build their confidence before their productivity becomes an issue. With enough breathing space, many children will eventually become sufficiently motivated to participate in art activities.

Praise

There are many ways in which we can praise children's work and behavior. Some forms of positive praise can be useful in motivating students; frequently, however, positive praise can have a negative effect. When I first began working with children I often praised my students liberally for their efforts, cooperation, and any other positive aspect of their performance. Everything was "excellent" or "wonderful" despite the fact that the children may have been displeased with themselves and their work. Soon, however, I realized that such praise was obviously false and very much resented by both special and regular children alike. Indeed, even the most severely retarded child seemed able to see such false sentiment as a form of coercion. One mildly retarded boy thoughtfully observed that I was pleased with "any old crap."

Attempting to deceive children into thinking that they are doing better than they really are compromises the trust bond established during the rapport process. Credibility suffers and subsequently motivation drops off. Even when a student is performing well, praise such as "Good job" or "You're a good girl" may have unfavorable effects. Such well-meaning comments may make the child feel good momentarily, yet ultimately nothing constructive has been said. The child is left with a vague understanding that somehow she has pleased her teacher. Nothing has been analyzed for the child and thus she cannot learn or otherwise benefit from such flattery.

False praise also has a negative effect on behavior. An early session with a class of behaviorally disturbed children taught me this lesson. I had praised the group's behavior despite the fact that at times they had been disruptive and uncooperative. The children decided to set the record straight, however, and began acting out soon after my misdirected comments. They effectively dispelled my illusion that they deserved such praise. They communicated to me, in case I missed something, that they were in fact very angry and unruly children, and I should recognize this anger in its full proportions and work with it, support them through it, but never ignore or lie about it.

When given too much praise or false praise, withdrawn, depressed or symbiotically-arrested children, often develop an unhealthy dependence and over-reliance upon the teacher or therapist. Their constant craving for approval may also cause them to solicit attention in inappropriate

74 ways. The child no longer is working for his or her own benefit, but rather to satisfy others. With such a lack of personal identification and emotional investment in the work, motivation ultimately falters. One child, who was emotionally disturbed with autistic features, constantly interrupted the session to ask whether she was a "good girl" and a "good worker." She was completely consumed and distracted by my real or imagined opinion of her self-worth. Although she was a good artist, her work remained stereotypical and ordinary. She could not concentrate on her art, but remained anxious, insecure, and unproductive until her problem was resolved.

Descriptive Feedback

Children are better motivated when they can take responsibility for their ideas and solve problems as individuals or within a group. If the children can handle such a responsibility in the artroom, I prefer to place myself in their midst and become a member of this "think tank" atmosphere. For instance, when I had the school carpenters bring in a section of a downed tree and bolt it into position as a prop in the artroom, many children excitedly asked me what I planned to do with it. In response I merely shrugged, asking them what *they* thought we could do with such an object. Initially, both regular and special-needs children were irritated at my lack of direction and authority. Thinking in concrete and pragmatic terms, some children insisted on simply being told what this enormous, incongruous thing had in store for them. However, I patiently waited for their tentative suggestions. One child suggested a small sitting platform; another wanted to hollow it out for a fort. I then asked, "How can we make art from this tree or use it as part of our work?" One child immediately said that she needed a place to hang her weaving while she worked on it. Another added she wanted to use it to suspend her ceramic chimes.

When I placed the children in a position of responsibility and authority (to a reasonable extent—one boy suggested that we make it a "hanging tree"), I succeeded in stimulating their own

problem-solving abilities and in turn, encouraged them to cooperate in the group process. Assuming this role as facilitator meant that my judgement became secondary to the thoughts of the group. I fielded suggestions enthusiastically yet in a carefully neutral way, taking care not to evaluate the students' ideas.

Descriptive feedback is a form of praise and attention which has a positive motivational effect on children. Rather than offering any judgment about the child's behavior or work, it merely describes them back to the child. In many instances the student cannot fully articulate his or her own ideas or reflect upon how they can be applied or implemented. In these cases, it is helpful to reinterpret the child's work pointing out areas of interest, for example, or noting certain design elements, or the use of emphasis and contrasts. If implemented correctly, this constructive feedback will enhance a child's motivation. When given positive acknowledgements and specific suggestions, students are better prepared to make sense of their own work and develop it further.

Descriptive feedback also recognizes the child's emotional relationship to the artwork and explores the process by which he or she is dealing with these feelings. When the autistic girl inquires anxiously whether she is a "good girl," I answer by describing how she is seated squarely at the table and is being attentive which will help her in her artwork. Should she remain distracted or anxious and her work display this, I respond by describing how we need to relax in our work and show care and concentration. If the behavior persists, then I know I must turn to more involved motivational interventions.

EXTENDING A CHILD'S FRAME OF REFERENCE

Building rapport is the beginning of "extending a child's reference." Lowenfeld (1957) used this term to describe the process of encouraging the child to expand his or her thinking, feeling and

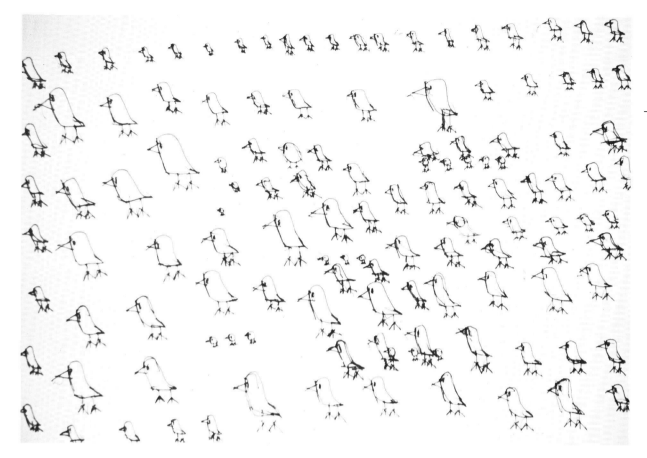

The obsessive repetition in this child's work posed a problem for the teacher who wished to extend the child's frame of reference and encourage him to incorporate different images in his work.

perceiving one step further. In other words the teacher must first communicate that he or she accepts the artwork the child has just created regardless of how impoverished or distorted. This acceptance then prompts a further step or point of departure for extending the theme or image.

Extending the child's reference should be cautiously and sensitively administered in ways that are least threatening or intimidating. The process may entail extending only the smallest aspect of the artwork, depending upon the child's capability to withstand change. This kind of motivational intervention aims to build visual ideas and images frame by frame, until they are supported by a momentum of their own.

For instance, children who draw stereotypical images in repetition can become *locked* into this mode of expression. Because of some cognitive or emotional deficiency, they have trouble breaking out of these rigid molds toward more personally and aesthetically meaningful work. Because this is a rigid defense system—one that the child is com-

pelled to rely upon—we must treat it with great deference. Yet to leave the child to such static devices means to abandon the search for his or her true potential. Thus, we intervene to motivate the child to move beyond the stereotype in a way that is minimally upsetting yet in a positive direction.

Three Case Studies
A deaf child with autistic symptoms drew nothing but little stereotyped birds for the first few months in my art class. He was quite resistent to changing any aspect of these birds. He refused to add color, alter their pose or change the scale. In fact, if I attempted to introduce a new medium or change the routine, he would begin to behave rather like a strickened bird, flapping his arms while making clucking sounds in an agitated manner.

Eventually this boy did expand his repertoire but only after he became acclimated to both the staff and the studio routines. The first indication of his willingness to expand the bird theme was when he accepted the suggestion to use his drawings in an assemblage. Even this extension of the boy's frame of reference, however, could only be considered precursory. Nothing really changed about the birds *per se,* only their arrangement (Henley 1989).

This is an example of the kind of growth the art educator or therapist can expect in the most difficult cases. Growth in special needs children cannot be understood in the usual sense of the word, but must be redefined to include indiscernible movements that can only be appreciated on a cumulative basis. It also includes highly irregular patterns that move forward, then regress, move forward again, then stagnate, at a sometimes excruciating, step-by-step pace. Thus, in assessing the child's progress in extending his or her frame of reference, the teacher must become an astute observer, one who is sensitive to every movement,

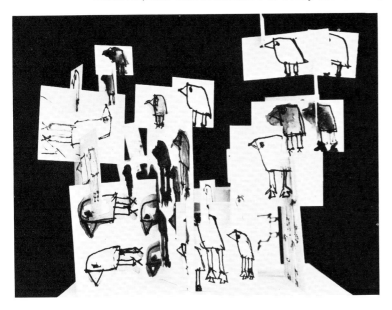

After arranging his mini-drawings into different configurations, this child created a bird assemblage, thus slightly extending his frame of reference.

always ready to implement appropriate interventions that motivate the child toward the next objective.

Using Lowenfeld's verbal motivation method (see Chapter 1), when my "bird boy" drew his favored image, I asked "Where is the bird? Is she on a tree? Is she sitting on a nest? Is she hunting for grubs?" and so on. Lowenfeld's method attempts to intensify the experience for the child so that the child may visualize the image in his or her mind. Once the image has crystallized, it may be projected effectively through the art medium.

By motivating the boy toward manipulating his bird pictures into a construction, I was able to extend his frame of reference toward increasing flexibility and experimentation. For several months I talked about his birds—"When do they fly? Do they ever turn around?"—using sign language and gesture to communicate these ideas. Although he could not effectively express himself through language, he did understand well enough to begin to slightly alter his drawings—first by site, then by adding color, then a sky, clouds, and trees for the birds to alight upon. After many pictures, he was able to use his favorite image in an expanded, dynamic way that retained his personal style.

My experience with a verbal, yet moderately retarded young man is another example of the use of verbal dialogue to achieve educational and therapeutic progress. Although he could draw interesting and intricate images, Gil had the greatest difficulty beginning his pictures. In the first sessions he would sit motionlessly over his blank paper, as if frozen with inhibition. After an uncomfortable period of silence and stillness, I casually asked him (without reference to the art activity) what he enjoyed doing in his leisure time. Gil replied meagerly "television." Intending to steer clear of a theme rampant with stereotypes, I changed tack, asking him about his work day—whether there was some aspect that he most enjoyed. This line of questioning seemed to arouse him enough to answer that he enjoyed the work crew, where he did basic yard and garden maintenance. I followed by asking what aspect of lawn work he most enjoyed

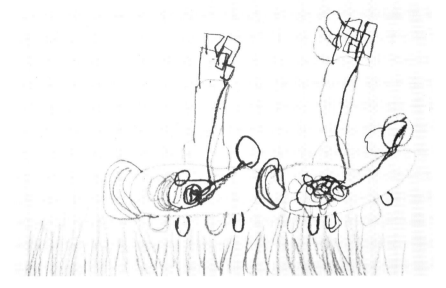

After lengthy verbal motivation, this mentally retarded boy produced a drawing related to his favorite activity — mowing lawns. His confusion about human and machine characteristics is reflected in his creation of a male and female machine "couple."

or excelled at. (Note that I am continually attempting to boil down Gil's generalized perceptions and feelings to elicit specific responses.) Gil then remarked that he preferred to mow the lawns using a power mower, that he especially enjoyed operating the machine and walking through the yards. I now had Gil beginning to articulate significant aspects of his experience: his pride in controlling a dangerous piece of machinery, his satisfaction from manicuring a landscape and the pleasures that his walks afforded. With Gil's imagination now fully activated, he was primed to draw this theme. He chose to portray the mower, which was to Gil the most important feature in the story. After drawing the mower, Gil again sat motionless until I intervened once more. I began again by prompting him to relive his experiences, and to increase his sense of self-identification—a crucial phase in the Lowenfeld motivation. I asked, "Who is operating the mower? Is it in the process of mowing or is it about to be put back in the garage?" (I was attempting to create an image of himself, as yet a conspicuously absent element in the story.) Despite the direction in which I was pointing him, Gil responded after another protracted silence, "I know, the mower needs a friend." He then began to draw a supposed female counterpart to the original mower.

At this point in the art process I began to interpret issues that addressed purely psychological needs. Presumably the child should have proceeded to draw the grass, garage or himself happily mowing. However, individuals with special needs often reason in aberrant ways. In this case, Gil's response reflected a deep-seated emotional disturbance. His thinking processes were at times quite disturbed. He related and identified intensely to objects (particularly machines) and in fact, once declared that he himself was assembled as a machine. Thus, instead of relating the mower to human activity, Gil equated it to a relationship between machines. My subsequent interventions addressed Gil's object relations as evidenced by his identification with machines as well as his impoverished self-concept and self-image. I stated to no one in particular after the second mower was drawn, "But it is Gil that operates the machines." "Gil also cooperates with his crew members." "The people appreciate having the lawn cut by Gil," and so on. These were still verbal motivations of the Lowenfeld kind, but they were not aimed solely at elaborating ideas. They were also concerned with directing Gil toward more reality-oriented object relations, where people befriend people, where people control the machines as objects, and finally where people are not machines. (In looking closely at this drawing, one finds a disturbing organicity in the two mowers. They might be viewed as transitional objects which bridge the gap between the mechanical and the human, acting as buffering agents between the two worlds.)

Gil's preoccupation with machinery is expressed in his box-like self-portrait, complete with tuning knobs.

After this line of interventions had continued for a time, Gil began to bring figures into his work. However, Gil's preoccupation with machinery remained an active element in his self-image. The human figure he drew is a rigid-looking appliance, complete with buttons that seem more like controls or knobs. The teacher looking at this piece may be satisfied that there are abundant details, enough to warrant a dramatic extension of the young man's original point of reference. However, looking at it from a therapeutic perspective, the work still indicates developmental arrest, an unhealthy identification and disturbed self-image which continues to place the child at risk.

Once, while conducting a day-long workshop for emotionally-handicapped children who were modeling clay figures, I observed a young lady standing aloof from her unruly classmates. She was meticulously dressed, manicured, and tastefully made

up, and stood well away from the turbulence and messiness of the art activity. Her teacher had advised me that she was electively mute and difficult to approach. He stated that she would in all probability not participate in the workshop. I nevertheless requested that she remain accessible to me in case I was able to draw her into the activity.

While turning my attention back to the students who were pounding and torturing their clay figures, I noticed that she followed the commotion closely, taking in everything. In response to her reticent yet intense interest, I arranged a separate work table adjacent to where I was working and invited her to sit and watch. After ten minutes had passed she slipped into this chair, folded her hands neatly and continued to watch the bustling clay work. After another fifteen minutes of being in close proximity, I spoke so that she could hear, "One of my favorite interests in life is working and being with animals. Birds, turtles, dogs and cats are some of my best friends." With this verbal intervention, I noticed that she made fleeting eye contact with me and seemed curious. After a while I turned to her directly for the first time and said, "I think you like animals, but I'm curious. What are your favorite kinds?" With this, her eyes lit up—I could see she was excited, her wheels were turning. I then slipped a piece of white drawing paper and pencil onto the table (knowing she would never touch the clay with her manicure) and said "I wish you would draw me your favorite animal." Without hesitation she began to draw an eloquent portrait of her cat, Keith, who was curled up on his favorite place on the couch. This remarkable sequence of events gives witness to the evocative power of art as a means of highly expressive and articulate communication. Despite this child's previous traumas or debilitations, she was able to tap into a deeply nourishing reservoir of ideas and feelings, then successfully depict her thoughts in an utterly charming drawing.

After a period of observation and caution, this mute child eventually expressed all kinds of experiences, preferences and emotions in her simple line drawings.

This student's capacity to create was tied to the interventions which served to motive her. The first problem was to establish rapport without intimidating or overwhelming her by direct discussion. Given the nature of her trauma, it is safe to say that the attachment to the material provider or protector had been at some point profoundly shaken. Subsequently, her capacity to trust had been similarly traumatized. A strategy for relating was required which did not reactivate these unmet needs, while also allowing her the space to communicate on her own terms. The establishment of an attachment needed to be cautiously pursued so as not to be construed as a reprobation or threat. To accomplish this, I used a verbal approach which constituted a kind of parallel play. Then I attempted to communicate to her by speaking to myself in such a way that I could be overheard. When the child made eye contact, she communicated that I could move to more direct, yet still cautious discussions. A non-threatening yet stimulating atmosphere enabled this child to take the creative as well as communication risks involved in creating her drawing.

DEVELOPING CHILDRENS' SELF-IMAGES

Warm Up Exercises and Modeling

Warm-up exercises prepare students for the art activity by first engaging them in physical movement (Cane 1983). After sitting stationary all day in their academic classes, children may need to loosen up both physically and mentally. Warm-up exercises allow for the controlled release of pent-up energy, so that the child is less rigid and more relaxed when it is time to make art. Stationary body movements such as stretching, neck rolling, finger shaking, and deep breathing are simple and fun to do. Such exercises provide a physical outlet and warm-up without becoming hyper-stimulating or confused with more robust physical education activities. Once the children are stretched and loose, the teacher may then find them a more alert audience and more responsive to verbal interventions.

Depicting the human figure is a major problem for many children with special needs. In many cases children may be unaware of their own bodies—especially the full range of movements or facial expressions of which they are capable. Individuals with damaged body parts or paralysis may overtly or covertly ignore that part of the body. This may contribute to a distorted sense of body image. Blind children are particularly susceptible to an incomplete perception of their bodies. They tend to view themselves as an arrangement of parts rather than an autonomous whole (Lowenfeld 1957).

An important part of motivation is to acquaint the handicapped youngster with the positive aspects of his or her figure and to promote a stronger sense of self-concept and self-image. Warm-up exercises are a good beginning to helping students become acquainted with their bodies. They serve also as a preliminary to life drawing and figure modeling activities in which the student takes the role of model as well as artist. By exploring action or still poses, the child activates an awareness of the expressive potential of any body—even the most handicapped. I have used costumes, period dress, even bed sheets to create comical and interesting figures for children to draw. This kind of posturing for life drawing or modeling seems to bring out the actor in children, where they become special and the center of attention.

Using Mirrors

Wall mirrors can be incorporated into the process of developing a self-image, allowing children to see themselves and each other from a fresh perspective. This may have a particularly favorable effect upon children who misbehave, since it enables them to view their antics from a distance and see themselves as others see them. Remember, however, that mirrors can also be destructive for certain children. Those who are deformed, overly self-conscious or autistic may be alarmed by confronting their own image.

An autistic boy with whom I worked avoided drawing figures for two years while slowly and patiently his self-awareness developed through observing and touching inanimate statues. On one occasion, I offered him a plastic mirror which he promptly smashed to pieces. I quickly stepped back to more indirect methods of motivation. Eventually he did spontaneously draw a self-portrait but without the use of a mirror. Instead, he relied upon haptic sensations as he systematically touched his body in search of its form.

In cases where the teacher is employing a mirror it is advisable to devise a buffer between the child and his or her reflection. Props such as capes, costumes, and other draperies can provide the needed barrier, while also providing a multitude of figurative forms that are interesting to draw. In this way, the teacher can present a life-drawing problem to a group of children in a challenging yet sheltered way, allowing the more delicate child an extra measure of consideration.

Using Videotapes

Videotape is another self-image motivational medium that prompts robust and immediate responses from children. Dancing, face mugging, even the most mundane hand wave can stimulate greater awareness in children of their own figures. Children regard television as a daily routine, yet it is something that remains awesome and distant. Seeing themselves on the screen, children become amazed and dazzled.

I have used video successfully with a group of moderately physically-disabled children who were

Video is a medium all children are stimulated by. The opportunity to work with this medium is relished by children who become fascinated by appearing on screen.

being introduced to life drawing. The process began cautiously, since several children were reticent about their handicaps and it was unclear how such an art project would affect them. These children tended to be very tense and constricted when they drew, building up tension in their wrists, hands and fingers. In order to release some of this tension, I encouraged them first to act out freely. They were then asked to rotate their arms from the shoulder like great propellers. This exercise, which was developed in Europe in the thirties, (Richardson 1948), encourages children to simulate the strokes used in sketching. By making these large, sweeping arcs in the air, my students were able to warm up to putting unrestrained lines and forms of great vitality on their newsprint pads. With freer, more relaxed sketching, their figures became more fluid and occupied the pictorial space with greater command. The children themselves seemed pleasantly surprised at the results of combining movement and drawing.

PROPS

Children are at their best when they are creating artwork that springs from the well of personal experience. Young children in particular take obvious joy in depicting significant life experiences as elaborate tales and arresting images. It is this special investment of personal meaning that makes the art of young children so rich and enduring. The naiveté and abandon with which they work will probably never again be approximated in their artistic lives.

As the child matures, his or her power of expression changes with experience and environmental influences. In some cases the carefree expression of early years becomes hampered with inhibitions. Adolescents' private worlds are often guarded places where adults, who are often disapproving, are not welcome. It is also during adolescence that children become self-conscious and embarrassed over the "childish" work of their formative years. They become determined to

In a warm-up ritual which preceded every art session, this autistic child played intently with his toy horse, which motivated him to experiment with the art materials.

abandoned their naive style and set about portraying things as they are perceived. This may entail the rendering of realistically drawn "action figures" or depicting accurate perspective.

This shift of emphasis is a natural developmental phenomenon and should be allowed to proceed unfettered by adult interference. However, this is also a crucial time for the teacher to respond with sensitivity and empathy to ensure that the child's drive to create is nourished and tended. As the needs of the child change, the teacher must stand ready to adjust his or her interventions, particularly those that encompass motivation. As children begin to try to create in a more realistic, mature style, the teacher must provide a rich and varied environment. The art studio should be an exciting, intriguing place, where a variety of stimulating objects offer ready inspiration. A healthy diversity of props improves the chances that the uninspired child will find something to spark his or her dormant imagination. Sufficient time must be built

into the art period so that such a child can unhurriedly walk around the studio and poke into corners and cabinets in search of the perfect subject. Having an overabundance of resource material will ensure that stimulation, inspiration, and motivation will be forthcoming. Although the teacher cannot cover every theme comprehensively over the years, an extensive collection of essential motivational props can be accumulated.

The key to using props as motivators is finding objects that are appropriate for the age and level of the child while also possessing sufficient aesthetic possibilities so that they don't become stereotypes. For instance, many children, particularly girls, enjoy drawing horses. The problem arises, however, as to how to provide a suitable model. A photograph or illustration does little to excite the imagination. Locating a real horse is, of course, logistically difficult. I have found a worthy substitute in a set of realistically modeled horses that are posed in different positions. They have proven to be popular as models for drawing and sculpting, and as toys.

In addition to being motivational for mature, higher functioning children, I have found that horse models often arouse the curiosity of more severely handicapped children. One autistic and visually impaired child made a very positive connection with one of these models. As part of his warm-up ritual, he would immediately reach for his favorite colt, animate it playfully, then set it up beside his art project for the duration of the session. Although he was too developmentally disabled to incorporate the model realistically in his artwork, it nevertheless developed into an important relationship and an indispensible part of his art program.

Another useful prop is a set of late nineteenth-century time-lapse photographs taken of horses in full gallop. Every stride of the horse is depicted in a strobe sequence so that the student can choose the exact position he or she wishes to portray. I also have on hand for student use a library of video clips in which footage of a galloping horse can be viewed as many times as necessary.

A crucial point in using props as motivators is incorporation. Once the teacher uncovers what really excites a child's interest, it is vital that the prop should be used purely for motivational purposes and not as the sole subject matter of the art activity. Props are not substitutes for the child's own ideas, but rather act as a point of departure for developing new ideas. For instance, if a horse was used as a model for a clay sculpture, the teacher might then follow up with a verbal intervention such as "Where is the horse running? Is he running wild or does he have a rider? Can you make the rider and saddle?" etc. In this manner, the prop is used as a point of departure and not an end to itself.

MAKING ART FROM ART

Another strategy that stimulates students' intellectual faculties in concert with their imaginations is the use of art reproductions as a means of extending children's frames of reference (Wilson, Hurwitz and Wilson 1987). Drawings by the masters, impressionistic paintings, neolithic cave art, folk art, graffiti and abstract expressionism can all be presented in exciting concert to most populations.

Copying artworks outright sometimes results in unique interpretations that ultimately bear little resemblance to the original.

Assimilating outside influences is a natural and productive part of the creative process. Children routinely draw upon images in their culture, such as comic book heroes and other media figures, for the subjects and themes of their art. Introducing children to art reproductions is a natural extension of this process—one that can be used as a stimulus to students' own originality and imaginative powers. By incorporating all or parts of the art reproduction, students are encouraged to leave behind their stereotypes and instead explore the form and style of a diversity of artists.

Many special needs children naturally work in a style that is reminiscent of Paul Klee, Miró or Franz Kline. Much of their figurative work and compositions parallel the images evoked in rock petroglyphs, Zen brushwork and Picasso's primitivist works. Thus, these artworks can be presented in ways that are meaningful for even the severest handicapped child.

Art reproductions can be used in several capacities. They can be incorporated into art instruction

84

purely as visual aids that expose the students to art history and art appreciation. Should the child be verbal and have sufficient language, a discussion of this material may prompt enthusiastic participation as a warm-up to making art. Sometimes the art can be copied outright. Having the student rework a print as a study model and vehicle for interpretation can prompt new directions in the student's developing style. Reproductions can also be manipulated for emphasis—cropped or exploded so that essentially a new work emerges. Again, this material should be used as a departure and not as an end unto itself. Assist the students in making creative use of this material, so that it effectively shakes up their existing stereotypes and injects new vigor into their work.

The success of this approach depends heavily upon the teacher's sensitivity to the individual needs of the student. Students should not be reworking artworks that are technically or develop-

mentally out of their reach. While challenges can be healthy, do not set the child up to fail by presenting artwork that may lead to increased inhibitions. Make every effort to match the student's capabilities and interests with an art form that will camouflage the student's deficits while complementing his or her style and ability.

A certain amount of strategy is involved in fitting the art reproduction to the individual. For example, when I introduced a group of normal, hearing-impaired students to reproduced material, the goal was to allow all the children to work with an appropriate artist or print at their own pace. The children with the capacity to do so worked with more sophisticated artists such as El Greco, Dürer, Wyeth, Dine and Warhol. However, a multiply handicapped child mainstreamed into the

Despite multiple handicaps, this child was able to use a Chagall print as a motivating device for her own pastel work.

group was incapable of approaching the styles of such artists due to her cognitive, sensory and developmental deficits. Her own figurative style was characterized by simplistic, floating geometric forms that invariably stood unadorned and unchanged.

The discrepancy in ability between the other children and this child was dramatic. It was also an issue in the social dynamics of the class. The regular students tended to resent this "incapable" student in their midst, since her presence accentuated their own handicaps and diminished their sense of self-esteem. To maintain a sense of parity between the students, I effectively camouflaged the multiply handicapped child's deficits by steering her toward an artist whose work complemented her abilities. The simplicity of form and color of a Chagall painting was well within her technical capability.

In this case the motivation did, in fact, result in diminishing the student's reliance upon her personal stereotypes. While her first attempts were essentially simplistic copies of the print, subsequent efforts were more improvisational and complex. Eventually, she was weaned from the print to the extent that she would study Chagall's work as a prelude to drawing on her own, creatively using the art reproduction as a vehicle for self-expression.

During the critique, it was important that I display the multiply handicapped student's work next to the work of the normal students. There was little indication of retardation or naiveté. Instead, there were numerous artists, art periods, cultures and artworks represented, with each student's solution being individual and age appropriate. Indeed, one of the more successful pieces was the Chagall—with the idiosyncracies of the original artist's style being fully complemented by the style of the multiply handicapped student. In this case, her natural tendency to distort and simplify constituted an aesthetic *strength*. Her previously stereotypical figures, once filtered through a new and enriching influence, exerted a favorable effect upon her developing artistic style.

USING STORIES, MYTHS AND NARRATIVES

Almost every child enjoys being read to, spoken to, sung to—being entertained—while learning something new. The spoken word, the dramatic movement and the song are all powerful generators of visual images and can be used as motivational strategies. Stories, myths, historical events, poems and descriptions can provide a reservoir of expressive material for use during the art process. While these are proven motivations used by educators and therapists in many settings, problems can emerge when applying them to children with diverse needs. These motivation strategies must be scaled to a mode of communication that accommodates the special needs of the child. Children who are hearing-impaired may be relying upon visual cues, signed language and body movement. Mentally retarded children may require simplified vocabulary and imagery to get the point across. The problem becomes increasingly complicated in the mainstream setting, where any motivation technique must have a broad, general appeal in order to include the entire group. Solving such a conflict involves making shrewd decisions as to the critical characteristics of the material we use. The storybooks I have used have a simple yet rich storyline. Illustrations, if used, should be striking, with the figures transcending the issues of age, gender and culture. Excellent authors for this purpose are Maurice Sendak, Edward Gory and Ralph Steadman. Their works are deceptively simple and defy typecasting or stereotype. They are expressive, not condescending, and make use of outrageous scenarios which prompt the students' imaginations.

I often have students create their own story and picture books. In presenting such a project to children with varying abilities in learning, language, social awareness and behavior, the motivation must accommodate many levels yet strike a common chord. The motivation in this case may entail reading and displaying a storybook. The students can be stimulated by the narrative and pictures, grasp the concept, and eventually improvise on the theme. The book may also need to mesh with a diversity of cultures and backgrounds within the group. Each child must additionally be able to relate to the age-appropriateness of the book, without feeling that it is infantile or beneath their ability.

Telling stories without the support of illustrations is another effective motivation method. I have done dramatic readings from a wide range of novels, poems and personal writing that serve to motivate students to manipulate the content, improvise on the theme or complete the ending. A favorite vehicle of mine is a Zen koan or haiku such as:

> A fallen flower
> returning to the branch.
> No it was a butterfly‗‗‗‗‗‗

Inspired by a haiku poem, a multiply handicapped boy made an unusually smooth transition from concrete ideas to metaphorical expression.

One response to this poem was created by a deaf/legally blind high school student who, because of his art ability, was mainstreamed with regular students in the art class. His usual subject matter consisted of airplanes, boats and other transportation themes that bordered upon being a personal stereotype. Listening to this poem prompted him to create this "fallen" butterfly. I was consistently impressed with the ability of students with such profound deficits to respond to motivations that demanded abstract reasoning and the ability to transform their ideas into pictorial form.

Another favorite narration of mine draws upon Victor Hugo's description of Quasimodo *The Hunchback of Notre Dame* as he rode his great bell. After listening with eyes closed to this gripping passage, the children from grades five through nine were encouraged to record their impressions using various art media. They were instructed to focus upon the most vibrant image that came to mind. The forms, movements and rhythms operating in this description elicited wonderful and powerful images in the artwork. While many of the children probably could not assimilate Hugo's choice of words like "tempest," "vertigo" or "winged crupper" they were able to take some-

thing from the passage that held meaning. Each child was able to work out images and ideas of surprising complexity.

Again, these responses cut across the lines of handicapping conditions, and, for the most part, functioning level. One special needs child who was predisposed to very concrete responses, visualized Quasimodo as the fly described in the opening passage. Whether or not this child lacked the conceptual capacity to grasp the metaphor remains unimportant in light of the effect upon her artwork. The goal of this motivation was to facilitate the beginning of the art process by inspiring images that prompt graphic expression. The fact that this special needs child lacked the faculty for abstract thought did not in any way detract from her solution to the design problem. While some of her peers were drawing more conventional figures riding the bell and other were more adventurously giving the bell equine characteristics, the special needs child had one of the most original responses of all. Again, the idiosyncratic nature of the special needs child enhanced artistic expression.

Working from music can also motivate children to go beyond stereotypes toward more unusual and expressive responses. Children of all ages enjoy

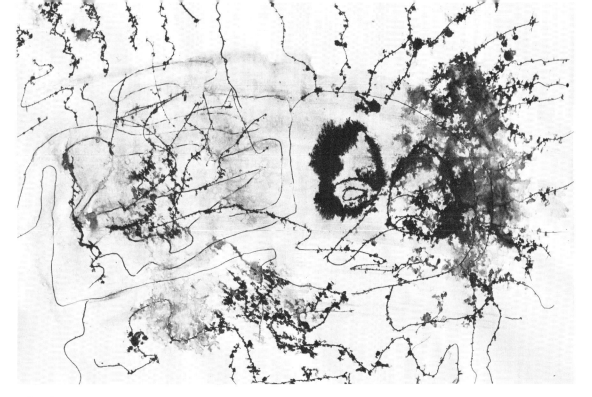

After listening to Mussorgsky's "Night on Bald Mountain," an eleven-year-old learning disabled boy created several expressionistic creatures that were inspired by the musical sensations.

87

sitting back with their eyes closed, encouraged to visualize the music. Reacting to the interplay of tones, rhythms and instrumentation can stimulate surprisingly abstract and impressionistic images. Whether it is Beethoven's Fifth Symphony or Pink Floyd's "Dark Side of the Moon," the response will invariably be original and diverse. Because music is a universal medium, one that touches us on a pre-verbal level, even the lowest-functioning child can respond.

Perhaps the most widely used musical motivation is *Night on Bald Mountain* by Mussorgsky. This powerfully expressionistic piece has been a Halloween mainstay for years since Disney used it in the *Fantasia* score. Children *delight* in envisioning the bursting graves, the soaring ghosts in the blackened sky and the magnificent Devil. Depending upon the functioning level of the students, some individuals will be able to respond purely upon the strength of the music, while others may require additional structure such as seeing clips from *Fantasia* to bolster conceptualization. In any case, musical scores such as these can lead to a multiplicity of responses.

ART MEDIA AS MOTIVATOR

Art materials invite a child to participate and experiment in a way that few verbal interventions manage. The sensory and manipulative qualities of the media answer the child's need for stimulation and expression in an intimate and personal way. This can be a very special relationship. Indeed, it is only this personal partnership between the media and the child that allows some with special needs to make a connection with the art process since many of these children are unable to respond to verbal instructions or even develop a normal relationship with the teacher.

Despite sensory impairments, cognitive retardation or emotional problems, many of these children will venture to squeeze the clay or brush the tempera spontaneously, thus making a crucial first step toward fruitful participation. A five-year-old autistic, deaf and legally blind child with whom I worked began his art experiences without any appreciable language nor was he able to relate sufficiently with his teacher to accept intervention. He was, however, fascinated with the possibilities of making colorful marks with crayon and pencil. He reached out to the world through the direct and immediate language of the graphic image. The art process in this instance played a crucial role in venting emotional tensions as well as building desirable behaviors and skills. This was achieved without the necessity that he function academically or even acknowledge the teacher's presence. During the early years of his education, art was a personal journey of critical importance.

An important factor when implementing a materials approach to motivation is to ensure an appropriate match between the medium and the child. Developmental arrest, physical limitation, cognitive abilities and emotional stress will always govern which media we introduce. These issues loom larger when the media is used as the prime motivating agent. Consider, for example, the case of a Down's syndrome child with language deficits and a cleanliness compulsion. How would one motivate such a child when using clay, for instance? First, one needs to rely upon the playful, manipulative qualities of the medium to arouse the child's curiosity. Still, one would assume that introducing a sticky, brown lump of clay to this spotless and hesitant child would hardly prompt enthusiastic participation. If the teacher is determined to work with this medium, it must first be adapted so as to resolve the conflicts that the material may awaken in the student. Using clean, dry plasticene or white, heavily grogged clay may address these issues. Once the medium is properly scaled to the correct developmental/sensory level and accommodates the child's emotional state, the teacher can then emphasize the pleasureful aspects of clayworking: how it can be smacked and rolled, carved and folded into a myriad of interesting forms and designs.

The same adjustments in the medium would be required when introducing color to a student with these handicaps. Few young, retarded or compulsive children will become motivated to paint if the tempera is excessively thin and runny or lacks the viscosity to stay loaded on the brush. The medium must be adjusted or switched to painting sticks and dry tempera cakes. When working with dry colors, pastels may cause problems for such a student, since they generate dust and tend to smear. Markers, Craypas or crayons may be preferred in this instance.

Populations such as adolescent boys, inner-city youths or vocationally minded students may not respond to the decorative aspects of the art media. These groups may need a medium that possess a challenge or possesses some great mystique in order for motivation to occur. These qualities may be termed "resistance" (Clements 1984) which refers not only to the difficulty of the material or techniques, but also to the characteristics that allow for heavy or robust physical involvement. This sense of physicality may also involve an element of danger or adventure.

One class of fourteen-year-old deaf students I dealt with was difficult to arouse with the standard graphic media. Even clay was uninteresting to this difficult group of boys. These children were obsessively "macho" in their demeanor—a self-image that was carefully cultivated and protected. Any supposed "feminine" activities—painting watercolors of flowers, for example—drew immediate refusals to participate. To gain their interest, I introduced pewter casting in cuttlebone, which necessitated the use of a propane torch, and other seemingly masculine tools and props. In presenting this project I emphasized how physically demanding and dangerous a project it was and that I ordinarily reserve it for older students. I advised them that it demanded teamwork and a steady hand, which only the most mature and competent students could handle. Interestingly enough, it was the most recalcitrant of the boys who demonstrated the most care in this instance. Being allowed to handle the torch was a prestigious position—one that had to be earned by good judgement and leadership.

In some instances, children function very concretely and have little use for projects involving abstract content or function. They want to know "What is it?" and "How can it be used?" and in some cases "How much money it is worth?" This situation demands a "product" approach to materials whereby the student is assured that some kind of object will be "manufactured" during the project. This approach will usually entail some kind of craftwork in a structured format that ensures a degree of tangible success. One group of inner-city vocational students who had never before taken a class in art or crafts resolutely refused to participate. Undaunted, I arranged that one day out of every other week would be given over to an art format which allowed them to work within their vocational specialty. Thus, carpentry students took a class in sculptural woodworking, welding majors worked in sculptural metal fabrication, data processors took computer graphics, and the upholstery class worked in soft sculpture. Within the confines of a secure and familiar environment, these high school students eventually acquiesced and began to explore their usual media from a new direction and different context.

When searching for projects that are adaptable for special populations, you need not rely upon gimmicky or novelty materials. Too often, prefabricated, commercially prepared media such as plaster molds, painting stencils, ceramic greenware and coloring sheets are used in the special education setting. Prefab projects require a minimum amount of participation and, because many of these projects are conceived by adults in an adult style, the products are usually foreign to the children who supposedly "create" them.

Kit/craft projects constitute a restrictive environment for the special needs child who, in most cases, is capable of planning and executing original material. The results may not be as superficially attractive or slick as the kit work, yet, in my view, anything is preferable to such abominations. As Kramer (1971) vociferously points out, aside from the aesthetic impoverishment of such work, motivation may be dampened. Children are seduced or misled by these "prefab" creations into a false sense of accomplishment; they become reluctant to create "imperfect" images and thus, remain greedy for new sensations. Needless to say they

are not substantially invested in these novelties and, thus, maintain a perfunctory, detached demeanor during the process, often losing interest or remaining unappropriative of their finished product.

Traditional media can be adapted to engage the child in a concrete, operation-oriented manner and avoid the creation of ugly stereotyped and impersonal work. The traditional art forms of drawing, painting and sculpture have successfully engaged artists of all cultures. Their possibilities for expression, variation and adaptability are virtually limitless. Given their flexibility and stimulating qualities, there is no compelling need for a novelty medium.

MOTIVATIONAL PROBLEMS

The art teacher will sometimes encounter children with special needs—and intact children—whose motivation to participate has somehow been interfered with and diminished. Getting started in the art activity may entail a great deal of stress for them and turn what should be a relaxed, enjoyable experience into a bitter struggle. There seems to be no end to the sources that will depress a child's willingness to create, and it is extremely difficult to isolate those specific factors that hinder a child's free expression. Most are bound up in several complex and subtly interrelated problems whose nature may be emotional, physical, cognitive or environmentally related. These factors may act as powerful deterrents which in their most intractable form, can prohibit the art process from ever taking place.

Depressed, withdrawn, hyperactive or insecure children are especially prone to problems of motivation. Confronting an empty drawing paper or an amorphous piece of clay can be highly imtimidating and anxiety-provoking. In many instances these children have suffered traumatic or sustained discouragement which has seriously shaken their confidence. Such children need a gentle touch and should be allowed sufficient time during the program to come out of their shells and work at their own pace without undue pressures of competition or productivity.

Conversely, aggressive, angry or hyperactive children may be initially overwhelmed by the stimulation provided by an art activity. These children may respond by rejecting, damaging or defacing the art project. In these instances, the students will need adaptations in the media, classroom set-up and teacher interactions so that productive and goal-oriented motivation can be established.

The most obvious source of motivational problems is a child's physically disabling condition. For instance, the cerebral palsied child may be self-conscious of spastic movements and be reluctant to manipulate a paint-laden brush. Paralysed students may not be able to imagine that adaptive procedures will enable them to create in the same manner as ambulatory children. For the hearing-impaired child, art may be thought of as an overly abstract process which possesses little usefulness or concrete meaning. The blind child may not have developed the needed environmental awareness that encourages exploration and creativity. In many instances the physical disability is compounded by feelings of inadequacy, self-consciousness or passivity. For example, a disfigured child may resist participating in life-drawing exercises, or a quadriplegic child may be consumed with anger and depression over his or her auto accident. Many of these variables can be amended by sensitively administered interventions based upon empathetic acceptance of children's feelings while exhorting them to surmount their disabilities through stimulating and engrossing art activities.

Cognitive deficits may also adversely affect a child's motivation. For instance, a mentally retarded student may not have had sustained sensory stimulation over the formative years. He or she may be locked into ritualistic, repetitive or other autistic behaviors that shut out much incoming stimuli and thus preclude participation in the art activity. There may be a lack of intellectual ability to grasp the concepts of technique, media manipulation or representation in the art process. Also, there may be difficulties in communicating these concepts due to the child's lack of receptive language or because of overriding emotional conflicts. In cases where there is a brain trauma due to an accident, the student's abilities may be severely impaired, yet on the surface appear perfectly intact and normal. To participate in the art activity may become a frightening, disturbing experience, since the depth of the handicap and its deficits will be clearly in evidence.

All children—exceptional or normal—are also deeply and positively affected by their surroundings: their family, school, leisure time and living environments. For example, the blind child who has had the advantage of an enriched and stimulating environment will display less trouble in orienting him- or herself, relating to others and conceptualizing objects. The same holds true for the mentally retarded, hearing impaired, autistic and other sensory-deprived individuals who have experienced early intervention and stimulation for arousal and subsequent motivation.

"Out of service/out of order" succinctly conveys the shutting down of this autistic young man. A bright, gentle child, his intense sensitivity to self and others often precipitated such autistic expression.

EXCEPTIONAL ART

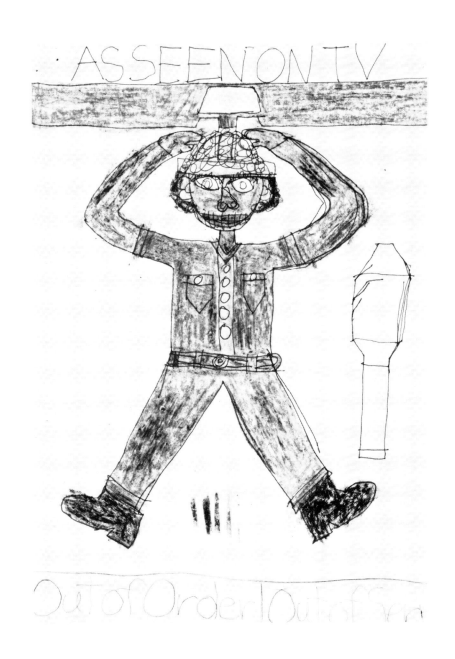

chapter 6

Drawing Development

Of all the art processes, drawing is the most familiar and popular. It is also the most demanding and intimidating. Drawing challenges a child to confront the unblemished whiteness of the paper and transform it by adding lines and forms that result in images. These images cannot aspire to the effortless forms and textures that are inherent when a child touches a piece of clay. Neither will they have the lush expressiveness of a colored brushstroke. Drawing marks stand alone, threadbare and vulnerable to a viewer's scrutiny.

In a drawing, many aspects of the individual come alive. The modulation of line, its thickness, its pressure, its freedom of movement, all reveal aspects of the artist and his or her process. Lines can be halting, jagged, flowing, loosely scribbled or precisely drawn with one perfect and economical line. Line thickness can be broad or razor thin. Varying pressure can produce lines that range from nearly invisible to pitch black. Content can range from the uncontrolled scribble and abstract design to images of near photorealism. The range of possibilities available from a simple graphite point can convey the artist's discipline, innate skill, sensitivity, temperament and mood with remarkable economy.

For children of varied abilities, the range of artistic possibilities in the drawn line is particularly diverse. Once experienced in the developmental sequence of drawing development, one can also

glean much information concerning a child's sensory, manual, intellectual and developmental capacities. In some cases, the content and the stylistic approach to the medium reveals emotional information as well. Because of the economy and austerity of the medium, this information is often blatantly evident. This is true not only of the special needs artist, but of seasoned artists as well. Because drawing is considered as something of a standard of measurement both in terms of developmental and aesthetic maturation, artists may be intimidated by it. Drawing demands enormous perceptive and visual motor skills, a developed aesthetic eye, perseverance, sensitivity, boldness and a range of other artistic attributes. Should just one of these attributes be deficient, it is immediately evident in the drawing. There is no rescuing a weak drawing, regardless of the embellishments that are ladled on to shore up the draftsmanship.

It stands to reason that special needs children will have enormous problems measuring up to all the demands of drawing. During the kinesthetic and early conceptual stages of drawing, when the child's insight and awareness of his or her work is still undeveloped, this may not be such a problem. Most children naturally enjoy making scribbles, doodling or making infantile pictures that represent the joys and wonder of their world. However, as a child matures to the point where social awareness, peer pressure and art criticism begin to come into

Drawing remains the most universal of art processes. In the hands of the exceptional child, the drawing instrument is often wielded with striking expressivity.

play, drawing inhibitions emerge. These inhibitions sometimes plague even the most gifted draftsmen throughout school and possibly their careers. When these inhibitions make their appearance the therapeutic art teacher must display utmost sensitivity, ingenuity and perceptiveness in order to enable the child to rise past stumbling blocks and inhibitions so that he or she can experience the satisfaction that comes from the drawing process.

In keeping with most theoreticians, I approach drawing development from a conceptual–perceptual standpoint. This means that before the chronological or mental age of nine to twelve years, the child is drawing from a conceptual perspective (See Gardner 1987, p. 19). The child renders figures and objects not as he or she sees them, but based upon his or her understanding and emotional relationship to what is drawn. This explains, for example, why at five years of age the self-portrait is the dominant figure in a composition, bigger even than a house, or a tree. At this stage a child is *egocentric,* or in other words, the world revolves around his or her needs, sensations, and feelings. Thus, the self-portrait will reflect this subjective relationship to the environment.

As children approach the age or level of functioning of a nine to twelve-year-old, they begin to make a cognitive and perceptual transition. They begin to display readiness to draw what they see or perceive. Identification with adult modes of perception becomes strong, with children abandoning their infantile stereotypes in favor of more realistic styles of drafting. This major developmental milestone is a pivotal one for the child and an important indicator of the type of art instruction he or she should receive.

Recent research has shown that intact children can indeed "beat" Lowenfeld's model of artistic developmental milestones by being taught to draw in a pseudo-naturalistic style (Winner 1982). Although such precosity may be impressive for the adult, art educator or lay viewer, it doubtless has little meaning for the child. Since it is an alien, inappropriate means of creating, the young child will not be sufficiently invested in the art. Subsequently, it will remain purely an academic exercise, devoid of expressivity or creativity.

In the author's view, young children, or those functioning at the conceptual level of a young child, should be encouraged to draw in the spontaneous, naive style of a child. Too often we push children to act precociously. Drawing should be left to children to express what they know about, how they feel, imagine or dream.

Children themselves will demonstrate when they wish to slough off their infantile modes of drawing and begin a more academic or discipline-based approach to drawing and artwork in general. In many cases the child will demonstrate the readiness well before actually making this leap. Some never make it, remaining forever mired as adults in the style of fifth graders. Thus, with intact and special needs children alike, the art teacher must provide moral support and technical guidance to work through this developmental milestone. With both intact and special needs students this can be an arduous yet gratifying journey.

My approach to the drawing process is decidedly developmentally oriented. Before the age of eleven, emphasis is placed upon spontaneous expression of experience, relationships, feelings and discoveries that naturally come with childhood. As the child begins to work in a realistic mode, however, my approach begins to emphasize art as an academic discipline. While I continue to use memory, affect and imagination as expressive and therapeutic factors in the process, I expand the emphasis to include art appreciation, art history, technique, experimentation, problem solving and critical or reflective awareness. From this point, I work with each child—even those with severe handicapping conditions—as a fellow artist, one who has seriously looked at art, learned to talk about the language of art, developed or been exposed to its techniques and ultimately brought something expressive to it from a wholly personal point of view.

EARLY DEVELOPMENT

A child's first marks are made when still a baby, through the smearing of food or other accessible media. Although this is a pleasureful activity, it does not constitute a drawing process per se, since the child has little awareness of the visual expression of his or her actions. Kinesthetic and tactile sensation are what fuel the process at this stage. The smearings that result from this tactile play do mirror, however, first markings made when the child matures enough to start wielding a drawing implement. At this point simple sensory pleasure is derived from manipulating, mouthing and playing with the drawing implement which may or may not make contact with a drawing surface. Should contact be made, the resulting marks will remain random scribbles indicating that visual-motor control is still in its rudimentary stages.

Regardless of what these early scribbles signify for the child or the adult, they are important links to later artistic involvement. This period coincides with Mahler's stages, when the drawing implement and the child's body are largely undifferentiated as both are used for kinesthetic pleasure and sensory exploration. It is also a period when the drives of sex and aggression are undifferentiated. Marking serves as a viable form of channeling drive energy, and these early joyful and robust experiences may be transferred later on into an uninhibited and powerful creative drive.

For children with special needs, however, the natural inclination to smear or scribble cannot be taken for granted. Disabled children might be slow, resistent or oblivious to this behavior. What should be a joyful, effortless exploration of babyhood may become a laborious, alien activity and be resisted. The developmentally disabled often become stranded at an immature drawing phase, such as scribbling. This means that it is possible to be working with a special needs ten-year-old—or a profoundly retarded twenty-year-old—on scribbling exercises usually meant for a three-year-old. Progress with students like these may remain stalled or only move forward in the smallest of increments. In other cases, a child may possess the readiness to make developmental artistic leaps, but not have been prompted or encouraged to do so. Just as any adult who has not drawn since childhood will draw in an immature style, the developmentally disabled languish in an arrested style until someone attends to their situation, recognizes their potential and gives them the needed shove to move them forward.

There are specialized problems that the teacher will encounter with different populations when trying to develop readiness and drawing skills. Children who are functioning at a regressed level may not possess sufficient cognition, perception or coordination to make a drawing. A crayon may be seen as part of the body, something to suck or break (Mahler 1975). Mark-making may be an incomprehensible activity for the child at this time. Sensory impaired children, such as the blind, autistic children and even psychotics, may find the idea of grasping and marking an alien, disagreeable process. I have observed young autistic children shriek with apparent horror as their peers color a picture. Perhaps they perceived this as an act of aggression, a violation or defacement. This reaction may be due to a lack of object constancy, which is to say the child has failed to develop a cognitive comprehension of the object (or the drawing implement) as well as a stable sense of self-boundaries. Blind children in particular may be fearful of grasping then striking outward with a

drawing object due to tactile discomfort as well as object disconnection. Orthopedically handicapped children may lack the strength to actually maintain a grasp and pressure upon the crayon, thus making a simple coloring activity a physical test of endurance.

In order to lessen this resistance, adaptations might be needed to prompt a child to participate successfully. Appropriate media and techniques are crucial for enticing resistant children to make their first scribbles. The first drawing instrument is usually a crayon. For young children or those with poor object relations, crayons with stout bodies and a flattened side to control rolling are most effective (since they stay put and are predictable). Crayons are colorful, thus stimulating, non-toxic and require only light pressure to register markings. Once a child's oral fixation is alleviated other media such as markers, colored pencils and pastels can be introduced. However, years of creative mileage can be achieved with a simple wax crayon.

In introducing this medium, I keep in mind a least restrictive approach, which allows the child to manipulate the crayon in any way that is safe and pleasureful. If a child is self-motivated and can spontaneously grasp the instrument and successfully wave it around, scribble and simple play, the art teacher's task is so much easier.

Should a child not respond to our enthusiastic demonstrations, verbal exhortations, or concrete examples, a hand-over-hand technique can be used. This involves assisting the child in the least restrictive manner, so that some degree of participation can be achieved. Hand-over-hand techniques may be as minimal as handing the child a crayon or positioning it appropriately within the child's grasp. If resistance is formidable the teacher might decide to 'motor through' the activity for the child. This means grasping the child's hand or wrist and manipulating the child's arms so that the motor patterns associated with the scribbling process can be assimilated. In some cases, it is only a question of time and perseverance before a child catches on. In other situations, when a child is resistant for some sensory or emotional reason, it can mean a protracted period of experimentation to see which approach works.

When teaching a child to scribble, I emphasize working in large, freely executed circles and arcs, with arm movements emanating from the shoulder and arm, thus loosening rigidity and inhibition (Cane 1983). This should be a playful activity which places little emphasis upon a product. The child must begin to enjoy this process or else further development will remain stifled.

Scribbling, as noted by many researchers, goes through a sequence of changes as the child matures. The disordered scribbles of a two-year-old coalesce into simple circular configurations by age three. By this time, the intact child may be naming or assigning significance to the scribbles. By age four the circular scribble evolves into a simple circle, drawn in one continuous contoured line. At this juncture the ubiquitous circle is not only a record of kinesthetic activity but a symbolic equivalent for something. Whether it symbolizes the

The disordered and circular scribbles created by intact three-year-olds and profoundly retarded sixteen-year-olds are often indistinguishable.

mother's face or breast, the sun or the universality of the cosmos, it clearly represents a concept which has some significance for the child.

This is a crucial developmental milestone which most children effortlessly achieve. For children who are developmentally disabled, however, this conceptual leap may not occur without the considerable effort of both child and teacher. The challenge is to assist in making the connection for the child between circle and face, to build a bridge between the kinesthetic and the conceptual. This can only occur if attention is paid to developing the child's self-concept and self-image, through a kind of awareness training. Before a face can evolve out of a circular scribble, the child must equate the circle with the shape of the head. The features within the face must also be comprehended as being part of the circle or head. Once the concept is formed, then symbol formation through the drawing process can proceed.

For instance, working with a fifteen-year-old, severely learning disabled girl, we drew circles for one entire year, then cut them out. Placing what was essentially a paper ring over my face, I would

repeat "circle-face!" Using dolls, mirrors and Polaroid self-portraits, we played at labeling the facial features, then I would draw them out on paper. After three months she unexpectedly mirrored my drawing and drew several small circles within a larger circle. For a developmentally disabled child, this was a significant conceptual leap. The comprehension of the circular configuration as symbolic of the face was probably rooted in Mahler's differentiation stage. The circle might have signified the child's awareness of the difference between self, transitional object (the paper), and me (the love object). The circular paper cut-outs functioned as a bridge between the child and love object, essentially facilitating the development of self-boundaries while retaining the security and comfort of the transitional object.

Four weeks later this same girl spontaneously drew two eyes, a nose and mouth, then surrounded the entire face with small bead-like circles as if to celebrate the circles within a circle. After six months she could draw the approximation of a face and even pencil in the hair. By the end of the school year, the face had sprouted limbs, hair, ears and quite an expressive mouth. During these nine months, I had not just "taught" her to draw. I had literally led her through Mahler's and Lowenfeld's stages of development from infancy (on a emotional basis) to three-year-old (cognitively speaking) to finally a five- or six-year-old level of functioning.

The following academic year, after several months of refreshment, this girl's figures had matured to the point of rendering the entire human figure complete with erogenous zones. The arms still sprout from the head and, curiously, the sexual parts are contained within yet another circle! This may point to the ongoing process of differentiation, as the different and significant body parts take on a separate identity of their own. Such splitting may never be unified into a cohesive and accurate body image given this child's cognitive limitations. Indeed, she did seem to plateau at this level. Although her ability to increase the *quantity* of details and embellishments continued, the infantile, idiosyncratic nature of her figures continued.

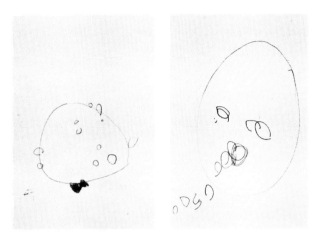

The development of a schema by a fifteen-year-old retarded student shows developing facial features and hair.

After six months of art education therapy, the figure is developed to the point of elaborating upon the sexual parts and facial affect despite its continued developmental immaturity.

98 It appeared that her potential had reached a kind of ceiling. At this point, I continued with developmental concerns, as well as increased the emphasis upon the aesthetic and self-expressive capacity of her art.

Making the Most of a Scribble

For children who are stranded in the scribbling stage, drawing can still be a viable artform which taps into personal experiences and reflects interest and issues which are important to the child. For example, a nineteen-year-old, mentally retarded young man, who worked in a sheltered workshop as part of his school day, collated button-like objects on an assembly line. His drawings remind one of Mahler's discussion of psychic organization—developing a general awareness, then sorting, separating and organizing. Such a composition might be considered a metaphor for this very process as a kind of motivational problem solving. In any event, we can safely say that grouping and organizing were important concerns for this child. Despite the limitations in his drawing capacity, the need to organize his world had reasonably invested in his art and contributed to an interesting variety

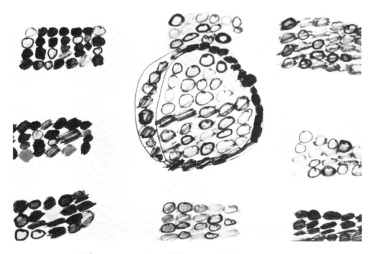

Like any artist, this retarded young man drew upon his life experiences to invigorate his art. His button-collating job in a sheltered workshop is reflected in this work.

of small circular motifs. In viewing a series of these works, one senses that subtle and quite complex aesthetic sensibilities were at work.

In another interesting case, a young man, also with mental retardation due to Down syndrome, created some bizarre grid drawings. In a convoluted weaving of lines, the controlled scribble is brought to new heights. For years he obsessively strung these lines together in complex formations. While such perseveration was obviously gratifying for this individual, his work was locked into a static, rigid mode of unvarying form and content. While I could not expect to move this individual through the developmental milestones to a schematic stage, I did attempt to develop his scribbling beyond a formula of obsessively weaving lines. I began by cutting out an eight-inch circle on white paper. Knowing he was also obsessed with baseball, I presented the paper to him as such, hoping the modification in the shape of the paper would affect positive change in his work. I believed that since it was presented as a ball, his emotional investment in the shape would prompt him to explore this unfamiliar pictorial space. Several sessions later he did just that, drawing in his usual grid format. Having to follow the circular form, however, resulted in several new, important modifications in his style. Most notable of these changes was the first instance when this young man voluntarily left unworked space in his pictures, in the form of two white eclipses arranged bisymmetrically.

Later works also used negative space increasingly which lessened the obsessive, driven nature of his designs. He was now allowing these seething masses of lines space to breath. Eventually he grew confident and relaxed in his work so that he could begin to explore different media. For six years, he would use only felt-tip or ballpoint pens; then, spontaneously crayon made its way into his pallette. The change in medium had the striking effect of negating the linework altogether. Instead of scribbling, there was now a softer, more flexible quality in his work. After the years of grid designs, such changes seemed to be a quantum leap for this

This powerful landscape, comprising thousands of interwoven lines, was created by a profoundly retarded young man of twenty.

A close-up of the preceding work reveals its intense complexity and ingeniousness.

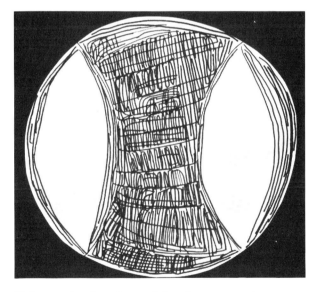

Using a circular piece of drawing paper, the teacher was able to affect changes in the student's artistic style after years of stagnation.

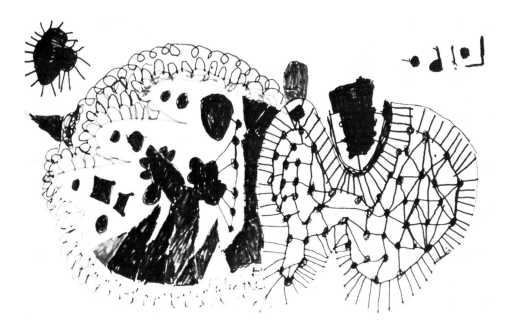

individual. Instead of tightly binding (and thus displacing) the intense tension and need for sameness, he was able to expand through the creative risks in his art. This relaxation of stultifying defenses is characteristic of precursory sublimative activity. Such an example is unusual given the low level of cognitive and emotional functioning of this individual, but it also underlines the potential of this population to respond to therapeutic art interventions (Henley 1986).

Preschematic Phase

The preschematic stage is characterized by the search for representational symbols and is often coupled with an increase in the conceptual activity of the child. At this point, the child has successfully achieved individuation as well as increased an awareness of his or her own ability to affect changes in the environment; these changes are indicative of the *practicing* stage in Mahler's scale. This process can be observed in the case of a child who had scribbled for a year, then began to work from nonobjective designs toward schematic representation. Strangely enough, the precipitating event in this particular developmental leap was the use of a live model. Since this twenty-year-old, visually impaired and retarded girl had previously been locked into nonobjective designs, no one thought to challenge her to draw from life. Once presented with a model of an Indian blanket, however, a schema emerged. This girl's rendition re-

This seemingly abstract design was drawn from life by a deaf/legally blind young woman who faithfully recorded the model's tie-dyed cape.

flects her conceptual awareness of the linear woven quality of the textile, using simplification, decorative borders and intricate interconnections to achieve an abstraction of unusual graphic interest and unity. This child's peers in the mainstream class never ceased to be amazed and interested in how she arrived at such startling designs using everyday objects as her inspiration. Little did they realize that this girl was grappling with elementary developmental issues which were camouflaged by the strategic use of the art process.

In this piece the human figure seems to be on the verge of taking form. Another drawing demonstrates a fascinating link between advanced scribbling and a pre-schematic drawing. Because this young lady had already formed sufficient object relations and developed a conceptual understanding of her subject, the therapeutic art education process unlocked her potential so that her drawing skills were brought up to her over-all functioning level.

An example of the schema finally evolved was drawn by a young man with Down syndrome. It is a conceptual representation that used a live model for inspiration. The figure is abstract, using both simplification and repetition as a means of interpreting the model. It was fascinating to observe the process by which he would block out the major forms (i.e., the head, body, bent legs), then proceed to elaborate not with representational features, but by dividing the model into the same bizarre kind of line grids used by other Down syndrome students. Despite the bizarre abstraction, the young man has effectively captured the sitting model, head arched back, hands at her side, legs bent underneath.

One more example of a highly abstracted scheme was also drawn from life by a multiply handicapped young lady of twenty-one. This piece depicts three standing figures. Using a compartmentalized, geometric format, she achieved a dynamic relationship between the elliptical forms and the triangulations that delineate the figures. Movement, gesture, bulk, body geometry have all been expressed with an economy of means reminiscent of the cubist tradition.

This schema drawn by a Down syndrome young man reveals the use of layering as a means of building up form.

Can you spot the three figures in this life drawing by a multiply handicapped young woman?

102 In both of these examples, it is interesting to note that the predominant design devices entail the separation of body parts and the attempts to unify them into a cohesive whole. When working with individuals at this developmental level, progress will often hinge upon the development of a body-image which is confining and secure—an element reminiscent of autistic or symbiotic union. For the two individuals above, the therapeutic art process entailed accepting these safeguarding devices while also encouraging the children to expand toward more advanced self-concepts and aesthetically pleasing design solutions. This was accomplished by using a modified Lowenfeld motivation, which aimed to increase the each child's awareness of him- or herself by investing the artwork with the power to signify and thus change their concepts of self and others.

The Human Figure Emerges

As a child matures there is a strong possibility that figures complete with recognizable features, limbs and other details will evolve. In the works of developmentally disabled individuals, however, these figures will usually be different from those of intact children. This girl from Great Britain is a striking example of a seasoned child artist. She draws constantly on a wide range of themes, all of which are accompanied by elaborate explanations or stories. The composition is complex, balanced and includes elaborate detail. The figure's affect is clearly expressed, its gestures are at once naturalistic yet also stylized and abstracted in an unusual way. The elements also are organized in a compartmentalized style reminiscent of the developmentally disabled individuals. It is possible that she too is dealing with issues of the body and its boundaries as described by Mahler's individuation process.

Awareness of sexuality is sometimes overtly expressed as soon as the figure evolves. One intact four-year-old was obviously exploring a range of gender characteristics in his artwork. All of the figures are hermaphroditic, possessing the genitalia of both male and female. Such work reminds us

A five-year-old's drawing reveals a typically egocentric self-concept with a conspicuous awareness of his gender.

that children are sexually aware from an early stage and that this is often expressed through artwork rather than verbalization.

Such attempts at reconciling gender issues works back to the rapprochement crisis. Mahler points out that a three-year-old's penis envy is often displaced onto the mother. However, it often surfaces in the art as a symbol of ambivalence over sexual identification and maternal conflict. In contrast is the early human figure of a developmentally disabled teenager drawn from life and embellished by customary make-up; this has the effect of lessening the demand to work in accurate realism. As discussed in the chapter on motivation, children who are unable to render in a naturalistic style must be given subjects which enhance their skills rather than draw attention to their deficits. Again, this is especially crucial when the child is attempting to function in the mainstream setting. In this work by a Down syndrome patient with mental retardation, there is a range of approaches that marks the individual's style of artmaking. Geometric designs, organic forms, rhythm, movement and gesture are used quite

This gifted five-year-old from Great Britain elaborates her figures with decorative embellishments which accentuate her egocentric world.

Even at four years of age, intact children are keenly aware of their sexual parts as evidenced by these little figures who possess the genitals of both sexes!

Loosely drawn from a classmate made up in clown attire, this outlandish portrait was created by a Down syndrome sixteen-year-old.

effectively. In a self-portrait by another Down syndrome young man of twenty-one, the broad gestural sweep of the arms are the center of importance, while the lower body is barely treated. The hugging gesture in this picture was significant. The student's drama therapist recounted that for the first time the student had reached out for an embrace. Previously this young man had an aversion to touching or being touched, a common trait associated with autism.

All of these pre-schematic figure drawings, whether from intact or developmentally disabled children, share certain characteristics. Each figure is depicted as the central, egocentric element in the picture. There is little concern over conveying realism. In each work abstracted, simplified or geometric forms overrule naturalism. This is a difference, however, between the drawings of the intact and the developmentally disabled that can be seen quite clearly. It has to do with the chronological age of the developmentally disabled artists, who have in some cases three to four times the life experience of the five-year-olds. This greater ex-

perience is reflected in their artwork by the idiosyncratic styles, bizarre design devices and use of a naive form of abstraction.

It is important that the therapeutic art educator strike a balance whereby the developmentally disabled be allowed and encouraged to develop their individual styles without constant interventions that pressure them to become more normal or developmentally advanced. As the earlier case accounts illustrated, most of these children and young adults may plateau at some point, with further normalization being a slow, uneven process at best. At some point in time, the therapeutic art teacher may begin to shift in emphasis toward a position that accepts bizarreness, distortion or naiveté despite developmental impoverishment. Young adults especially may need to simply keep making their art, developing their styles and enjoying themselves at something which is an appropriate, creative and productive use of their time.

In an embracing gesture, this mentally retarded boy records an important breakthrough that occurred with his drama therapist.

SCHEMATIC STAGE

Intact children from the ages of eight to eleven are usually able to create images which explore themselves and the world around them, with insight, knowledge and skill. Personality characteristics, details of the environment and a relatively realistic usage of color now replace the pre-schematic, rudimentary, egocentric image of the child. Now exciting stories unfold, with detailed images to accompany the child's narrative. Teachers can now challenge their students with problems to solve and more demanding applications of the drawing medium.

In order for special needs children to advance to this stage their self-concept must be advanced enough so that they can begin to relate themselves to the environment. They must comprehend and act upon the fact that they can influence or affect things in the environment—peers, family, flowers, pets, etc.—by their words and actions. If the special needs child has not advanced to this developmental milestone, his or her figures will remain as egocentric as pre-schematic figures. If this is the case, the program emphasis must continue to center upon developing the child's awareness of self and environment if schematic expression is to be achieved. Using Lowenfeld's motivation techniques, as well as other resources such as audiovisual aids, natural objects, the artwork of other artists, can all intensify a child's relationship to the self and the world.

The first indication that the child is now functioning at the schematic stage is the emergence of a baseline. The baseline infers that the child has discovered that the figure is now rooted in space and is poised to affect something or be affected by something in the environment. An early example of this is the tree and person composition created by an intact, precocious four-year-old. The child can take enormous pleasure at this stage in relating a story or conjuring up fantastic images. As in the other stages, the first schemes by developmentally

The preschematic image, drawn from imagination by a five-year-old, composes elements in their order of importance without the benefit of a baseline or realistic scale.

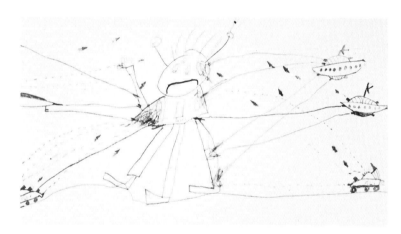

At age seven, the figures become increasingly animated and narrative. This imaginative scene is elaborately detailed, with ships and tracer bullets caught in motion.

106

Using a baseline and progression of figures, this picture demonstrates this multiply handicapped ten-year-old's freshness of vision.

This spontaneous and energetic sketch attempts to solve the problem "Draw Yourself at Home." This legally blind ten-year-old captured a routine yet poignant moment of time.

disabled children are less developed than their intact counterparts. In the first schemes by a severely learning disabled child of ten, the figures parade across the rolling baseline, colored in a colorful, eccentric style.

A fascinating drawing from life by a sixteen-year-old emotionally handicapped child captures the dancing pose, the fluidity of movement and the affective joy of the two models. Responding to the problem "Draw yourself doing something in school that you enjoy," another emotionally disturbed boy of eighteen drew himself hard at work on the potter's wheel. The elaboration with which he depicted the mechanical works of the wheel receives far more attention than the schematized figure. When asked to draw himself at home, one visually impaired young man of eighteen drew not only a portrait of himself standing outside his apartment building, but a veritable voyage of stars, moons, messages and numerical symbols, all of which possessed great significance for him, and gave him enormous gratification in communicating. For a

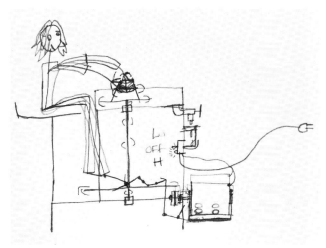

For a young man with autistic object relations, elaborating the mechanical works of the potter's wheel supercedes the details of the human figure.

Caught in a frozen pirouette, this Down syndrome and emotionally handicapped sixteen-year-old animates his figures with poignancy and naive charm.

A simple problem of depicting yourself at home generated a wealth of figures, buildings and imaginative symbols by an eighteen-year-old multiply handicapped young man.

cerebral palsied young man who spent much of his time passively observing his environment, a mail truck stopped at a traffic light provided a suitable theme. Although unable to draw with his spastic hands, he was remarkable at drawing with his feet. For someone so sheltered and with limited experiences, simple things in life take on great significance, in this case driving this child to record his impressions using an astounding adaptation. A talented child can sometimes break through developmental expectations by way of a unique approach to drawing. One six-year-old dispensed with base-lines, narratives, egocentric emphasis and other conventions of the pre-schematic phase. Instead he created a veritable jazz riff of improvisations and variations on the theme of "aliens." One senses that this child could have continued creating these ingenious characters had the paper been larger.

Although drawing with his feet, this young artist is able to capture details with amazing control. This process is, however, an exhaustive one. This piece took four one-hour sessions to complete.

This gifted second grader spins off a series of ingenious celestial characters with superb draftsmanship without concern for narrative or other conventions expected from six-year-olds.

For some individuals, the human figure is not the favored theme. Depending upon their interest or emotional state, some students may include alternative figures in their compositions. The work of a visually impaired teenager centered exclusively around animals. Her compositions invariably have several figures who seem to relate to each other as if they were human. Another emotionally handicapped child worked exclusively on houses, each with a labeled room. His only figures were birds or an occasional tree or shrub.

Throughout the developmental sequence, the art of the special needs child does not fit snugly into the orderly stages associated with intact children. In normal child development, the visual schematic drawings retain the infantile features of earlier phases but use more elements to elaborate the setting, story or idea of the picture. One intact eight-year-old's response to the story of Johnny Appleseed essentially used an elaborated, pre-schematic figure in a descriptive context—a story can be gleaned from the picture beyond the figure's announcing that "I am here." In contrast, older yet developmentally disabled or sensory-impaired children often show elements of advanced, realistic stages in their art. For example, the boy who depicted the potter's wheel is quite schematic in his human figure drawing, yet the wheel is done with the realistic detail uncharacteristic of this phase. Essentially his human figure is commensurate with a nine-year-old, while the treatment of the mechanical equipment confirms that this is the work of a high school student. Although done in a scribbling style, the boy tucked in bed uses perspective and foreshortening, devices which are associated with higher development. These inconsistencies will follow the art of special needs children through their drawing development. Observing and plotting this graphic record of maturation is among the most fascinating aspects of working with these individuals.

A unifying aspect of the art of this stage, was that it is often elicited most effectively by using Lowenfeld's motivation techniques. In almost all of the previous examples, the children were en-couraged to draw something about which they were interested and in which they were emotionally invested. Few projects are based upon "Draw what you see" concepts; instead the children were exhorted to launch into those themes that excited their sensibilities.

Dawning and Pseudo-realism

Many art educators lament the onset of the realism stage, for they maintain that the child's art loses its naive charm and spontaneity. As children mature, they inevitably become self-conscious and guarded against revealing their feelings or ideas for fear of ridicule or humiliation. They take very few creative risks; individuality is replaced by peer-group values. Most twelve-year-olds do not want individual attention. Praise is as potentially uncomfortable as criticism. Lowenfeld terms this the "crisis stage," when rigidity, self-consciousness and stereotypy are prevalent in the artwork. Maturation is commonly uneven during this stage of transition, with vestiges of infantile or childish artistic styles combining with more adult imagery.

For special needs children, this transitional stage can be painful in many ways. From a social standpoint, they are often the first to be excluded, teased or harassed. Peer pressure can assume grotesque proportions for any child who is physically imperfect, culturally different or emotionally vulnerable. From an artistic standpoint, drawing is the most unforgiving of media. Children at this stage are increasingly expected to put aside their childish styles and aspire to some degree of naturalistic realism. If one cannot manage this advancement it becomes painfully obvious to everyone that "so and so is still a baby!" In light of these circumstances, being withdrawn—or aggressive—can be viewed as less an emotional maladjustment than an adaptive survival response.

This transitional stage is also a period when artistic and behavioral maturation is accompanied by periods of regression. Therefore, the therapeutic art educator must adjust his or her expectations in accordance with the individual child and his or her current state of emotions and ideas. It is not un-

A drawing problem involving the story of Johnny Appleseed prompted this narrative piece by an intact eight-year-old.

House after house was created by this autistic child who habitually labeled each room and often elaborated upon the floor plan by adding an architectural layout.

The merging of these two imaginatively stylized bird figures, created by a multiply handicapped twenty-year-old, is indicative of this young lady's emotional development, as the symbiotic attachments between herself and significant others were of paramount importance.

common for a child who has worked in a wholly original style until this stage to slide back to stereotypes or other less-imaginative imagery due to peer pressure or self-consciousness. For example, this is the stage at which girls often become preoccupied with drawing cartoonish dog faces, horses or other animals, either in a stereotypical style or one that approaches realism. At a time when sexual feelings are stirring yet self-consciousness is at its highest ebb, what better theme is there for the twelve-year-old girl than the horse—muscular, handsome, brimming with hot-blooded sexuality? For reasons that are unaccounted for, autistic children who function at this stage also draw horses, often in fantastic styles. The most well-known of these is the Ukrainian child Nadia, who lives in Great Britain. The deft and energetic draftsmanship of Nadia's work is indicative of a mature artist, not an autistic child functioning at a pre-verbal, mentally retarded level. (Although the scribbling surrounding the figure contradicts this.) Nadia's drawing prowess appeared to transcend the normal developmental milestones. Inexplicably, she created countless horses, roosters and other animals in her supernatural style but when it came to figures, Nadia's work was regressive. In keeping with her autistic symptoms, Nadia avoided or was inhibited with people, especially those who demanded academic participation and interpersonal relations. Thus, just as an intact twelve-year-old avoids expressing her burgeoning sexuality in overt human figures, so did Nadia create safe symbolic equivalents for the few joys in her life.

Boys at this stage also take refuge in stereotyped preadolescent themes. Cars, weapons, superheroes and other "macho" subject matter are common preoccupations with nine- to twelve-year-olds. Such themes also allude to aspirations of adult male functions. Driving a powerful car, wielding an elaborate gun, possessing supernatural strength, all allude to the male's emerging sexuality without expressing it overtly. As with the girls at this stage, self-consciousness usually inhibits direct sexual references—at least when working in the school artroom.

In the case of autistic savant Nadia, precocious realistic draftsmanship coexists with regressed chaotic scribbles. Such dual functioning is exceedingly rare and unique.

Issues of displacement and sublimation are particularly significant at this stage, as the themes of power, aggression and sexual innuendo emerge in their most graphic form. As the boys wrestle with the effects of preadolescent restlessness and impulsivity, it is important that drawing activities allow for the venting of drive energy in aesthetic-minded and socially appropriate ways. While the art educator will encounter constant scenes of blood and gore, such themes can be steered toward less-violent images which entail the same vigor and excitement. Themes involving action, physical challenge, fantasy or mythology are all appropriate vehicles for exercising the ten- to twelve-year-old's need to symbolically act out his feelings.

The dawning realism of a ten-year-old intact boy can be traced through his drawings in which displacement gives way to sublimation. Firebombers, gun ships and seige machines assault a fortress defended by figures mounted on mythic dragons. It is noteworthy that there is a discrepancy in this drawing between the overtly aggressive content and the diminutive style. The scene is quite elaborate on one hand—with many fine details carefully drawn—yet it seems forced to the bottom of the page with a vast area of pictorial space unused. The figures are lightly drawn, with seemingly fragile little bodies drawn with the most delicate features. This contrast between the wish for omnipotent power and the reality of vulnerability and fragility is common in ten-year-olds.

At eleven, the figures have become more formidable, yet there is marked ambivalence over depicting the hands and face. Hands are difficult to draw, as are faces, yet there is more to this than draftsmanship. The hands may be seen as metaphors for exercising control over the environment and self-control for the individual. The face permits the viewer to read the intent and character of the figure. Often though, distortions and omissions occur, resulting in aborted attempts to work through ideas which start out grandiose and end in frustration.

At twelve, however, the child's skills and emotional levels have advanced so that the discrepancy between wish fulfillment and the demands of reality are brought to closer proximity. Drives are still displaced using omnipotent figures rooted in fantasy, yet the physique is more in accordance with truly human potential. The figure is dynamically drawn, reaching confidently in a foreshortened pose, poised for action. Finally at age twelve and a half, this same child has begun to carry through his concerns for power and aggression, yet they have begun to expand. The next drawing presents a departure which now incorporates the same omnipotent powers of superheroes in a sketch of a wolf. This creature of mythical powers is drawn quite sensitively and accurately in a pose of strength and grandeur. As is characteristic of sublimation, the same qualities ingrained in the previous works have been carried through, only now in more reality-based and expansive terms. He has satisfied the demands of the drives, yet transformed them through the faculties of cognition and aesthetic sensibility into a mature work of considerable power.

For special needs children the path through developmental milestones is an uneven one, with progress often being accompanied by periods of regression. For example, an emotionally handicapped boy of eighteen was engaged in drawing cars from life at the urging of his instructor. As soon as he fulfilled this obligation, he quickly reverted back to his preferred mode of drawing from memory or fantasy, creating several whimsical, child-like vehicles. Although he was capable from a perceptual standpoint of drawing from direct observation, his emotional needs dictated that he draw more in accordance with developmental level of a much younger child.

Adjusting Structure
If the transitional stage child is to be prodded past the stereotype, drawing activities must reflect adjustments in structure. No longer can the ten- or twelve-year-old be allowed to work exclusively in the infantile fashion Lowenfeld describes or to draw upon memory, imagination or fantasy mate-

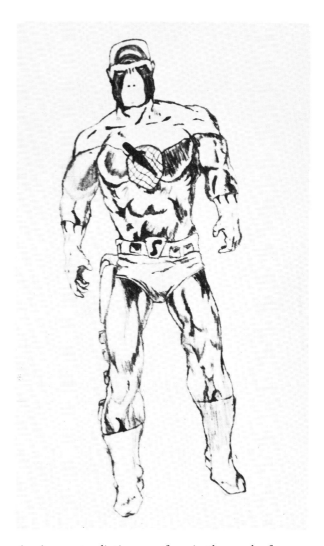

Again, contradictions surface in the work of an emotionally disturbed young teen. While forcefully rendering the figure, this boy neglects the figure's affective features while a knife menacingly sticks into the figure's chest, calling into question his invincibility.

Drawn from imagination, the wolf presents a forceful and dignified figure that reflects this boy's burgeoning "machoism."

Although able to draw skillfully from life, this autistic boy quickly reverted to his favored imaginative style of drawing vehicles.

rial which make up the typical preadolescent's preoccupations. If the drawing activity is to transcend stereotypy, and break new ground in terms of maturational and aesthetic growth, the structure may need to become more directive. Drawing activities which blend memory and imagination as stimulated by the Lowenfeld's motivation techniques should be combined with more academic approaches, including working from observation or life studies and drawing from artifacts, artwork or popular culture, as well as exercises in style involving the processes of abstraction and nonobjective design work. By integrating both subject and object approaches to drawing, the preadolescent stands a better chance to expand his or her visual vocabulary, break out of stereotypy and learn new concepts as well as camouflage areas of deficiency or immaturity.

Memory

Students functioning at this beginning realistic level should continue to have an opportunity to explore and process personally relevant experiences through their art. While a child might be somewhat inhibited about drawing from memory at this point, since the imagery will be characteristically more childish than if drawn from life, experiences continue to constitute a vital wellspring of subject matter for drawing.

Sometimes an innocent drawing problem can elicit disturbing material. Here the theme "Draw a Moment from your Past" resulted in this Vietnamese child's experiences as a refugee.

Stirring up memories with emotionally or physically handicapped children can become more than casual recollection. A compelling example of this occurred when I gave a group of twelve-year-olds the problem of recounting an interesting event in their lives. This prompted a Vietnamese refugee, who spent months at sea as "boat child", to recall this traumatic event in his drawings. This memory called forth feelings of exasperation and isolation, as well as exhilaration at gaining freedom from his bondage.

A visually impaired young man of nineteen solved the same problem by recalling a trip to an amusement park. At first, we might assume that such a memory was simply a pleasant recollection. However, for a sensory deprived young man who lived a sheltered lifestyle, the experience of a roller coaster was probably both exciting and terrifying. Who can imagine the sensations of wind, movement, vibration and height for an individual whose sensory apparatus is defective and distorted. Such a memory may be more than a simple recollection; it may be an extraordinary, supernatural experience.

This intensity of recollection is also reflected in drawings by a psychotic young man of twenty. After working on plant propagation in the art studio, he created a series of drawings a month after the project was completed. For an individual who was obsessed with mechanical objects, this investigation into the life cycles of living things was indeed a breakthrough. The obvious pleasure with which he recalled each phase of the project suggests an almost vicarious re-experiencing of the process of differentiation and maturation—a fitting metaphor for the changes occurring both within the child psychologically and in his artistic development.

After a trip to an amusement park, this mildly retarded and visually impaired high school student captured his ride on the roller coaster with vividness and precision.

Although severely emotionally disturbed, this young man took great care in depicting his observations in his art. This series, drawn from memory, recounts his amazement at following the growth cycle of a plant.

This twelve-year-old gifted child had no problems tapping his imagination in creating this drawing montage. Later he wrote a short story to accompany the images.

Working From Fantasy

Although a child's fantasy life is certainly active during this transition stage, it is often suppressed and guarded in its overt expression. However, given effective motivation students can create drawings that depict the most fantastic images. A twelve-year-old, underachieving gifted child chose his images from a predesigned list of elements. These included action-oriented themes such as skeletons, pirates, volcanos, tornadoes, islands, dinosaurs, caves, flying saucers, jungles and so on. Given these stimuli, he arranged the elements in a kind of montage instead of a visual narrative type of composition. In contrast to this sophisticated solution, another child, diagnosed as clinically depressed, described the story of dinosaurs who steal reptilian bird eggs, murder their parents and then are, in turn, killed by the violent eruption of a volcano. Narratives can also take a cartoon strip format. One young man who was visually impaired fantasized of romance and wealth, depicting scenes of opulence in his sequence of fantasy drawings.

Fantasy figures play a large part of the children brought up during the *Star Wars* generation. Films, games such a *Dungeons and Dragons,* and toys all have—for better or for worse—an important place in the art of the preadolescent student. While the teacher may decide to de-emphasize these themes due to their propensity to become stereotypes, he or she must also can appreciate and accommodate these attempts at recreating figures of fantasy. Usually, however, children of this stage will only draw such figures while at home during their leisure time. And, just as any reading material, whether it be a *Mad Magazine* or a comic, is considered growth-inducing, so too are the myriad of superheroes, space figures and fantasy kingdoms that will dominate leisuretime drawing.

Fantasy remains a powerful tool for eliciting

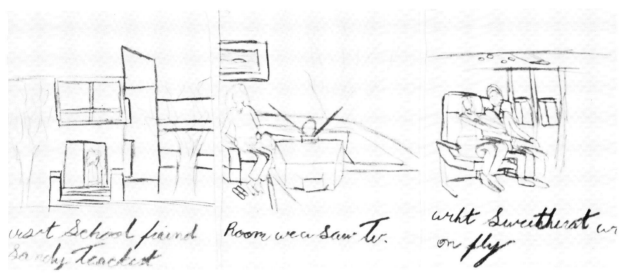

visit School friend
Sandy Teacher

Room were Saw tv.

wcht Sweetheart on
fly

images. The task for the teacher centers upon stimulating and guiding the images so that their expression can be therapeutically and aesthetically productive.

Although virtually blind and deaf, this young man was able to sequence his visual elements in a narrative format using his memories in an imaginative way.

Working from Life

As I have pointed out in numerous instances, life-drawing can be a demanding and difficult process for children with special needs especially when involving self-portraiture or figure study. Because the ten- or twelve-year-old's self-image is in a state of volatile flux, drawings may reflect distorted self-perceptions. One such disastrous attempt occurred when a twelve-year-old learning-disabled boy drew a self-portrait using a mirror. He started out fine, drawing an accurate contour of the head, followed by features which yield a strong and sensitive likeness. Yet, as each pimple was noticed, as well as the failed haircut, the less-than-stylish shirt, the weird glasses, the child became more and more agitated until he began to deface the portrait and distort it even further. Finally he pronounced himself "ugly and a fag," as the caption reads. He promptly discarded the piece (which was later retrieved and reworked).

There are ways of defusing or camouflaging a weak or distorted self-image, thus softening the

Drawing self-portraits during puberty can be an unsettling, even painful experience. This drawing was going along fine until the artist kept finding imperfections which led him to deface the drawing and throw it away.

This drawing shows quite a maturational leap from earlier attempts. Note the dramatic exchange of pencils, symbolizing the kinship between this autistic artist and his new-found friend, the art therapy intern.

confrontational aspect of life drawing. Often the frozen frame of a video image can soften and abstract the figure sufficiently so that poses can be chosen which do not demand absolute naturalism. Instead, it is the gesture, the color tones, the figurative elements in the composition that beg to be rendered without having to focus upon the student posing.

Other devices can be used to defuse or displace the intense self-consciousness of the preadolescent. With lower-functioning or younger children I have already mentioned the effectiveness of outlandish costumes, make-up and other props. These are less effective with more mature students, since they tend to increase self-consciousness and acting-out. When working on the human figure with a transitional stage group, I often ask for gestures, skeletal structure or simply the essence of the figures rather than shaded realism. With its focus purely upon the surrounding shape of the model, contour drawing is one method of approaching the figure simply as a design element. To work with gesture, I often thread a colorful piece of bell wire around the model. One continuous line that travels up the legs, torso, arms and head is bent to the

configuration of the model to elucidate the basic elements of the pose. Plaster casts can also be used in lieu of live models in either a contour, gestural or shaded detail drawing.

Often children can explore relationships, process feelings and work through developmental milestones through posed life drawings. For instance, a composition drawn by the boy who earlier rendered himself at the potter's wheel reveals that, a year later, skill at rendering the figure has caught up nicely with his facility with mechanical objects. The figures show appropriate affect as well as a relaxed, casual pose. The subjects include an art therapy intern who had worked with him and had established a close working relationship. The other figure is himself, complete in potter's apron, perched atop his wheel. This is more than a casual life drawing, however, as evidenced by the drawing of the poignant exchange and meeting of their respective hands. A vital connection has been illustrated in this drawing, one that confirms the bond that has been cemented between the student and intern. As evidenced in these drawings, the issues of separation and individuation are again brought to the fore. One can plot the process by which this young man (who was still mired emotionally between the autistic and symbiotic phases) began to separate out his own self-concept from that of the animated machine (the potter's wheel). Subsequently an attachment was made through intensive one-to-one work with an intern which brought him through to the symbiotic stage. During the course of both individual and group work, he was guided to maintain his own identity, by encouraging him to draw himself from life, securely surrounded by the objects of his affection. The final piece powerfully demonstrates the intensity of this attachment, its successful resolution and the subsequent individuation (Henley 1991).

AGE OF REALISM

For the special needs child, high school can be a last desperate attempt to make up for lagging developmental milestones, to resolve preadolescent conflicts and to develop a firm sense of self-identity. It is a stage when an emotional relationship to the artwork increasingly gives way to a relatively detached academic approach. Students at this point become stimulated by themes or subject matter on the basis of their aesthetically challenging properties. Art, for better or worse, is no longer simply an expression of the child's self, but an academic discipline requiring conscious effort and desire in order for naturalistic and expressive results to be attained.

Problem Solving

With students who are functioning at an adolescent level, I often use the problem-solving format. Students are given a challenge—one that has parameters to contain their search but is sufficiently open-ended to allow for idiosyncracy, expressivity and,

for special needs students, a degree of camouflaging. Problem solving can be scaled to a range of levels, from severe learning disabilities through gifted and even genius levels. A mainstream class can work on the same techniques, with similar media, yet be addressing different problems which match their particular needs. In this way, similar projects can have quite different emphases. An emotionally handicapped child may be attempting to solve the problem of the expression of sexuality without drawing pornographically, while a gifted child may be using Seurat's pointillist techniques with different grades of graphite. Both students can stand side by side, grappling with their specific problems without overly burdening the art education teacher with problems of logistics.

The goal in devising an appropriate problem, whether it be for a group or individual, is to integrate the art experience so that it fully taps a child's resources. This includes both technical mastery and personal expressivity. Take for example, the student working on the pointillist technique with different grades of graphite. She may have studied Seurat, Van Gogh, Sisley and the monochromatic landscape painting of China. After researching and practicing the technique, she may well be proficient at working with pointillist or short-stroke method. Yet my next critical concern would be "What of herself has the student brought to the piece?" I do not mean the technical innovation or sensationalized imagery one sees in much of the competitive artworld, but some aspect of the self, regardless of how naive.

As teachers and therapists, we must exhort the student to not only gain technical mastery but to use it as part of an emotion and thought process, so that once the images emerge, they do so with freshness, clarity and power. Just as the preadolescent boy who drew himself at the potter's wheel spontaneously evoked his feelings for his teacher, a student's work should go beyond infatuation with technique and style. Not to do so can have a deadening effect upon not just student art but that of mature, even celebrated artists. One need only read Dubuffets's *Manifesto* (1986) denouncing the

This gifted child from Taiwan spent months of disciplined work on skulls as a drawing project. Here he has given the figure a wash in India ink. He later incorporated his drawings into pottery and other multi-media works such as origami.

safe harbors of "attractive" art or Kepes' thoughts on realism as being a "dead inventory of optical facts" in *Language of Vision* (1944).

A case in point was a gifted Chinese student who enrolled in an independent study course in my therapeutic art program. He chose skulls as the subject on which to focus his work for most of the semester. He researched the skulls of O'Keeffe and scoured books of scientific illustrations, as well as observing specimens which were on hand in the artroom. After months of doing an exhaustive number of studies, he grew proficient in rendering these objects, but he also became bored and exasperated. Sensing his frustration, I finally gave him a new problem: "Tell me what you know about bones." With such an ambiguous problem following such concrete study, he seemed at a loss to respond. In asking him what he knew about bones, I was not requesting another technical/scientific illustration. I was exhorting him to show what sensibilities, what intrinsic truths he had internalized about the bleached remains of these creatures. For two sessions he sat bowed in contemplation as if I had posed an unanswerable Zen riddle.

During the second session however, he began playing with paper, drawing out patterns, cutting

them up and redrawing them countless times. After his third two-hour session, he presented me with his solution—perfectly constructed in paper: an origami deer skull, complete with fissures, tooth sockets and brain case. Twenty separate pieces were meticulously connected. On the forehead he brushed a haiku in a brisk, spontaneous calligraphic style which translated "Left after death, the shell of a jewel lives forever."

Not all students will be as brilliant as this one, nor will all be as tenacious at sticking with a problem and seeing it through to completion. I intuited, however, that this particular student could stand the heat that demanded a transition from technical prowess to original, creative thinking. As a truly gifted child, he could handle being pushed and prodded to extend his limits to arrive at this extraordinary solution.

The problem-solving format must of course, apply to children with diverse special needs. This can be accomplished by structuring a problem so that it engages a child from a point of strength. Drawing might only be one aspect of the problem to solve. Integrating art history, appreciation, reflection as well as multi-disciplinary areas such as science or computers can be emphasized as part of the project. For instance, a class may be encouraged to borrow the style of a famous artist as a drawing project. This would include being exposed to these works via visual aids, observing the instructor's demonstration of how such a style is accomplished, and then the actual execution of a drawing which reflects this particular style.

For most high school students, this is a straightforward problem, engaging technical skills, art appreciation and perception as well as a creative element of interpretation. For a learning-disabled child, however, this problem may be too broad and overwhelming. First, the teacher should select an artist whose style bears a relationship to the student's own manner of working. This will have a camouflaging effect upon the interpretive aspects of the student's artwork. One such child I knew worked in a kind of geometric style, with hard-edged figures reminiscent of immature schematic drawings. The natural style for this child was Cubism. As a visual reference, he was provided with reproductions of Picasso and Braque, which he then studied and discussed alone with the rest of the class. Adaptation was necessary to support him through the interpretive process. Looking at Picasso's works, he was encouraged to first select a piece that interested him. Being a music student, he chose Picasso's musical instruments. His task has further narrowed down by providing him with a viewfinder to isolate just one or two of the instruments. We then analyzed these elements, thus setting him up to begin his first drawing—a copy from the Picasso print. For his second drawing, he was asked to bring in his own instrument and break it down into a geometric composition. The finished drawing stands up to the majority of the other drawings created in this sophomore mainstream class.

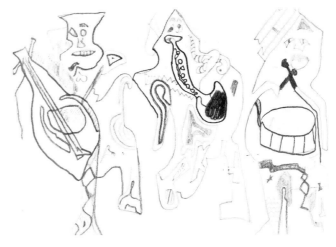

After studying Picasso's The Three Musicians, *this learning disabled boy improvised upon the theme, resulting in a bizarre yet fascinating study.*

Despite having retinitis pigmentosa, this young man works quite effectively when provided with a strong lamp, scrap paper to practice on and a visual aide from which to improvise.

Using a free association technique of improvising on words, these two gifted high school seniors worked within the metaphor of garbage, *with fascinating results.*

Another popular art project is "word" problems. A list of words is handed out to the students; these are then rendered either from life, imagination or memory. Two gifted boys depict different responses to the word *garbage*. They spent hours staring into waste bins, meticulously rendering the refuse in a naturalistic still life. An emotionally handicapped child frets over the nuclear threat in his response to the word *future*. Another emotionally handicapped child took a free-form approach in illustrating the word *think*. Ordinarily a very concrete, literal child, she was prompted by the problem to create an emotionally energetic, abstract solution.

The Creative Still Life
Unless made stimulating, exciting or somehow personally relevant, still lifes can become a mere technical exercise for students. To insure student motivation, assemblages should be prepared individually by each student. Thus, the drawing project begins with a construction of objects fabricated by the student using glue, so that the composition remains stable over the period of study. By individualizing the still life, the teacher can better match content with each child's ability or manner of working. For example, a visually impaired, mentally retarded young woman of twenty began with the rather mundane objects of a pillow and cardboard backdrop to which she added a zigzag of bent bell wire and two eyes cut out from a magazine and pasted to the pillow. The resulting composition is a surrealistic figure of remarkable ingenuity and draftsmanship. Another emotionally handicapped, hyperactive girl of nineteen put herself into her still life. In this ambitious production, she first draped butcher paper in a corner of the room, painting a decoration over its surface. Then, in her intensely energetic way, she added a stuffed fish, suited up in an old gown, set up a mirror and drew herself into the composition with pencil and a watercolor wash. The result is an outlandish solution to the personal still life problem.

Responding to the word future, *this emotionally handicapped boy reflects his anxiety over nuclear proliferation. Note how the subject matter stimulated him to act out in profanity.*

Abstraction can be challenging for students with special needs. This drawing makes use of inventive nonobjective elements, although they mirror the emotional turmoil that characterized this twelve-year-old with Attention Deficit-Hyperactivity Disorder.

Although multiply handicapped, this eighteen-year-old girl put together an astounding assemblage of objects, then rendered them with great facility and boldness.

Always in action, this hyperactive young woman surrounded herself with props then drew a self-portrait/still life using a mirror to capture the entire composition.

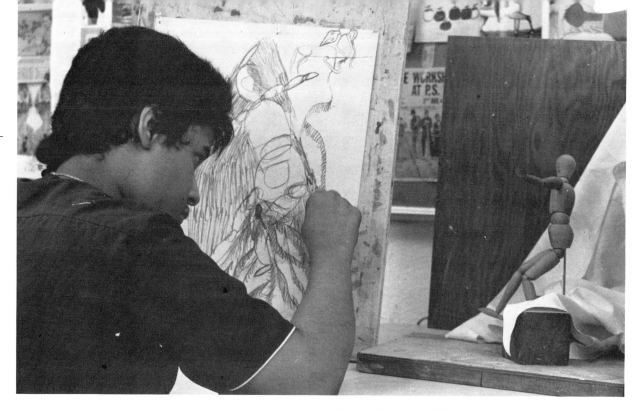

The traditional still life challenges students. This hearing impaired young man concentrates intently on his composition.

Drawing in Series

Artwork works best aesthetically and critically, when created in series. Problems that require a progression or transformation in a sequence of pieces produce a more comprehensive impact. Students can better reflect upon each work in the context of interrelationships and dynamics. Because mature artists work in series, the student can be encouraged to emulate their example.

One sequence that I often employ uses a photographic approach to deriving abstraction from representational imagery. In this project the student selects an object which is then cut bisymmetrically and drawn realistically. Organic objects, such as walnuts, peppers, rotten wood or even minerals, algae and other microscopic images, make excellent subjects. Subsequent drawings in the series can then move in many increments or directions, depending upon the level of the student (Shames 1969).

Beginning with a simple orange, this sequence by a gifted, hearing-impaired high school junior entailed enlarging the cross section, then simplifying it toward greater abstraction. Although matted together, each drawing can stand alone as an integral piece. Yet when they are seen together, the viewer is taken on a journey from the mundane, everyday object through a series of processes, where scale, value, realism and context are all manipulated so that a fresh perspective has been gained. On an affective level, this young woman's imagery alluded to her budding sexuality. Much of her work involved moistened and curvaceous forms, whose maternal and erotic sensuality were celebrated through sublimation.

In another example, a gifted, yet troubled, high school student blurred the line between representation and abstraction by focusing upon the designs inherent in the family car. By a skillful use of cropping, working from unusual angles, and by alternating between tight and loose drafting, the expressive possibilities of another mundane subject were sensitively explored. The investment in this object was more than casual, however, since it was in this car that the young woman had a serious accident when first learning to drive. One can safely assume that both the trauma and pleasure associated with this object presented a powerful stimulus for her, one which also was resolved through successful sublimation.

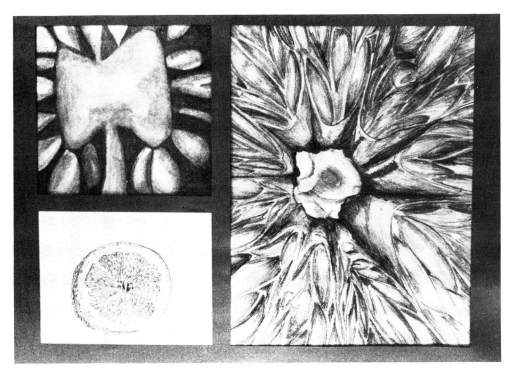

These pieces reflect a sequence of steps whereby the student studies an object realistically, then proceeds to abstract it by magnification, cropping and distorting. This gifted young woman has effectively expanded the visual definition of what comprises a simple orange.

Creative matting enhances this series of auto design studies by a talented sophomore. Design problems that require concentration, consistency and improvisation may challenge gifted students who respond to greater challenges but lack discipline and structure.

chapter 7

Painting

Painting is among the most emotionally charged and expressive of all media. In the hands of children, paint seems to possess a life of its own as it spreads, bleeds and saturates the pictorial field. Because of paint's viscosity and vibrancy of color and the physically robust movements associated with the painting process, children often become highly stimulated. Unlike drawing, which is relatively controlled and usually employed in a representational mode, painting essentially breaks all the rules. Where realism, perspective and detail are expected in drawing, the painter can play with abstraction, impressionism and minimalism. The grey austerity of the line becomes a bold stroke laden with vibrant color. While drawings are deliberate and pragmatic, the nature of paint encourages spontaneity, mystery and chance. Painting can set a child free to loosen up, experiment and act with vigor without the usual inhibitions. Moods, impressions, tensions, gestures can all be expressed with exuberance and passion.

Because of the universality of color, paint offers an immediate connection that is lacking in other media. Somehow painting arouses a child's most deeply seated sensations and associations, unfettered by the laws of language or even reason. The visceral, emotive quality of paint invites chaos and action. Its propensity to drip, slosh and bleed demands a certain amount of impulse control to handle it. Emotions which may have been previously repressed or sublimated may be unleashed through the paint's vibrant colors and viscous texture (Kramer 1979).

Thus, painting is inherently a powerful, expressive, therapeutic tool. It can prompt active participation, while also inviting the possibility of behavioral and emotional regression. It is the task of the teacher to know paint's properties and to modulate the degree of sensory and affective stimulation it generates. By adapting or tempering its properties and adjusting tools and set-up, the medium can be handled by a wide range of children.

EARLY INVOLVEMENT

The first marks with paint roughly parallel that of the drawing process, with disordered marks, scribbles and circles characterizing the work of young or retarded children. With paint, however, these early marks can take on added expressivity, since the nature of the line can be modulated from the narrowest to the broadest of strokes. The stroke is also laden with color which may spread, drip, bleed and inexplicably change regardless of the child's intentions. The inherent sensory qualities of the medium allow even the most handicapped child to exert strong effects with minimal participation.

Painting often stirs the emotional and visceral side of the child. This sensitive portrait was produced after reflecting over a family album, focusing upon a photo of this child's grandmother taken during WWII.

MEDIUM

In order for the young or retarded child to be able to handle the painting process, a materials approach must be taken. Beginning with the paint, a decision must be made whether a child is capable of handling liquid medium. If a child is reticent for fear of becoming soiled, or if the teacher feels that excessive spillage and chaos might occur, then it may be appropriate to begin with dry medium. Dry tempera in large cakes may be excellent for this purpose, since it offers a large target for the brush, while also easily mixing to extend its expressive qualities. If it is warranted, the palette may be limited initially as well, to a single color or to the three primaries, so that the child does not become confused or overwhelmed. However, in keeping with the goal of a least restrictive environment, I begin by introducing a full palette to children until they demonstrate an inability to handle the range of choice. I am often amazed at severely retarded individuals who relish sampling a range of colors; although they may be oblivious to their compositions or designs, they do respond strongly to the sheer vibrance of the colors.

Should liquid paint be introduced, initially it is important that it be of a thick, dripless consistency. Tempera is the medium of choice because of its brilliant opaque colors. Powdered tempera can also be used if economy is a consideration in the program. In mixing the medium, the powder should always be added to the water, and allowed to slake overnight to insure even saturation. Mixing or agitating the paint will lessen the colors' brilliance, due to excessive oxidation. If too thin, the paint will be dull in intensity; if too thick, it may flake off once applied. To thicken paint or give it a creamier consistency, additives such as starch, soap or matt medium are effective, although if over used, they will also cause flaking when the picture has dried.

In distributing paints to young or retarded children, it is advisable to use weighted containers or to secure containers to the work surface. Aside from minimizing spills, the secured paints reassure reticent children that the material is under control despite their poorly coordinated movements. Particularly with autistic or emotionally handicapped children, objects are least threatening when they are predictable and stationary. Both paint and water containers should have wide bases and be shallow enough to slide a brush in over the lip yet deep enough to contain the paint or dirty water. Muffin tins, margarine containers or heavy, shallow ashtrays are ideal for this purpose. Their placement should reflect the sequence of movements and the student's dominant hand. For a left-handed child, the water container should be on the left, with the paints ringing the upper edge of the table or easel. Place the containers to minimize dripping on the picture.

The painting work surface can be either a horizontal work table or an easel. A flat table usually is most effective, especially with younger students, since the child can be squarely seated and tucked into place with the medium and tools spread around him or her in an organized and inviting fashion. An easel tray may also contain the medium effectively. Needless to say, however, when a canvas or paper is hung vertically, dripping is the inevitable result. Nevertheless, there is something painterly about an easel even for young children. It challenges them to exercise greater control, while also allowing for robust, unrestrained movement while working. (Using easels with young children usually calls for a student/teacher ratio of one-to-one or two-to-one for effective monitoring.) The painting surface should be large enough to permit vigorous brushwork. Heavy-duty absorbent paper will resist dripping and stand up to heavy brush pressure while wet. It is sometimes advisable to tape down the painting surface so that wetting does not roll the edges and strong brushstrokes don't wrinkle or tear it. However, many young children will need to turn their papers around freely as they work so as to reach or concentrate on different areas.

APPLICATORS

The application of paint can take a wide variety of resourceful forms, depending upon the effects desired or the adaptations needed. For uncoordinated children, I may try a stout, thick-handled brush such as is often used in stenciling. Children may drive a brush's ferrule into the paper, damaging the surface. A stiff-bristled brush will offer enough resistance to prevent digging. Stenciling brushes hold less paint than regular brushes and thin paint may run. Other brushes, such as squirrel-haired mop brushes, hold pigment well but offer no resistance to pressure. House painting brushes are often excellent choices, especially if large surfaces are to be covered. Disposable sponge brushes have also become popular; they are cheap, versatile and come in several widths.

Should a child's disability stand in the way of manipulating a brush, adaptive applicators can be used. Deodorant roll-ons, shoe shine applicators, condiment squeeze bottles and barbecue/bottle-brushes will all apply paint without having to actually dip into the paint.

Some applicators can be selected for their ability to vary the application of paint so that unexpected effects are produced. Sponges can be easily manipulated by young, retarded, autistic and some orthopedically handicapped children. I encourage children to brush, scrub and pat with the sponge, using different concentrations of water and paint to increase the variations. Rollers can also be effective applicators, especially if the child has difficulty with motor control. They are available in different shapes, widths and textures and can be further varied by attaching materials such as burlap, mesh and even carpeting. Especially for the youngest or most regressed children, they afford an experience that is akin to pure kinesthetic and rhythmic play. With children working out of wheelchairs, I have used long-handled household feather dusters, whisk brooms, and even small mops as alternatives for paintbrushes. With these applicators, the pictorial surface is reached and covered quickly, thus increasing the weakened child's sense of power and self-confidence.

Spray painting is another possibility, with airbrush gun sprayers. Even water pistols are interesting tools for those children who can effectively depress a trigger and shoot in the right direction. I have used a professional quality airbrush with very young intact children, deaf and blind children, and the mentally retarded, all with excellent results. All that was needed was a secure yet unobtrusive helping hand. The delight of a little deaf and blind girl feeling the spray of clean water onto her hand or a three-year-old's fascination with the soft veil of color she created more than compensated for my having to direct and operate the equipment.

RESISTS

One of the most straightforward and aesthetically interesting techniques for varying the scribbled paintings of low-functioning children is to use resists. By blocking off parts of the picture with wax, latex, frisket or crayon, the expressive and aesthetic qualities of the painting are automatically enhanced. Fields of color can be broken up, with more dynamic forms and spaces emerging between the interplay of paint and resist. With special needs populations, cold wax or crayon are the media to start with, since they are non-toxic and easy to apply. Even the most obsessive scrubber or scribbler can find a safe, enjoyable outlet because the thicker the wax build-up the more effective the resist. The child should be monitored so that the entire picture is not covered. Some negative space should remain to accept the paint medium. For those children who will not ingest or smear, liquid latex is an excellent resist which can be painted onto a surface, then peeled off after painting. Many children relish this picking and peeling process.

Before working in the resist technique, one multiply handicapped child habitually scrubbed every square inch of the paper with either crayon or paint. With this technique, he was encouraged to

The dynamic interaction between the contrasting black linework and the soft washes of watercolor make for a superb example of resist in the hands of a severely retarded, autistic boy of ten.

break up his surface treatment and allow some breathing space to modulate his compositions. The result was a large-scale use of the resist process in which bold figures, freely drawn lines, arcs, scribbles and blocks of crayon color interact nicely with the light wash of tempera.

In keeping with the emphasis upon camouflaging, the resist process can transform a disordered, improvised scribble into a vibrant free-form design. It is not a decorative process which depends upon a gimmick, but a straight ahead process which relies exclusively upon modulating positive and negative space and adequate application of the medium. The results are often aesthetically pleasing without being trite or condescending.

STENCILS

Stencils can be used much in the same way as resists. Untreated areas of paper are blocked off, allowing the child access to only portions of the pictorial field. Using tape, cardboard or acetate, a child is free to slosh paint back and forth without saturating the entire work. Stencils can be cut in random shapes by the teacher for the children to choose among, or the students can cut, tear or fold shapes of their own if they have the necessary skills. Often a theme is useful for the stencil, to make the transition from nonobjective design to a semblance of representation. For example, to encourage the feel or suggestion of a landscape, horizontally shaped stencils can be overlapped and placed in different combinations. The dividing lines between stencils create contrasting values and organic forms, resulting in pleasing juxtapositions.

I often use simple geometric stencils to encourage a child to paint a circle, square or other shapes which are introduced in the academic classroom. Props as basic as a roll of masking tape can provide the needed structure so that a child can plunge the brush into a well-fortified object, scrub the brush around and come up with a fairly intact colored form. Changing the placement or size of these circles results in a simple yet pleasing composition of floating, overlapping colored spheres.

SPONTANEOUS PAINTING

The young or lower-functioning child usually does not need to be provided with a design problem, or a theme when painting, since the medium itself suffices as a motivation and stimulus. As the child experiments with the materials, concepts such as color, balance, rhythm and design will be developed. Just as with mature artists, constant exposure and experimentation will assist even the youngest painter to develop aesthetic sensibility. Decisions about the next brushstroke, the contrasting color or the curved line will all eventually be faced and dealt with after the child has worked freely and intensively over a sufficient period of time. Paintings created in this way will communicate ideas, feelings, moods and reactions to the environment regardless of the child's capacity for representational imagery. The teacher can accom-

modate this process of self-discovery by being available to monitor the child during the painting process. Although most children throw themselves vigorously into the medium, they often need someone who can intervene when the process breaks down, becomes chaotic or is in danger of becoming overwhelmed. Because many young or lower-functioning children often overwork and saturate their paintings, close monitoring is required to ensure that objects and figures are not obliterated. Since colors often become muddied, the teacher should change wastewater containers often and exhort the children to keep their colors clean. Since splattering, spilling and other accidents often ruin artwork and prompt peer conflict, sufficient space should be allotted to the activity. If tables are not accommodating, then the floor can be pressed into service. Lunchroom trays or other surfaces with borders can serve to protect paper from spills while also maintaining firm parameters within which the child can securely operate.

At this level one can expect that the stimulation provided by the painting process will overshadow the need for a finished product. The sensual stimulation provided by the medium will sustain a child's interest more than the expected results. It is important, then, that paper, illustration board or other painting surfaces be plentiful and generously provided. Children may work only minutes, then call a piece finished. In many cases it is indeed a complete work and warrants new paper, regardless of how much time it took. One is reminded when watching young children at work of the Zen painter whose calligraphic brushwork occurs with little deliberation and with total assurance. The stroke is quick and loose, with great intensity and concentration, similar to that of the child.

One multiply handicapped boy's approach to the medium was physically robust, intense and self-absorbed. Working with tempera, then later student-grade acrylics, he worked with large blocks and planes of saturated colors which he sometimes arbitrarily mixed on a lunch tray palette. With his assorted house painting and stencil brushes, he applied his pigment quickly, spreading it over large

This large, color field painting was done by a boy with multiple handicaps. Paintings such as this are often created in a single session, with the child beginning new work on top of the still wet, finished canvas.

The creator of the previous painting often required a referee during his intense bouts with paint and canvas. He often raked over the whole piece with a scraper to essentially erase the image because he was too impatient to wait for a fresh canvas.

expanses of canvas, often covering it over, reworking and then covering it over again. Contrary to what might be expected, this boy became calmer rather than more stimulated when he switched from drawing to painting. He became less impulsive and more thoughtful and reflective in front of the canvas. However, close monitoring by the teacher was needed while he worked, despite his intense self-initiative and motivation. He would often mix all of the colors on the palette together in one great grey mass. He sometimes reworked to the extent that there might be three or even five paintings atop one another, with the artist never slowing down enough to harvest a product. Despite these problems, he essentially worked, acted and looked like a painter—intensely preoccupied, temperamental, vigorous—a person whose style was highly developed despite severe handicapping conditions. While his work was somewhat obsessive and limited in imagery, his style was instantly recognizable, unusually fresh and eccentric. What was most fascinating, however, was the manner in which his work evolved. Just as a mature artist works in series, so did this child, with five to ten paintings, for example, being strictly interior color-field landscapes. The next series would seize upon one element of the previous works and then improvise, extend or play around with this one element until a new, yet related breakthrough was achieved.

This case is instructive in that it encapsulates both the problems and potentials of young, retarded or otherwise immature child painters. While emotions are aroused and senses stimulated, they can be effectively channelled through the art process. Elements of design are explored in ways that provoke great intensity and pleasure and are not simply academic exercises. Ventures into scale and other stylistic experiments come naturally without pretension, and they have a liberating and invigorating effect upon the child's expressive ability.

PAINTING WITH HIGHER-FUNCTIONING OR MATURE STUDENTS

Painting activities with higher-functioning children inevitably mean a transition from simple, schematic figures or nonobjective designs to imagery that is representational. It is a formidable challenge facing the adolescent painter to preserve the freshness and vitality he or she had as a child. The spontaneity and expressive character of the medium must be expanded with greater control and complexity. Whereas realism is relatively easy to attain through a drawing medium, it is far more difficult to achieve with paint. As is the case with young or lower-functioning children, impulses and emotions are stirred and possibly become agitated by the sensorial qualities of the paint. Between this loosening of affect and the difficulties in controlling the technical aspects of the medium, the adolescent painter has his or her hands full.

At this stage in development, the child may be especially self-conscious and in fear of being embarrassed or humiliated by failure. Given the high possibility of failure, students functioning at an adolescent level may be reluctant to extend themselves or take risks in paint. Thus, painting must be presented with supportive strategies which allow the adolescent to persevere with representation while also allowing the child within to play, explore and express. Regardless of the handicapping condition, these issues of self-consciousness and inhibition can dominate the painting studio at this developmental stage. Therefore, projects in painting must attempt to balance a sense of security with a sense of adventure in order to elicit the wonderful art this age group is capable of.

PAINTING TECHNIQUES

Advanced painting techniques should possess the intrinsic capacity to camouflage weakness and put all students on equal footing. Emphasis should be upon using basic, traditional media in ways that

unlock expressive possibilities. While string painting and Rorschach-type prints may be quick and superficially attractive, there is no substitute for the dramatic wash of a watercolor or the startling hard edge of an acrylic form. With such an approach, the teacher can hope to elicit art which is honest, raw and vigorous, in a style which allows the process to speak for itself.

Watercolor

Few media have the expressive potential of watercolor. Most children can work with this medium, if given the right materials and adaptations. The easiest form of watercolor to handle is the semi-moist cakes which come in a pan with a selection of different colors. Only the sequencing of the brush to the water, to the paint and then to the paper is needed. Given a few lessons in technique, the child can immediately begin to experiment with the expressive qualities of the medium.

The first technique that I demonstrate is wet-on-wet washes. The rich colors that grow pale as they melt onto other shades is an exciting, pleasurable experience for all children. I have seen mentally retarded children sit transfixed as their red hues explode into orange and purple sunsets. Although the concept of sunset probably eluded them, the sheer sensorial pleasure in the textures and contrasts inherent in the process held their attention for unusually long periods.

This process should begin with a robust warm-up in which the child paints plain water onto a stretched sheet of heavy watercolor paper. Stretching can be accomplished simply by taping down the entire perimeter of the paper with wide masking or drafting tape. Once the paper is wet, I encourage the children to blend complementary colors onto the wet surface to see what kind of effects are possible. After a period of trying different color combinations including black on clear water, I may show them reproductions of artworks to further expand their frame of reference. The monochromatic brushwork of the Chinese artists effectively conveys active and spontaneous brush techniques. Winslow Homer's Caribbean pieces

show how simple floods of diluted color stand for a tropical sky. J.M.W. Turner's landscapes also demonstrate how mood and drama are evoked in a soft, transparent wash of atmospheric color.

Once students see how seasoned artists rely upon the same techniques they are using, they become motivated to improvise upon the basic technique. Additions of salt or alcohol into the wash can impart unusual textures and bursts of color. Dropping color or plain water into these washes also makes dramatic bleeds. Scratching the surface of the paper will create contrasting linear designs as the colors are absorbed into the crevices, creating darker values. Color can also be lifted off during the wet or damp stage by rolling toilet paper onto the paint; this results in cloud-like forms. Textures can be created by wrinkling the paper, or by crumpling it into a ball, soaking it in paint, then restretching the paper. The network of lines which absorb the darker values creates an abstract, gently modulating the surface and creating soft, feathery, cloud-like forms.

Once the wash is dry, students can continue to work from a representational standpoint or with free-form expressive techniques. Using a dry

Wet-on-wet techniques make use of accidental bleeds and blots that enhance abstract landscape design. This learning disabled boy of fourteen was too hyperactive to patiently mix and match colors in a traditional way.

brush, damp sponge or toothbrush, color can be glazed over to wash in the greatest detail. At this point, students may be shown the works of Andrew Wyeth, a master of dry brush techniques. The textures of foliage, rock, wood, metal and skin can be effectively approximated given ability and practice.

This process can become as complex as the child can handle. A severely learning disabled boy of fourteen created a painting in a field near school using experimental wet-on-wet techniques to represent his impressions of the environment around him. With a minimum of contrivances, using only a mop brush and tissue as a blotter, he created this landscape with only verbal assistance. Although this boy usually had grave difficulties following the sequences of a technique, the watercolor posed few obstacles. Only four steps needed to be sequenced: taping the perimeter of the paper, wet-

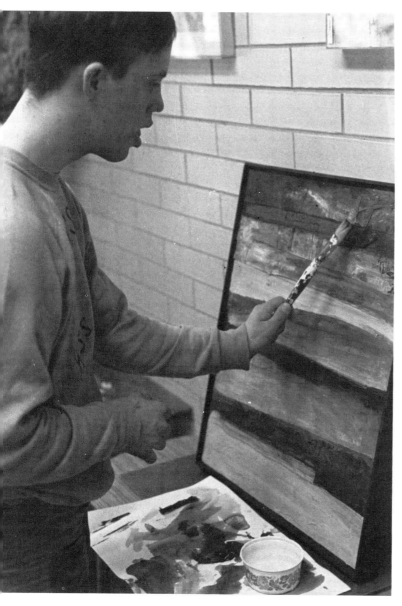

In contrast to the feverish pace of many handicapped artists, this Down syndrome young man meticulously applied masking tape to masonite board, then applied modeling paste in a variety of textures. Here he finishes up with acrylic glazes mixed with matt medium.

ting down the paper, choosing the first color, and experimenting with brushstrokes, droplets, sponging and lifting. Using a task-analysis format, and visual-aids to overcome his learning and perceptual problems, the technical objectives were quickly met. He was soon able to concentrate upon the expressive qualities of the medium, using experimentation, observation and decision-making which, in turn, developed aesthetic sensibility.

Acrylics

Children are clearly more motivated when they are allowed to use "real" artists' materials and techniques. Despite a studio full of colorful tempera, many adolescents will clamor for acrylic paints. Perhaps it is the homogenous, viscous consistency of the paint or the fact that it is squeezed out of tubes that make it so appealing. In any case, children relish using this silky smooth medium and their art certainly benefits by it.

For lower-functioning students, many of the adaptations discussed earlier will apply to acrylic as well. Hard edge paintings are particularly popular with children who still cannot render figurative images. Using geometric or free-form designs delineated by masking tape and/or stencils, lower-functioning students become surprisingly adept at creating flat, colorful images which are concrete, yet quite complex. In a similar mode, a Down syndrome student created a hard-edged painting using horizontal bands of masking tape of different thicknesses. Using the flat blade of a painting knife he applied mixtures of thick acrylic as if he were icing a cake. Instead of spreading, he attempted to use sculpturing strokes. He finished off the raised impressions with contrasting colors using a brush, which allows the under painting to show through and contrast with the overglaze. This is a fairly complex project, yet one which this child, who functions in the upper-severe range of mental retardation, accomplished with only minimal direction.

Paint can also be poured in a controlled yet lively process. In one case a group of young men routed watered-down acrylic paint in veils of translucent washes. Just as Morris Louis or Paul Jenkins would, the students used poles, and their bodies to change the angle and direction of the flow. The resulting work is a flood of colors which, if not overworked, can create interesting and vibrant effects. Poured paint is also useful as a backdrop for detailed dry brushwork.

Objects can also be painted. Putting paint on familiar objects offers the child an opportunity to alter context and assign new meanings through the artwork. One thirteen-year-old boy was fascinated by the surface and forms of bones. A skull offered him an excellent point of departure from which to work in colors and patterns suggestive of Native American designs. The skull also allowed for interaction between painting and sculptural aspects of the piece. Once again, using unexpected and unusual props facilitates motivation. There are limitless possibilities among the objects that can be incorporated, all of which create a sense of parity and opportunity for camouflaging in the mainstream artroom.

Working in a group, these mentally retarded young men experiment with pouring translucent washes of acrylic down chutes of canvas. Control was achieved by adjusting the height and angle of the pour, using sticks and other basic tools.

A learning disabled boy decided to paint a deer skull brought to him by his dogs. After a brief soaking in bleach and gesso, it offered an excellent vehicle for free-form experimentation in acrylic.

Each mentally retarded child was taught one particular stroke to make for this large-scale landscape.

Learning disabled children find this sort of activity well-suited to their own style of working. Those who were put off by relatively abstract objects like the skull, used more concrete and familiar objects which in most cases, elicited memories and experiences. One severely learning disabled child painted an old plastic model of an oceanliner he had once made. Now slightly broken, it offered an excellent field to paint upon, with its numerous fine details and dynamic form. In its finished form, painted in pinks, blues and silver and mounted on the wall, the piece recalled Brancusi's sleek birds. It was as strong and abstract a piece as any in the class.

Many children are fascinated with the impressionistic mode of Seurat's pointillist techniques and Van Gogh's use of bold brushstrokes. A group of Down syndrome boys who functioned in the severe range of mental retardation, created a four by eight foot mural using these techniques. I orchestrated the painting of this piece by giving each child one color and one stroke that he would use exclusively. Each child was directed where and when to execute his stroke. I then called up two or three students at a time. The mural managed to come off in a fairly orderly and systematic fashion, despite nine boys milling around impatiently to do their "Van Gogh act"! The finished piece attests to the cooperative and graphic abilities of supposedly, lower-functioning fifteen-year-olds.

The expressive qualities of acrylic paint can be greatly extended by experimenting with the painting surface. Masonite, wooden planks, plaster reliefs, collages, ceramic plates can all hold paint in unusual configurations. A particularly effective painting surface for all populations is the shaped canvas. This is created by impregnating unprimed canvas with white glue, or matt medium. The canvas then can be shaped by dropping it over armatures, such as balloons, cardboard, wire, Styrofoam or other light materials. Fitted over these armatures, the canvas forms geometric or organic shapes which are rigid and durable.

Expressionistic and abstract works done with these relief techniques allow children of every functioning level equal access and success. While this activity prompts a vigorous, active approach to painting, it also primes a child for working in more representational modes. Students often go on to paint realistic textures of wood or the subtleties of cloud and sky after a period of free-wheeling experimentation. Once the expressive possibilities of the medium are discovered, confidence and enthusiasm often fuel a child to tackle new challenges.

Figure Painting

Figure painting is one of the more difficult problems facing the teacher with higher-functioning or adolescent students. Most children at this functioning level are painfully aware of their inabilities. Even intact children at this age become inhibited, self-conscious and resistant to take any chance where failure and humiliation are a possibility. Thus, in painting figures, the teacher must attempt to take fear of failure out of the project through shifts of emphasis and restructuring.

For example, a group of high school students

who were emotionally handicapped and learning disabled were working on a still-life painting project. This is usually not the most exciting project, yet through several adaptations, the students eventually enjoyed and succeeded in the project. They first chose then glued together the objects they wished to draw. Using models they themselves had created increased the chances that their interest could be sustained. The compositions were drawn from life in a style which focused upon form and contour without obsessing over details. Following the sketching process, the students were exposed to Fauvist painters who used shocking, outlandish colors in relatively realistically drawn compositions. These students delighted in painting their fruit in shades of blue, and their wooden cubes in gold with polka dots. It essentially let them off the hook of having to draw realistically or paint with accurate colors. The activity had the effect of loosening their style, allowing for humor, absurdity and playfulness in contrast with fairly rigid, traditional still-life techniques.

The degree of technical mastery needed to achieve a credible likeness in a figure painting activity will be beyond the grasp of many special needs children. However, it can be attempted by populations whose motor and intellectual capacities are relatively intact, such as those with emotional or conduct disorders, learning disabilities, and orthopedic or hearing handicaps as well as with certain mildly retarded students. The major difficulty, aside from first creating a decent contour drawing on the painting surface, is modulating colors to denote the changes in the face or body. This can be accomplished in the initial project by painting over a photograph or computer printout.

A severely retarded girl of fifteen drew and painted two models from life. The models were posed in draped material, creating fascinating yet simplified forms and colors which were easy to render. In contrast, a child of similar ability worked from a postcard depicting a navy ship. By cropping the image drastically and by assigning a strange color scheme to the figure, a work of unusual abstraction was achieved. The two paintings

Impregnating unprimed cotton duck with white glue allowed this communication disordered thirteen-year-old to form-fit his canvas over different objects (in this case Styrofoam) to create a painted relief.

This retarded girl painted two life models with great sensitivity and control.

140

This tropical landscape evokes a calm and serenity that belies the intense process that brought the work into being. This multiply handicapped woman of twenty furiously scrubbed layer after layer of oil paint on the canvas, until the image she had in mind emerged from the thick impasto.

By cropping drastically, and by viewing her subject from below, this multiply handicapped yet gifted painter achieved great evocative power in her abstract interpretation of a ship.

illustrate how two quite dissimilar projects can be going on, each involving the painting of a figure: one in watercolor, the other in acrylic; one from life, one from a visual aid. The two projects are similar enough to keep logistical problems to a minimum, while also maintaining a sense of community, of a painting studio where artists gather and focus on their own work in their own style. Neither piece alludes to any exceptional treatment or modification, nor is there any indication that severely handicapped teenagers created these works.

Painting with the Neurologically Impaired
The post-traumatic work of a college freshman who had sustained a brain trauma due to a stroke is characterized by an intensity of feeling and visual acuity that is almost hallucinogenic in nature. The artist attributed this intensity to dealing with the struggles that came with returning to the studio after enduring prolonged hospitalizations and therapy. She endeavored to portray her depth of feeling for a life returned to her after having faced the possibility of life-long brain damage and incapacitation.

This case is instructive because it illustrates the common presenting problems in working with brain trauma victims. It is also of particular interest given the high degree of artistic training this young woman had before her stroke. Her rehabilitation required that both the objective and subjective aspects of her condition be addressed by the art specialist. Cognitive retraining was required in order to reteach her how to mix colors, stretch canvas, sequence layering of pigments, etc. Equally important therapeutically, however, was

restoring her creative vigor and motivation and providing much needed support to build sufficient self-confidence and energy for her to confront the white emptiness of the canvas. Because she had been trained in an academic, realistic style, which was part of her left brain functioning that was now impaired, she required support in making the transition to a new, more impressionistic style. Such a more "forgiving" style did not, however, compromise her expressive capacity as an artist. Indeed, some have observed that her art is now more vibrant and artistically mature. It was our task, however, to convince her of the merit of her changed style.

This remarkable work was painted by a college art student who had suffered a series of debilitating strokes. Due to her extensive brain damage, she had to adjust to a more intuitive, expressionistic style that contrasted sharply with her earlier academic work. This transformation was a difficult, painful process that liberated powerful emotional expression in the process.

142

Painting with the Physically Handicapped

One young woman's cerebral palsy was so debilitating that only her neck muscles could function with any control. Using a helmet and stylus, the teacher was able to fit almost any kind of brush, depending upon the project. Because the woman only had a lateral range of motion, only horizontal compositions were possible. Usually in cases like this tape would frame the entire picture, leaving no exposed edges to tear. However, in this case, in order to affect vertical movement, the paper had to be removed from its masking tape moorings and slid upward, downward or sideways to remain within reach of the brush. By changing the type of brush, modulations in surface lent further diversity to the work. Despite these profound limitations, this student was able, through sheer tenacity and a few adaptations, to create arresting landscapes and abstract works.

Numerous other adaptations can be devised, depending upon the disability and the project. Paralyzed painters often work with brushes in their mouths or feet. Astounding control can be achieved after years of practice with this technique for those with some control over their arms or hands. Many adaptive devices are available which attach the brush to the hand, wrist or elbow. Often an occupational therapy department can provide assistance or consultation on fabricating specialized devices.

It is important that a painter working in a wheelchair have a barrier-free workspace in which to paint. A lapboard can be fitted to the chair and a table easel mounted on it. Care must be taken to secure the easel firmly to a surface so it can absorb even the roughest pounding. If at all possible, I prefer to have the child leave the wheelchair to work in a regular chair or on the floor. While it may demand some heavy lifting and patient assistance, children are often thrilled to leave their chairs behind and take their places as any other art student.

Although severely spastic and paralyzed, this young woman possessed extraordinary stamina and tenacity. Although her art was limited by her inability to move, her creative vigor and sensitivity made her a model for other students to emulate. This text is dedicated to her memory.

Painting with the Visually Impaired

Just as visually impaired children enjoy drawing and coloring, they can also become enthusiastic painters. For those with some residual vision, straight painting techniques can be used with only minor modifications. For instance, colors might be confused, thus containers that vary in size or shape may ease identification. The paint containers, water jars and paper or canvas should remain secured to the table surface and their placement should be consistent and predictable.

For those children who are blind, paint must possess some tactile quality. Acrylic is ideal medium because it leaves a discernable raised line when squeezed out of caulking guns, plaster bulbs or bottles. Various aggregates can be added to the paint to leave a variety of textures. To make the paint gritty, sand can be added. Sawdust, woodchips, aquarium gravel and even sugar will add an interesting tactile dimension to the medium. Spoons, spackling knives, painting knives and hands, can all be used to apply materials to a surface. Some teachers add associative scents to the paint for easier identification, i.e. cinnamon for brown; lemon for yellow; licorice for black, etc. In other situations the children might be encouraged to associate specific colors on a language or symbolic basis, such as red being the color of anger, or being green with envy.

The theme or subject matter does not necessarily need to be curtailed for the visually impaired. Often completely blind children will request a certain color despite the fact that they cannot see or even conceptualize color. In many instances their request is based upon a desire to do normal things, as a regular classroom member.

Sometimes the extent of a student's visual impairment is not easily assessed, due to secondary deficits such as mental retardation or autism. One young woman of nineteen I worked with was considered functionally blind. She was fitted with a cane and was often led around by sighted aides. What we didn't know was that she could see at very close range. Given a paintbrush for the first time, she astounded everyone by painting an interesting version of a tree. The canopy of her tree is unremarkable since she simply cannot see enough to care about it. But the massive trunk is another matter, reflecting her desire to have that tree stay put. Blind people cannot take for granted where things will be the next instant or the next year. Common to their art are images that center around predictability and stability. Once again, if the teacher takes the time to perceive what issues the child is bringing to the artwork, he or she can take these cues as most rational and effective references for accommodating the exceptional child's needs.

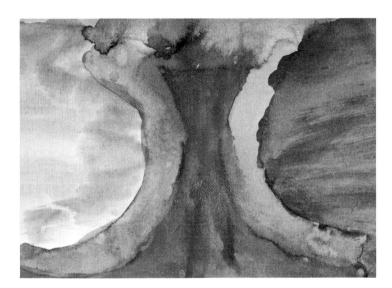

Painted by a visually impaired child of ten, this piece overemphasizes the roots of the tree to underline the importance of its stability and predictability. Note the tree's canopy is given scant attention because the child cannot see it.

chapter 8

Printmaking

Of all the art processes, printmaking is perhaps the easiest and most productive technique to adapt to special populations. It is essentially an interdisciplinary medium which allows the special needs child to use the skills of drawing, painting, design and even sculpture. Because printmaking draws upon these familiar processes, children are apt to experiment and cross over into different media with less resistance or confusion. It is, however, not just the familiarity factor that popularizes printmaking. More than in any other process, deficits such as immaturity, physical handicaps, emotional disturbance and other problems can be camouflaged in printmaking. For example, drawing styles which display developmental arrest or distortions due to psychiatric illness can thrive when simplified as monoprints or distorted through woodcuts. The pathology does not seem to filter through as blatantly due to the inherent design characteristic of the printing medium. Indeed artists such as Dubuffet and Miró have chosen printmaking most often when working in a naive or bizarrely figurative style.

Parity is then achieved among special needs and mainstream children due to printmaking's flexibility of style and approach. Children who are not able to work in a realistic, detailed style can shift to abstraction or a nonobjective mode without depreciating the aesthetic worth of their work. From a kinesthetic standpoint, young and lower-functioning children especially thrive using the techniques which involve the rolling with brayers, scribbling into the ink, vigorous rubbing, then anticipating the magical moment of pulling the print to reveal their designs. Cause and effect are solidly introduced in this way, as well as prompting more abstract processes such as learning to modulate color values or working with positive and negative space. For older or more mature students, the process can be as sophisticated as need be, with lithography, etching or woodblock printing enhancing a child's representational drafting skills.

MONOPRINTING

The most direct and exciting printmaking process used extensively with immature or physically handicapped students is the monoprint. This process requires only scribbling skills from the artist, along with robust physical involvement. The process can be approached in several ways. Using water-based ink, the child rolls the medium onto a flat, flawless surface, such as tempered masonite, Plexiglas or a cafeteria tray. The surface should have a protective border that contains the spread of the ink. The child then draws into the ink, using implements such as erasers, cotton swabs, discarded markers or the edge of the brayer. This creates the negative space in the design. All the child

Printmaking can be structured so as to engage groups of children in robust yet cooperative activity.

Monoprinting can support the need of high-level students to work representationally without losing spontaneity and immediate gratification. In this variation, the ink is still applied to the plate, but before drawing on it a piece of paper is placed over the ink. A design is created by drawing onto the paper with heavy pressure, using the back of a pen, a broad pencil point or other hard stylus. Once the drawing is completed, the student pulls the print revealing the drawing's lines which have registered as the darker values due to the pressure exerted from the other side of the paper. The surrounding areas also come in contact with the ink yet, because the rest of the paper was not rubbed, they register as mottled values that contrast with the dark lines of the drawing.

In both techniques a second print can often be made using the same inked plate. In most cases a second print is necessary because children habitually use too much ink despite the closest supervision. Excess ink will drown out any finely drawn lines. It is the second print which registers the most modulation of color and surface texture and crisper resolution of line work.

Once pulled, prints should be assigned an edition number and placed on racks especially made for drying them. Prints are sticky and will be damaged during the flurry of printing activity unless placed safely out of the way to dry. Once the prints have dried, students might be allowed to

needs to do once the drawing is completed is to place a sheet of paper on the plate and, without letting it shift, rub the paper down with a wooden or stainless steel spoon, the palm of the hand or a commercial barren. After some vigorous rubbing, the moment of truth arrives when the child carefully pulls the print off the plate, accompanied by the "Oohs" and "Aahs" of peers and staff alike. Not only will the negative space and lines contrast with the colored inked areas, but wonderful textures may be achieved. Texture may result from an inconsistent thickness of the ink on the plate, uneven rubbing pressure or other "happy accidents."

Several prints can be pulled off of the same monotype plate. This compensates for the common problem of students' overinking.

Dramatic effects can be achieved when monotype prints are made on different kinds of backdrops. Old drawings, magazine illustrations and photographs can all create an interesting field of negative and positive space.

add detail work to their relatively simple designs. Drawing, pen and ink, markers, watercolors and charcoal can all be worked into prints which need added embellishment.

The type of printing paper used can also add another dimension to the printing process. Background surfaces can include newspapers, old watercolor paintings, photographs and textiles.

Printmaking also lends itself to studying, comparing and working in the styles of other artists, from the paleolithic hand printers to contemporary printmakers such as Baskin, Mirò and others whose style may be comprehended by children with special needs.

COLLOGRAPHS

The next logical step in the printmaking process is to devise a composition using positive elements and adhere them to a rigid surface. Figures, landscapes and nonobjective designs can be cut out of cardboard, or self-sticking linoleum and then mounted. Ink is rolled onto the designs and then printed, using the monoprint procedure of rubbing paper over the plate. Because ink often spreads over the borders of the raised forms into the negative areas, an unusual halo effect occurs. The positive forms retain the darker values with the background receiving lighter more mottled tones. Using a linoleum cutter to add fine lines and cross-hatchings will lend another element to the composition.

As long as a child can cut using heavy, serrated utility shears or aviator snips, he or she will be able to accomplish this process. Those who lack the control or strength can work under the closest supervision with a paper cutter. Using the cutter with a shield which separates the handle from the blade, such children can use gross motor movements to sheer strips of linoleum or cardboard. While the use of such a dangerous tool with an incapacitated student may cause you to shudder, keep in mind the least restrictive approach which allows each child to use his or her own resources to achieve parity among intact peers. With proper modifications, the paper cutter can offer the weakened child an opportunity to cut with force and precision without assistance.

BLOCK PRINTING

For students whose motor capacities are intact, block printing allows the same robust physical activity as sculpture or carving. When working with a razor-sharp whittling tool, students are expected to rise to the occasion: to control their impulses and to maintain an awareness of safety. In my experience with special needs children, I have encountered many children whose behaviors were often disruptive or even assaultive. When they were given the responsibility of working with an "adult" process, however, they handled the situation remarkably well. Although close supervision was critical, they often worked with great self-absorption and unusual productivity.

In printing with linoleum or woodblocks, the child begins by developing a design or sketch which will lend itself to being broken down into positive and negative elements. This is the most difficult phase of the project, since children may be used to working with contour drawings or shading techniques with modulated values. I often begin with a warm-up exercise using black construction paper to simulate the positive and negative concept. Students are instructed to cut out basic figures and other elements which are then pasted onto white, grey or silver paper for contrast. This is followed by redrawing the paper design onto the block. The block can be commercially prepared linoleum mounted on plywood or clear soft wood. Both are easy and quick to cut. The drawing is transferred to the block and then color-coded by shading in the positive elements with black marker to remind the child what to leave and where to cut. At this stage the teacher will be besieged by students who declare themselves ready to cut when their designs are not fully resolved. Children who have limited attention spans, are hyperactive or suffer impulse control problems will have a ten-

Rolling objects through a press is physically stimulating for all exceptional children, and is particularly suited to cognitive efforts.

dency to rush the planning stage in order to get on with the exciting part of gouging and cutting. Unless there is some compelling reason to yield to their impatience, I usually send these children back to the drawing board so that they will not falter when cutting up their block.

Once cutting begins, several safety rules must be considered before the student is allowed to participate. First, each block should rest against a bench fence or, better yet, be secured with a "C" clamp. Secondly, children must first be taught and then practice making the thrust of their cutting motion away from their bodies and limbs. (Students frequently turn the blade toward themselves rather than taking the time to loosen the clamp and turn the block. When a student does this repeatedly, I enforce a time-out.) With time and practice students will learn to instinctively cut away from themselves. If students do not learn this after repeated demonstration, practice and cueing, they are not sufficiently mature to handle this technique.

Printing the block can be accomplished in the same manner as in monoprinting and collography, or the block can be run through a press. The press should be securely bolted to a bench with ample

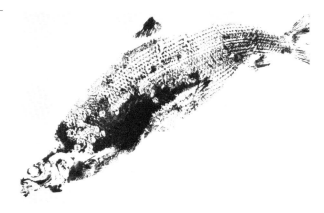

Many three-dimensional objects can be printed. This fish was inked, printed and the print worked on with colored pencil. Often prints are handed back to students for embellishment, which reinforces skills and gets added mileage out of materials and projects.

room to wind the print through. In order to insure the correct pressure upon the block, the teacher should do a test run before inviting students to participate.

One variation which elicits strong responses is gyotaku. Developed by the Japanese, this process uses the textural element of the fish's body to create a relief print. I took a group of physically handicapped children to the market to select their specimens, which alone caused great excitement. Although more than a few were initially tactile defensive and alarmed by the fishy odor, soon most dove into their carcasses with enthusiasm and were quite enthralled with the wonderful prints their fish evoked. This project maximized physical participation while camouflaging handicaps and producing aesthetically pleasing results.

JIGSAW PRINTS

With advanced students who can operate power tools, I have often used the jigsaw technique for a block printing variation. A fine-bladed band saw or a jigsaw are versatile power tools for students functioning at a middle or high school level. They are timesaving, exciting to use and, with the proper supervision, among the safest power saws.

This activity begins with a drawing which delineates the outline of element in the composition. The drawing is transferred onto one-quarter inch tempered masonite and then cut up into puzzle-like pieces using the jig or band saw. The students must realize that most designs require that there be no waste—that each piece cut away is part of the puzzle. Once cut apart, the jigsaw puzzle is reassembled within a masonite frame. Once assembled, individual pieces can be inked. This is where the jigsaw process is versatile and exciting for students who have only worked within the monochro-

Masonite is easily cut by a board saw which is one of the safest and most easily controlled power-tools. The pieces are later reassembled forming a jigsaw puzzle that can be inked and printed.

The cut pieces are then reassembled and inked using a brayer or painted with tempera or acrylic paint. Different pieces are easily inked in different colors, adding an extra dimension to the process.

The same free form pieces are reconfigured into another design illustrating how added mileage can be obtained from one single process and design.

Pulling the print is an exciting event for children of all levels.

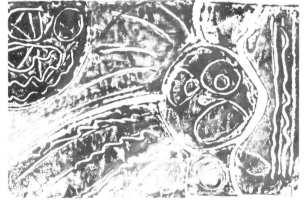

Expressive imagery can be elicited using the same jigsaw plate by drawing free-associating figurative forms into the ink using rubber erasers. This loosely drawn print aptly conveys emotional expression.

matic limitations of block printing. Each piece can be inked in a different color since, instead of one block being printed, the jigsaw is made up of numerous blocks which register perfectly in their puzzle. As long as the ink stays wet, students can meticulously ink and print their pieces, creating relatively complex and well-crafted designs.

EMBOSSING

Embossing is one of the most popular and enjoyable printmaking processes with all levels of students. It is quick, easy and immediately gratifying. Since there is so little investment in planning or technical preparation, students can be robust and spontaneous. They become remarkably self-motivated, enthusiastically exploring and experimenting with a vigor that is sometimes uncommon with the more handicapped special needs student. This is an ideal process to use when more complex projects are completed and children need a fun-oriented respite from more demanding work. Although embossing is fun for kids, its value as a serious process is in no way diminished. As with the other processes, it can be sophisticated, as artists such as Salvador Dali have demonstrated, or it can be scaled to the lowest-functioning child without sacrificing its aesthetic integrity.

Embossing is a process whereby relatively flat objects no thicker than a quarter are passed through the rollers of a proof press. The objects are sandwiched between a masonite board and a piece of felt; the pressure of the rollers impresses the shape, lines and textures of the objects into the surface of the paper. All a child needs to do is place the objects in a composition on the board, cover the objects with printing paper, place felt on top, then feed the sandwich into the press and run it through to the other side.

Many kinds of objects can be embossed. A high school student arranged keys and washers in a composition that used rhythm and repetition in a bold graphic way. The gears and works of an old clock are also ideal objects. Springs, metal washers, coins and wire will all pass through the press.

A child with an obsession with keys created an interesting embossed surface that is enhanced by freely scribbling with graphite sticks.

These brass gears and wires have been carefully inked with metallic pigments, then wheeled through the press by a group of severely learning disabled boys.

While the younger or lower-functioning students will randomly place some objects on the board, more advanced students will exercise excellent compositional awareness. One hearing-impaired boy did the bulk of his figure drawing in embossed relief. He would form bell wire into a figure in the style of a gestural drawing, capturing a continuous contour of the body. This he would squeeze through the press and wait excitedly to see if the pressure would change the figure's position in any way. Often the figure would indeed distort, making for more "happy accidents."

Most often embossing relies upon the clean white relief form for its aesthetic appeal. This is indeed an ideal approach to the process for it is the subtlety of the form and its play against the whiteness of the surrounding pictorial field that makes so strong a statement. Yet the objects can be just as easily inked to create a collograph embossing.

chapter 9

Sculpture

The impulse to manipulate, arrange and construct is present in even the youngest child. Materials which are easy to grasp, visually stimulating and invite stacking or arranging will prompt even low-functioning children to participate. Smoothly sanded blocks, colorful wire, large easy-to-handle feathers, string, beads or rings are all excellent media for construction purposes. It is possible to work within a broad range of functioning and developmental levels with this medium to create pleasing yet serious sculpture.

A young or mentally retarded child's first experience with construction techniques may come through working with wooden blocks. The smooth, clean, geometrical shapes invite a child's manipulation, exploration and problem solving. As children move through the developmental milestones, their play with blocks becomes increasingly sophisticated. Random touching or teething leads to grasping, then manipulation. As manipulations become more controlled, then matching, sequencing and arranging occurs. Configurations lead to stacking until free-standing rudimentary structures emerge. Through block-play, a child begins to explore three-dimensional design, as the visual and tactile senses experiment with form, balance, composition and scale. The kinetic, temporary nature of block structures engages children. The stack teaches exciting, suspenseful proportions, then the structure finally tumbles dramatically to the ground.

Watching one multiply handicapped boy create his structures epitomized the drama and exhilaration of block play. Methodically he would stack the shapes, often cantilevering portions which added a kinetic sense of balance to his pieces. His constructions rose with great sureness as he deftly dropped both the expected and unusual shapes into place. As the structures grew top-heavy, I could sense his mounting anticipation. He would begin to push the limits of the construction until, finally, the glorious collapse would take place. As the pieces tumbled downward, he too would fall, finally coming to rest among the rubble of his fallen tower. Watching him lie on the floor, his head hidden away in mock (or real) anguish, one appreciates how he and the structure were inextricably tied. Such intensity of emotional investment and identification with the art process is usually found only in mature artists.

SENSORY STIMULATION CONSTRUCTIONS

Some lower-functioning or infantile children, such as the young blind, the autistic, the mentally retarded or the multiply handicapped, may require sensory stimulation techniques as a precursor to actual artmaking. Many young children need to be gently stimulated with tactile, olfactory or visual sensations. For instance, the child might be ex-

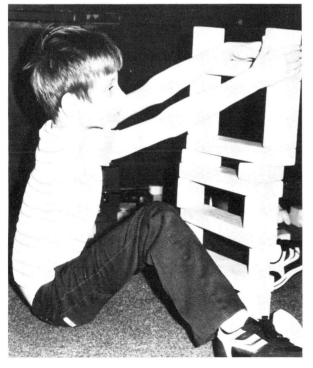

Blockbuilding is serious business for this multiply handicapped child. He pushes the material to its limit and becomes part of the action as his towers and facades crash to the floor.

posed to a feather, with the teacher waving it to create a breeze or brushing it against the skin. The next step beyond this passive experience is for the child to begin to manipulate it. Malleable wire can be used to attach the feather as an element in a free-standing stabile or in a mobile. Elements such as wooden rings, bells or other colorful objects can be added as the child increases in attention span and motor control. Care should be taken to insure that objects are non-toxic, too large to swallow and without sharp or abrasive edges.

SIMPLE WOODEN SCULPTURES AND TOYS

A logical extension of block play and sensory stimulation constructions is to fabricate toys. With only minor modifications, usually made by the instructor, toy constructions can be assembled by young children regardless of their disability. Sawing, sanding, assembling and finishing can all be accomplished, given adaptive modifications of tools and work space. For instance, when students are sanding, clamps should be used to secure the work and the students should wear protective eye gear and aprons. One developmentally disabled child needed a hand-over-hand approach to get him started painting his toy train. Eventually this support was diminished as he learned to control the enamel paint. Once the train was assembled, the construction process was reinforced for this student in a most positive, pleasurable manner—by actually playing with the fruit of his labor.

SHADOW BOX RELIEFS AND FREE-STANDING SCULPTURES

Shadow box reliefs provide yet another art medium which can effectively camouflage developmental disabilities. Using works by Louise Nevelson for orientation and motivation, I conduct this activity with all ranges of children. Only grasping, arranging, simple gluing and proper sequencing are

Real work gets done with real tools and equipment.

required to produce dynamic compositions. Wooden shapes, often scrap from the wood or plastic shop, are ideal elements with which to experiment. I can compensate for the motor deficits by providing a box-like frame which gives even the youngest child a secure, discernable structure within which to place the elements. To cover sloppy gluing, I have the children spray their reliefs in one color, usually black or white as Nevelson did.

Although behaviorally disturbed, the boy who assembled the train thrived on having his own workbench, vise and materials at hand for his exclusive use. Actually, the child could not be trusted to work with tools around the other children. However, emphasis was placed upon the

This construction required that this hyperactive child be provided with his own work station away from the other students wielding their own tools and lumber. The shadow box is a Victorian dresser drawer with bow front, salvaged from the garbage.

positive which, in this case, highlighted his special work station. The shadow frame for this artwork was a drawer from a discarded dresser, complete with finished wood, dovetail joints and even a bowed frontpiece which lent extra interest to the composition. Notice how the student bent birch dowels into the space creating interesting arcs and horizontals which echo the shadow box frame and create an extra dimension of tension and movement. These concepts were not taught, but were the result of an extensive period of spontaneous experimentation.

No one is permitted to use glue until several sessions have been devoted exclusively to arranging and rearranging the dry elements. Such a project encourages robust physical activity. The tools, medium and process yield a kind of positive resistance and sensory stimulation which allow the behaviorally disordered child to act out aggressively and energetically, yet productively. Such outlets are imperative if the teacher is to redirect these impulses.

Another variation of the shadow box theme is the personal collection relief. In this project, therapeutic and art educational goals effectively integrate to create an aesthetically powerful and personal statement. Again, the works of mature

artists can be employed as a motivational device. In this case Joseph Cornell's work is an ideal vehicle for conveying the concept of constructing a personal relief as well as for teaching compositional awareness and fabrication techniques using a variety of media. A successful finished product is in no way dependent upon a child's mental or physical condition. Every child has objects, photographs or favorite themes that can be combined in the three-dimensional collage format. In most instances the shadow box itself is prefabricated and the child need only arrange the composition.

In one case in which a child was quadriplegic, I completely installed the elements myself using the verbal direction of the paralyzed artist. This intervention constituted a least restrictive approach, since the child could neither grasp nor arrange, yet could verbally instruct with great articulation; she knew exactly what she wanted. The fact that I acted as her motor apparatus did little to diminish her sense of self-satisfaction in regard to the finished product.

LARGE SCALE WORKS

Large scale works offer an opportunity to experience monumental constructions, depending on the child's physical capacities. Students enjoy creating works larger than themselves. Even children in wheelchairs have taken part in group projects where their ability to design, stabilize an element or assist in the finishing process has contributed substantially to a piece's success. Working in a large scale need not require enormous quantities of material, specialized equipment or technical expertise. Scale is more a matter of relationships between the maker and the setting in which a piece is installed. A child in a wheelchair may consider any object that is placed above his or her eye level a large scale work. It is the presentation which accounts for much of the exhilaration and awe of a piece, not its true size.

For instance a group of middle schoolers created a modular ceramic sculpture which reached almost five feet. In creating this piece, several wheelchair-bound children rolled innumerable coils, which were then forced into large hemispherical plaster molds. Once the hemispheres were coil-built, the halves were then welded together to form a full sphere. A base was constructed using coils which were stacked inside a 16″ Sono tube (construction pillar mold) to create a large cylinder. A hemispheric piece was used as a cap for the cylinder. As a buffer between the spheres, students devised a series of slab-built plates which functioned as horizontal spacers in the composition. Finally, designs were worked out for a small, delicate sculptural element to cap the piece. It was a cerebral palsied child's piece, a loosely pinched together series of coils formed into a dance-like figure. Inside the finished piece a steel pipe acted as a stabilizer and armature. While it took several able-bodied children to combine these elements (and a competent ceramics technician to supervise the construction), the orthopedically handicapped children nevertheless played a crucial role in its creation.

Modular sections of ceramic cylinders allow for different kinds of participation. The base sections were coiled by a robust group of hearing impaired middle schoolers, while the top pieces were pinched by cerebral palsied and multiply handicapped children.

Bending redwood boards helps delineate expanses of space which can be textured and colored by inserting different materials such as crushed shale and black dirt. Children with different abilities contributed to the different facets of the project.

ENVIRONMENTAL CONSTRUCTIONS

To most young or handicapped children the idea of manipulating large environments is an overwhelming, often incomprehensible prospect. How can a blind or immobilized child effect artistic changes in a large room, playing field or backyard? I feel it is important for these children to realize that they can indeed have control over both the immediate spaces of their wheelchair lapboard and a 1,000 square foot courtyard. This is precisely what occurred when I tackled the rehabilitation of a school courtyard which had fallen into disrepair. The area was overgrown with weeds, its pond filled with sludge, its fences broken. The first phase of the project was to create an environment by working with organic elements such as shrubs, flowers, water, fish, sky and stone as part of the landscape design. To this end, paths were cut, batter boards were laid, retaining walls built and lawns rehabilitated. At this stage, labor was provided by physically intact but economically disadvantaged high school students hired for the summer on a work study program. Once the flower beds were built, physically and mentally handicapped children were

integrated into the labor crew. Both intact and handicapped students worked together in a least restrictive setting, at tasks suited to their individual needs. Although these tasks were sometimes segregated, their utility and function were in no way discounted. Although a deaf/blind young woman was severely handicapped in terms of freedom of movement and intellectual ability, she proved to be an excellent and valuable gardener. In fact, because her obsessional behavior manifested itself in manually arranging and rearranging things in her environment, she became a one-woman rototiller, working and reworking the soil with her trowel with great joy and determination. For this blind individual, feeling the texture of the soil, the pleasure in scooping and pouring, and sensing the fragrance of the flowers was all profoundly important as sensory stimulation. Other children—some in wheelchairs or on crutches, some sensorially disabled, others mentally handicapped—all found equally stimulating and useful tasks in this project.

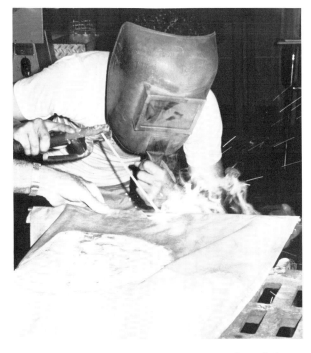

Vocational classes can become art studios if the art teacher collaborates with the shop teacher on a cooperative basis.

Installations integrate different aspects of children's abilities. Each element contributes to the different dimensions of the space and allows for different interactions.

An entire year was devoted to landscape design and construction. As this first phase neared completion, attention was turned to the second phase—the integration of student-made elements into the composition. Again, scale became the most important principle in the composition. How could both small and large scale artworks have impact on such relatively enormous space?

We began by constructing a ring of banners which circled the pond, echoing its circular shape while also connecting wind with ground and water. We used batik to create the banners. Students who could safely handle molten wax carried out the wax resist process. Using stencils, the students created a series of designs which revolved around stars, planets and space. Each composition used a large sphere as the central element. The wax was applied, then students of all levels were invited to brush on dyes, crumple up the waxed material, then send it back to the waxworkers for a new layer of resist. Once completed, the banners were sent to the metal working shop, where steel T's were brazed by learning-impaired vocational students. Students enthusiastically mounted the banners and marveled at how the swaying, colorful pieces interacted with the environment (Caprio-Orsini 1987).

Soon students began to donate other forms of art to the space. Small ceramic reliefs were tucked under juniper bushes. Welded flowers were placed alongside steel-colored Dusty Miller annuals. Plaster castings were submerged in the flower beds as if they were undulating creatures living just under the earth's surface. Large scale, pieced-steel reliefs were installed. After the second year, many student-made creations were mounted in both conspicuous and unobtrusive fashions. The interplay between the overt and covert sensibilities of these pieces imparted a feeling of drama, playfulness, self-celebration and modesty. Each student who contributed felt an impact had been made, especially when viewing before-and-after photographs. There are few indications of disability or functioning level in this environmental piece. It remains a statement about how input is needed at every ecological level. Without such contributions, the piece would not possess balance and a sense of closure.

A child with extreme hyperactivity found an outlet for his energies by submerging this plaster cast into the ground.

A collaborative sculpture between the vocational and art departments at the New Jersey School for the Deaf, 1986.

The finished space: sculpture garden, performance area, meditative retreat. New Jersey School for the Deaf, 1987.

An environmental artwork designed by James Pruznick was videotaped as children interacted with it. The values of the translucent material changed as moving darkened bodies blended with the white tones.

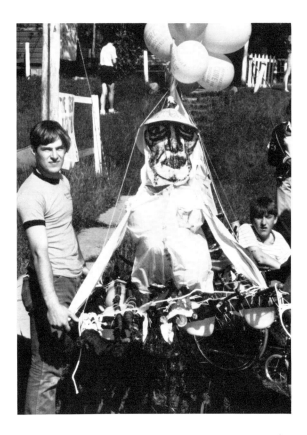

An annual arts festival was held in the finished space, with children from the school as well as other institutions participating in workshops, viewing the artworks or simply feeding the fish in the pond. As an extension of the concept of environment art, we constructed another sculptural piece out of a parachute draped over an aluminum frame. Students were invited to view the piece as sculpture, interact with it as an environment, and manipulate it as if it were a game or enormous toy. Some adolescent students were resistant or even hostile: to them such an incongruous object was in fact neither sculpture, game nor toy. In accordance with their concrete modes of relating, it remained purely a draped sheet which created much unwarranted fuss. For the younger or handicapped children, such resistance was not apparent. Being less set in their ways, these children unabashedly interacted with the piece. The sensory-handicapped children especially felt secure in its cozy space and delighted in feeling its silky textures, its gentle breezy movements, its transparent, moving images. Despite its provocative nature, such a work is important for children to experience. It has the effect of shaking up their stereotyped concepts and ideas about the nature of sculpture, architecture, playgrounds, parachutes and their environment in general (Pruznick 1987).

The video camera can add a dynamic element to large scale installations or environments. By documenting a piece on tape, the art object expands to include those who are interacting with it, and thus becomes as much performance as sculpture. Any event which involves movement, sound, environments and costumes can be recorded and viewed as a piece in itself. Such an enterprise does not require sophisticated production techniques; all that is needed is a lively, multimedia approach to artmaking.

This performance project by Sharon Hyson A.T.R. and her clients was floated across a lake to a sister camp.

One wildly funky construction was created by Sharon Hyson along with her clients with multiple handicaps. It was made to float on water and sent to children on a neighboring campus as a performance gift. As they anticipated its arrival across the lake and observed the construction's interactions with water currents, fog, etc., the children developed a heightened sense of empowerment and creative capacity. Recording the whole process on video intensified the work's aesthetic and interactive qualities, while preserving the event for posterity.

This construction of 2-D and 3-D elements is manipulated by these students of different levels of functioning. Photo: Sharon Hyson.

Grouped together, these Down syndrome students become a performance piece as their costumes create designs in motion on videotape.

CASTING

Casting provides a range of experiences for all levels of children. The process lends itself equally well to working on small scale, technically basic processes or monumental modular pieces of great complexity. A variety of media can be used, including plaster, paper, clay and metal. By working with a negative mold, children can exercise both their perceptual and problem-solving abilities. Rhythmic and robust movements, motor coordination, figure-ground perception, depth and texture are all touched upon during the mold-making and casting process. While the casting process is usually associated with high-level technique and material, there are several processes that can be modified for use in regular school or treatment programs. It is the high-level nature of the casting process, however, which intrigues and prompts young people to experiment with these techniques. Children can rarely contain their excitement upon cracking open a mold to finally view their design, magically now cast in its finished form.

First Experiences

An initial experience with the casting process for very young or developmentally disabled children often comes in the form of food—molds in which gelatin, cake, ice, pudding or bread can be cast in a variety of shapes, textures and colors. Working with Jello or pudding provides a good first exposure to the process of casting. Lively, interesting materials, such as water, food coloring, cream or eggs are stimulating to young children. Spatulas, mixing bowls, blenders and ovens all arouse a child's curiosity and encourage energetic participation. The process of baking, chilling, releasing the mold and decorating the product are all valuable skills and constitute a developmentally appropriate introduction to more advanced casting techniques. Indeed, these activities can be considered precursors to what any sculptor would undertake in the atelier.

With such a colorful and harmless medium, there is little concern over the young or retarded

child ingesting the media. However, I do not approve of actually encouraging children to eat these materials, since this confuses them as to what is an edible food stuff and what is an art medium that should never be eaten.

Sand Casting

Most children have experienced activities such as sand or water play. Scooping and pouring (and in effect, casting) are all natural activities in the sand box, thus it takes few adaptations to bring these activities closer to a true art process. By replacing the sand with plaster, children can still make playful impressions yet their images can now be preserved.

The tactile sensations provided by playing with sand set the stage for more production-oriented casting techniques. This autistic child finds endless pleasure in simply feeling the sand sprinkled and sifted onto her body.

When casting plaster in sand, the sand should be clean, damp and compacted. Fine detail is difficult to attain in this process, therefore the emphasis should be on bold, contrasting forms and textures. Once cast, the piece should be inspected to insure that all edges are smooth and rounded. A rasp or file will refine the casting so that the child can safely handle and decorate the piece.

Casting in Clay
Sand casting is one of the most powerful techniques in the curriculum. Few techniques are able to accommodate such a far-reaching range of functioning levels or disabilities. While it is essentially a simplistic, unfettered process, works of great complexity and sophistication are also possible.

Casting in bas-relief uses the same concepts as casting in food materials and sand, yet offers infinitely more flexibility and sophistication, particularly for higher-functioning or more mature students. It can however, be easily scaled down for the youngest or most regressed child. The child uses any means possible to make an impression in thick slabs of clay. Stamps, natural objects, household utensils, even finger or hand prints will register detailed impressions of rhythm, movement and pattern. Once the composition is created, borders around the slab are constructed to contain the plaster. If I need a slow setting time I use Hydrocal plaster which takes twice as long as plaster of paris to set. Sometimes the goal is to create a modular panel or mural. If this is the case, I use identical cardboard molds or frames to insure consistent dimensions and shape. The pieces can then be combined and mounted together. A rigid frame also provides the child with firm parameters in which to work. Once the plaster medium is poured into the mold, a child need only wait moments before seeing the finished casting. It is a dramatic moment when a child registers the fact that the robust stampings and slashings actually resulted in an object.

Painting, or staining can then proceed. Usually, I prefer children to paint a thin coating or stain over the piece and then wipe it down to almost

A deaf/blind high school student created this sandcast plaster rubbed with oxides and sprayed with a matt medium.

A multi-media construction with plaster cast from a direct clay negative mold. The piece was later sprayed a matt grey to unify the elements.

This bas-relief was cast from a clay negative in the form of a cave wall. This learning disabled middle school student is rubbing black iron oxide into the plaster, drawing images reminiscent of the paleolithic bison and other beasts.

clean. This causes each detail or texture to emerge in startling contrast. A finish coat of spray fixative can then be applied to give a gloss to the dry colors.

This process, of course, is most rudimentary. More complex creations can be achieved by using larger amounts of clay and plaster. Reliefs on a larger scale, however, require extensive reinforcement and armatures to support their greater weight and bulk. Dramatic forms can be created just by casting directly into a clay negative. Several students created a bas-relief by impressing a variety of found materials, anatomical castings, various bones, rubber balls and texture tools. Students also integrated formed and stiffened canvas as an additional element in the relief. Plain white glue was used to freeze the folds and draped forms, which interact nicely with the cold white images of the casting. Several of these group pieces were installed in our sculpture garden. Implanted in the flower beds, they seemed like living landscapes, writhing under and above the earth's surface.

Different colored paper pulp was patted into simple designs by an emotionally handicapped and hyperactive fifth grader.

Cast Paper

With a modicum of technical expertise, a teacher can extend the possibilities of direct plaster casting by using paper pulp. Papermaking is an interesting process, especially since the medium is so ordinarily taken for granted; children are rarely aware of its origins. Pulp can be prepared by pulverizing plants or the inner bark of trees. If such an energetic approach is beyond the teacher's resources, then cotton rag can be processed. This involves cooking and washing the material, then beating it to a pulp so that the fibers are thoroughly softened and engorged with water. Despite this pulverizing, the cellulose in the fiber retains its essential strength as a casting medium. Like the simplest kitchen-art food molding processes, papermaking is comprehensible and enjoyable by even the youngest or lowest-functioning students without sacrificing aesthetic or technical sophistication.

The paper casting process can be accomplished in several ways. I prefer the "patty-cake" method which is essentially a daubing action. The child grasps a handful of paper pulp, squeezes out the excess water, then pushes the material into the surface of a plaster negative mold. Care must be taken to insure that the plaster mold has no undercuts and that it's been given an application of mold release, such as a liquid dish soap. Any relatively flat plaster relief can function as a mold, so long as it allows the paper cast to pull free. Designs can be culled from simple objects such as rubber balls to create spheres, wooden blocks for geometric shapes or organic objects such as people's faces, old radios, sea shells or other shallow surfaces. Separate colors and designs can be integrated by applying globs of different colored pulp to different areas. Found objects such as leaves, twigs, bark and other organic objects can be imbedded in the pulp. Once the cast is complete it is allowed to dry with a coat of glue or even fiberglass to create a stiff backing. Straight watercolor, acrylic or enamel are other possible finishes. A fifth grade learning disabled child demanded a clearly defined structure and cooperation in each phase of the operation. He was mostly entertained by the kinesthetic, kitchen-play aspect of the process. He reveled in the mushiness and plastic qualities of the pulp and thoroughly enjoyed mashing it exuberantly into the molds. Some of the other children were able to plan out the distribution of their colors by drawing partitioning lines on their molds. One actually cut small pieces of plastic, which were set on end to provide fine borders between forms and colors.

The recent work of Frank Gallo is a useful motivation for paper casting, especially for secondary school students. His figurative torsos of seductive women are flawless in their surfaces, with the pleasing expanses of bleached white form interacting nicely with cascades of hair and other textures. Although such a technique is fairly complex for a student, Gallo's images gave birth to several powerful portraits which used students' death masks as departure points for experimentation. Unlike plaster relief, these pieces hang lightly and effortlessly on the wall. Paper is strong and resilient which lessens concerns over weight and strength.

Casting pewter into cuttlebone is an ideal introduction to the casting process. Cuttlebone is effortless to carve while pewter is simple to melt and pour with relative safety. This hearing impaired student is pouring the metal into the mold.

The mold is cracked open to reveal the finished cast.

Presentation contributes to the aesthetic effect of these eighth-grade pewter castings.

Metal Casting

Casting with metal is also an exciting process, especially for pre-adolescent boys. The manipulation of molten metal encourages cooperation, impulse control and serious concentration. It is an activity which children associate with adult processes, and therefore they are eager to participate. One of the easiest and most interesting methods of casting metal uses cuttlebone as a negative mold. This material is the shell of a squid-like marine animal. It is easily carved and refined, yet it takes the heat of a torch quite well. The process is simple. The bone is sliced in half to reveal the soft, inner material. The students transfer their designs using a sharp, hard pencil. The negative space is then carved away using a small spoon, knife tip or an X-acto blade. When the negative impression is refined and ready for casting, the two halves are jointed with wire, or an elastic band and a channel for the molten metal is carved. The casting metal is torched until molten, and poured using a black iron ladle. The metal dribbles freely into the mold and is allowed to cool and solidify. The finished casting is removed when cooled. The piece can then be filed, hammered or soldered, then buffed to a polished finish. This is a very popular project—one that is at once technically simple, yet because of the danger element it is seemingly advanced. It is a straightforward casting process which thrives upon original ideas and designs yet yields concrete products. For this reason I use it as a break between fine art processes such as life drawing and landscape painting and as a way of providing quick, object-oriented gratification.

While this project does not ordinarily elicit provocative or stirring images due to the craft-like, technical nature of the process, it is a powerful stimulus in eliciting different behaviors. Metal casting intensifies the dynamics of the group. A conduct-disordered child may become utterly unbearable doing such a project due to the danger element, or paradoxically the same child may assume striking leadership qualities, choreographing the entire casting process. Cooperation and team work are needed in such a project, in which one child pours the metal while another operates the torch and another steadies the mold. Observing this process many times, I am consistently struck by how children can rise to the occasion and find resources and self-controls that were not evident under less challenging circumstances.

CARVING

For those children who can handle tools, carving or subtractive sculpture allows for robust activity and often yields interesting artwork. With only basic tools such as chisels, gouges, rasps and sandpaper, surprisingly complex and sophisticated work can be created. Students who experience behavior, motivation or attention problems are often captivated by sculptural technique. The element of danger and level of intensity needed for the activity exerts a powerful attraction. In exchange for their being allowed to handle tools in aggressive actions ordinarily denied them, students must control their impulses. The opportunity to pound away with a heavy wooden mallet or whittle and shave with a razor-sharp chisel allows a child's aggressive energies to be sublimated through appropriate and productive means. It is the teacher's responsibility, however, to see that the student does not become over-stimulated by the process, allowing emotions to gain a destructive upper hand. This can be accomplished, even with the most difficult children, by allowing them first to prove themselves with less dangerous tools such as rasps or Surforms.

Using soft blocks of insulation brick, pumice stone or other commercially available materials, three-dimensional forms can be formed solely by filing and sanding. With different shaped cutting or

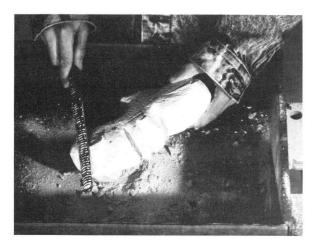

abrading surfaces, a wide variety of designs are possible. Convex, concave, V-grooves, square channels, round holes and flat planes can all be achieved simply by selecting the proper rasp. The "automatic design" element of these tools is crucial if lower-functioning or physically handicapped children are to reap results from this technique. Simply by running a rasp back and forth, a bold, interesting form will result. Adaptive devices, such as a movable track to guide the rasp's movements, can assist in controlling poorly coordinated students. Two strips of lattice wood placed on top of the stone block will serve well as a guide. The rasp can then be changed to vary the designs being produced. Because of the softness of the insulation brick, the weight of the steel rasp is sufficient to grind away the material. Often however, dust is a problem with this technique. Placing the entire project within a cardboard box (with one side removed for access) will contain most of the cinders and dust. Ventilation in the studio is an important consideration when working with this technique.

Once a student has demonstrated that he or she can handle working soft brick or commercial material, then mallet and chisels may be introduced. An extended practice time should be allotted to learning basic safety procedures, such as keeping hands behind the forward thrust of the chisel, insuring that all cutting is away from the body and that the block is securely held in the jaws of a vise. Physically handicapped children can participate in this activity if given sufficient time and practice.

Another approach to the subtractive process is the use of a flexible-shaft machine. This tool operates in a similar fashion to an electric drill, only the heavy body is connected to a flexible, cord-

Subtractive carving is easiest using a soft material such as this insulation brick. Using a vise bench, the piece is held securely while this eighth grader saws out the major forms with a key-hole saw. Sculpting is best controlled using a rasp or Surform tool, and final refining with fine sandpaper.

like wand which has the chuck at the end, similar to a dentist's drill. Children who are unable to grasp and maneuver a rasp or chisel can often safely hold and control a flexible-shaft tool. Using grinding stones in a variety of shapes and sizes, a range of lines, forms and textures can be effortlessly achieved. Work in relief, using plaster, wood, stone and even bone, can be accomplished with this flexible cutting tool. A visually impaired child often "drew" his pictures in relief on slabs of pinewood and black slate. A quadriplegic girl with a bare minimum of strength and coordination in her arms often used a plastic wrist support and a Velcro strap to attach the tool to her arm. She was able to use her gross arm movements to carve blocks of wax, wood and eventually soapstone.

Presentation of the finished sculptures is a crucial phase of this process. Children who have only managed to rasp a few grooves or grind off some rounded corners need to feel that their work has worth and integrity. Once, when the group was viewing Brancusi's kissing sculptures, one girl wryly remarked that his work was not that different from her own minimally embellished cubes. Only the scale and a city plaza as a mounting space were missing from her works.

The base of a sculpture can complete the work. Sanded wooden blocks can calm down an intricately textured or painted piece. A dramatic piece of driftwood can embolden the minimalist cube. Steel rods can raise a piece impressively in the air to change its scale and impact. A clean white plywood or sheetrock cube can lend a museum or gallery air to even the most modest scratchings. Once the artworks are seen away from the dusty mess of the studio, mounted atop their bases, children get a fresh perspective and new respect for their work.

An excellent sculptural tool for special needs children is the flexible shaft. This relatively safe and effective tool allows the child to work with fine details with little physical exertion or control. Different cutting tools can be used in this machine, much like a drill.

169

Despite being severely crippled, this young man has learned to use a mallet and chisel with excellent control. Few modifications are needed in this program, given his tenacious drive to succeed.

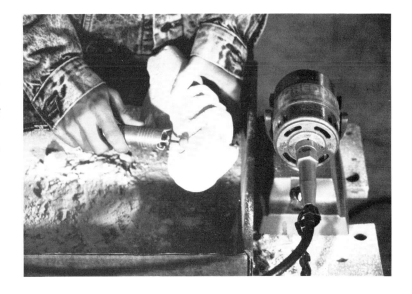

170 **COLLAGE**

Once a child has progressed to the point where grasping, placing and arranging elements is within his or her ability, an effective and exciting next step is to introduce the technique of collage. There is enormous flexibility in this process, which makes it ideal for adapting to specific handicapping conditions as well as working within a mainstream setting. The possibilities for camouflaging disability through this technique are also excellent. The range of media, techniques and expressive effects offer numerous alternatives to representational depiction. Collage is inherently a manipulative medium. Students can arrange prefabricated elements or create their own. It is in many ways a concrete operation which lessens resistance due to inhibition or failure of the imagination. There are of course, exceptions. One child in a class I taught had busily cut apart some pictures quite expertly. When I next observed, I found that he had reconstructed the pieces back to their original form! This, in his rather concrete estimation, was a highly rational solution to the problem!

In one situation I encountered, collage was used to articulate the feelings and ideas concerning a child's handicapping condition. A well-meaning, yet naive researcher had encouraged a group of hearing-impaired children to make art in response to the question "What is it like to be deaf?" Almost all of the children balked at this request, responding that being deaf is "normal." This is not an uncommon response from any congenitally handicapped child, who knows no other way of functioning. One child from the group, however, had lost his hearing due to a fever at age four. He had memories of the hearing world and was in this case surprisingly all too willing to cooperate. Being a bright, artistically gifted child, he was indeed a perfect subject for this researcher's study. His response was not a drawing, but a collage. In only one period, he pored over the catalog of images, then leafed through a stack of old *Life* magazines, assembling images. In this piece, the child's affective concerns are clearly projected. Body dis-

A hearing impaired student created this sensitive and provocative collage, exploring the feelings and ideas associated with his deafness.

tortion, anxiety and the loneliness are all overtly expressed. Clever juxtapositions of images, worked up in an unusual vertical format, lend additional interest to the piece. A brand of black humor, unusual in a fifteen-year-old deaf child, is also evident in a play on words—Falling on Deaf Ears—as well as in absurdist combinations of animals, humans and abstract elements. In the hands of this bright, yet emotionally fragile child, collage proved to be as malleable and evocative as the best drawing or sculpture medium.

Collage can be effectively adapted for children of different developmental levels and physical abilities. Spastic or paralyzed children may need to have raised surfaces or thick backings for their elements. Pieces of masonite, Styrofoam, cardboard and plywood are often used as backings for magazine images. Scraps of tree bark, carpeting, corduroy and woven mats are all lightly textured and easily adaptable to the orthopedic child. Patterns, textures and brightly colored elements, which are reminiscent of puzzle-play, should be emphasized with young and lower-functioning children. Materials such as thread, colored tape, seeds, buttons or other found objects can be incorporated. Projects dominated by these materials, however, forfeit any camouflaging possibilities if they are used with older children in mainstream settings. Beans, macaroni, etc., are strictly associated with primary grades and are used mainly with children who might ingest their media. Emphasis should be placed upon finding elements which are least restrictive and socially appropriate, yet also conform to the exceptional child's need for adaptations and accommodations. With this medium, there is no reason why the special needs student can not be working with cut figurative images, abstract colors, shapes and textural elements while the intact child works on a more complex level. If skillfully structured by the teacher, this process provides parity and challenge to all children.

Collage is a stimulating process which in this case promoted manual dexterity, design awareness and a strong possibility for success.

Discarded canvas scraps, corrugated cardboard and old pieces of wood were all that was needed to arrange this effective design. This assemblage was constructed over an old painting on masonite, which had been salvaged from a garage sale.

chapter 10

Ceramic Arts

Clay is among the most therapeutically dynamic art media. The sensory properties of the material invite children to manipulate and build with it, regardless of their functioning level or mental condition. While some students may initially find it unpleasant or disturbing to the touch, given the proper adaptations and support, the medium usually wins over even the most defensive or obsessively clean child. It is the highly plastic quality of clay which arouses the urge to touch, squeeze, roll and eventually build. Its solid, malleable presence offers a concrete point of departure from which explorative manipulation naturally develops into more complex modes of subtractive or additive sculpture. The medium can be worked simply by hand, or it can incorporate a range of adaptive equipment, allowing even the most handicapped children to work on a large scale with quantities of material and to operate with great force and power.

Given its dynamic quality as both a fine art and a craft medium, clay often forms the cornerstone of many art programs. Although it is a resource-intensive medium, requiring an investment of a space and basic equipment, it is among the most viable investments of the program. It has a capacity to sustain a range of students, from the very young and low-functioning through aspiring sculptors and future professional potters. (See Kramer 1970 and Silver 1978). Given its capacity for sen-sory and emotive expression, clay is among the most useful media for therapeutic work. Its accessibility and capacity for camouflaging developmental disability makes it particularly suited for work with special needs populations.

THE STUDIO

Admittedly, ceramics programs demand much in the way of resources. Some allocation of funds will be required to set up even the most modest studio, although much equipment and other paraphernalia can be salvaged or fabricated through resourceful recycling. Basic to a ceramics studio is a partitioned space to contain the inevitable dust and slime that is often a byproduct of working in this medium. It can be considered an activity center to which part of the artroom is devoted.

The ideal studio encompasses about 300 square feet and accommodates ten to fifteen students, including those in wheelchairs. The basic furniture requirements include work tables, sufficient counter space, under-counter storage for tools and supplies, two or more sinks and a protected and secured cabinet for greenware.

Furniture
All ceramic work should take place on a heavy-duty table with a smooth, even surface. Two sepa-

Installing his monumental coil-built sculpture in the school courtyard was a particularly satisfying moment for this physically handicapped middle schooler.

rate covers should be fitted to the table to accommodate the different phases of the ceramic process. Unprimed canvas should be used for the hand building method. This prevents the clay from sticking to the table's surface, while also imparting a pleasing texture to the clay slabs. A plastic cover is used for the decorating phase, allowing for considerable spilling and dripping during the glazing process, while also facilitating cleanup and preserving the finish of the table top. The table should be heavy and sturdy, enabling students—especially those with coordination problems—to vigorously roll, pound and throw slabs of clay forcefully to the table. Table height should be sufficient to provide clearance for wheelchairs to fit comfortably underneath.

The use of plaster bats is problematic in programs that service children with special needs. Plaster tends to crack or chip and will break apart under the strain of heavy use, possibly damaging the ware during the firing if allowed to make its way into the clay body. Wedging or drying boards can be cast in plaster if they are constructed within a wooden or metal frame, thus protecting the edges. A twenty-percent addition of Hydrocal or Hydrostone plaster to the plaster mix will toughen and harden the cast, thus increasing the durability of the wedging board.

Tools

The modeling handtools used with special needs populations should be kept basic and safe, with few sharp edges or points. Loop tools, fettling knives, cut-off wires with heavy toggle handles, natural wool, elephant ear sponges and a professional rolling pin are essential tools for the clay program. While a professional type of rolling pin may appear a luxury item, it is actually an economical investment that will withstand the roughest treatment and heavy-handed pressure from poorly coordinated or spastic students. The extra weight enables the slightly built or physically handicapped child to exert a minimum of energy while maintaining enough pressure to effectively roll a clay slab. Banding wheels are another essential tool, enabling the handicapped to reach all sides of a pot with minimum manipulation. They promote even coverage of glaze or slip by providing a spinning work surface for applying decoration or brushwork. The banding wheel also allows the child who self-stimulates an opportunity to spin an object appropriately, thus encouraging more adaptive behavior in the mentally retarded or autistic student.

Equipment

The potter's wheel is central to the ceramics process, and although it is technically difficult to master, it can be adapted to all types of children for productive use. I have even used a wheel with young blind children, allowing them to feel the spinning, slippery form within their hands. I have also trained high school students to eventually become potters' apprentices. Such is the versatility of this machine.

If there are orthopedically handicapped children in the art program, it would be advisable to purchase an electric wheel that has been specifically designed to accept wheelchairs and can be operated by both hand and foot. A centering jig is also advisable, so that this most difficult phase of the process can be mastered with a minimum expenditure of time and frustration. Wheel heads should be fitted to accept wooden or plastic bats, since

The ceramic ware cage is a secure area for storing and drying of unfired ceramic pieces.

the removal of the finished pot from the wheel is critical in this process. After the arduous effort of throwing a form, the child may mar or distort the work unless the whole bat can be removed, allowing the pot to dry unscathed. The bat should be fitted to the wheel head by two bat pins which automatically align and secure the bat to the wheel.

The potter's wheel should be powered so that sufficient torque is supplied during the throwing process. Underpowered wheels which sport high r.p.m.s often break down under constant use or when pressure is applied to the clay. It pays to invest in a high quality, institutional-grade model which will supply years of trouble-free use.

A clay extruder is another useful piece of equipment that can be effectively operated by almost any child who has the use of his or her arms. Clay is loaded into the barrel, then compressed through a variety of dies, creating a continuous extrusion in either hollow or solid forms. These tube forms can then be manipulated into sculptures. The extruded form can act as a departure point from which the student can alter, elaborate or combine the basic forms to create original ceramic pieces.

This electric potter's wheel is accessible to wheelchair-bound students, featuring both hand and foot speed controls. This cerebral palsied young man has become quite adept at centering one-handedly.

For those who cannot center, a jig can be purchased or fabricated. This aluminum bar is brought down upon the clay using different angles to effectively bring the clay to center.

An extruder is an excellent tool for manufacturing clay parts such as coils, tubes, cubes or other custom shapes. By plunging the arm downward, these boys are extruding long tubes of clay, saving hours of tedious fabrication time. They then work together to fashion a sculpture using their extruded forms.

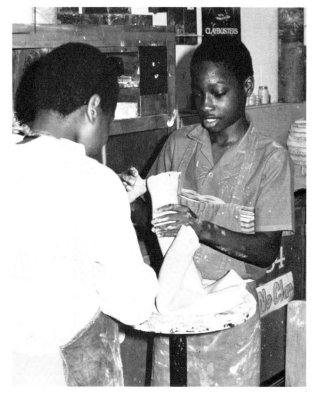

This planter was extruded as a long cube. Once laid on its side, the ends were attached and the top wall pierced to create this interesting vessel.

For instance, a square form could be placed upon its side, pierced with a fettling knife and turned into a planter. Small-scale hand extruders can also be employed to create a limitless variety of decorative effects such as strands of hair, flower stamens or clay string.

Slip casting is a ceramic process most often associated with special education programs or sheltered workshops. In this process liquid clay is poured into a plaster mold to create the ceramic piece. The usual products are stereotyped figures or stylized objects of little aesthetic value. However, when employed as a point of departure, slip casting can be a versatile, creative process. Cast spheres, cubes, faces, birds or fish can be added to existing handbuilt or extruded forms to create a whimsical, realistic or funky effect.

The ceramic kiln is perhaps the only piece of equipment in the school studio that is not operated by the ceramics student. This is unfortunate, since the kiln can be a most flexible and accessible tool that essentially extends the creative possibilities of the clay process. A kiln can take many forms and be fired by a number of fuels. The most useful and common in the school setting is the electric kiln. This type of kiln is limited in the creative effects it can generate, since the oxidizing atmosphere produces glaze and clay body tones that are rather uninteresting. Yet the ease of installation and economy of operation makes a well-built, automatically-timed electric kiln a mandatory investment for the school setting.

Cleanup
The studio must be well ventilated to prevent the inhalation of hazardous clay dust and fumes. Sanding dry pottery or sweeping the floors or tables should be avoided in favor of vacuuming with specially designed machines that trap all of the clay dust in the filter. Only fully protective dust masks that are approved by the Bureau of Mines should be used while cleaning the ceramics studio. The ceramics kiln should be located in an adjacent room and be fitted with an exhaust hood to evacuate the harmful gases. Cleanup should be accom-

plished in a large holding tank of water, preferably one fitted with casters for convenient relocation. A heavy-duty, fifty-gallon plastic refuse container is ideally suited for this application. The washing of hands and tools can be accomplished in this tank, sparing the sink from clogged drains and unnecessary mess.

The recycling or reclaiming of scrap clay should also be avoided, except on a very small scale involving maybe one container specifically used for this purpose. While it is ecologically sound to recycle, it is a difficult procedure to monitor and the clay is liable to become contaminated by foreign objects, such as paper towels, sponges and possibly even needles. With the cost of clay literally dirt cheap, it is much more economical to discard the bulk of the studio's clay refuse and tightly monitor any clay that is worthy of being reclaimed.

PROPERTIES OF CLAY

A vital aspect of this artform involves the properties of the clay itself. Many classroom teachers have encountered clay that has an extremely short working life. The material dries prematurely and becomes too weak and brittle to work with. This lack of plasticity and tensile strength is sometimes further aggravated by noxious chemicals in the clay body, making the material unsafe and inappropriate for student use. All of these concerns point to choosing the correct clay body that will offer optimum working properties under the most difficult artroom conditions. A suitable clay for children of all levels is the same professional formula used by studio potters and their advanced students. These clays are designed to provide excellent plasticity despite overworking. They include a reasonable amount of sand or grog to insure good "tooth," the texture that contributes to strength, support and increased chances for survival during the firing. They do not include materials such as asbestos or extremely strong coloring agents. Excess iron or umber as a colorant in the clay can stain skin and clothes while also emitting a foul odor that can be quite irritating for a sensitive child. The preferred clay body should be a white or buff stoneware or earthenware that has a broad firing range, so that there is flexibility in its application. Finally, the clay should be moist but not sticky. An effective test for the correct moisture content in the clay is to roll out a 5″ coil and bend it into a closed loop. If the clay leaves residue or sticks to the hand, it is too wet. If the loop cracks, the clay is either too dry or not properly aged. Ideally, the clay should be aged in twenty-five pound blocks and stored in airtight plastic bags for at least two months before use.

Plasticine is a form of clay which can be particularly useful in situations where there are no firing facilities. This material can be molded or sculpted without the usual dust or dirt that regular clay produces. It is an excellent choice for the obsessively clean child who is repulsed by the sensory properties of regular clay. The range of colors available in this medium also acts as a stimulator with resistant children. Pastel shades from blood red to pure white are available. Mixing or matching them often produces a lively interplay of forms and vibrant contrasts, making it particularly useful when working on figurative sculpture with young children. It is important when using Plasticine in therapeutic programs that the material be worked and warmed up before presenting it to children. Initially it is quite hard and does not invite robust manipulation.

Self-hardening clay is another option for programs with scant resources. This material has the properties of regular clay but will harden and take paint without firing. (Or it can be fired in a regular kitchen oven.) Although an excellent innovation, self-hardening clay often contains caustic salts which make it impractical for children who are sensitive to chemicals or might actually ingest the clay. However, since its first introduction, suppliers have continued to improve upon this product, making it more viable for institutional programs.

FIGURE MODELING

As with figure drawing, figure modeling challenges the special needs child to work representationally. It is a difficult process; the margin of failure is greater than with other projects in which the attractiveness of the media compensates for poor workmanship or design. Basic manipulative abilities and an understanding of the human or animal figure is required. However, there is enormous potential here. Unusual abstract creations often emanate from the hands of handicapped children.

The first attempts at figure modeling usually consist of rolling out coils and balls of clay and stacking them into a "snowman" configuration. As the child matures, coils are added for limbs. Once the child is at this stage, I demonstrate how to cement the elements together using the slip and score technique. Although clay will adhere when in the wet stage, upon drying, pieces will simply fall apart unless they are slipped together. Making slip involves mixing water with the clay in either a mortar or blender until a consistency of pudding is reached. Then the solid clay elements are incised or scratched at their contact points using a comb, needle tool or plastic fork, depending upon the level of the child. The slip is liberally dabbed onto both contact points and the two elements are squeezed together allowing the slip to gush from the joint. The excess slip can later be sponged away. Once this process is learned, a child can create figures which have great strength and flexibility.

As the child increases in manual dexterity and figure awareness, the simple snowman can become increasingly embellished and detailed. As with the drawing process, the thrust of figure modeling centers upon prompting the special needs child to elaborate his or her ideas and to create scenes and figures which are personally meaningful. Despite the fact that the figures may still be at a schematic stage, the profusion of objects, figures and settings can be quite expressive and meaningful for the child. One young ceramicist's ensemble illustrated the symbolizations that children project in this medium. This child had just relocated from an extremely rural area where he was used to a relatively primitive lifestyle without television or a comfortable household. His sculpture alludes to the wish fulfillment of his current home which sports these modern conveniences. This boy invested his memories, longings and feelings in his art despite his relative youth and immature artistic development.

As awareness of the figure increases further, greater advances in form, elaboration of detail and animation occur. Although the method of construction does not change dramatically, the sculptures do become more complex regardless of whether there are handicapping conditions at work or not. One such figure was created by a visually impaired, mildly retarded child. While not realistic in conception, the abstract interplay between the body and its painted embellishments creates a figure which is reminiscent of Peter Volkus's expressionistic figures. Although its representational

quality is poor, the fluid use of the clay and highlighting of the face, creates a fanciful and strong figurative presence. Landscapes in sculpted relief also allow the child to represent scenes or experiences. One student used precise glazing to color figures in contrast to their background.

More advanced students should be able to aspire to sculpted figures with some degree of anatomical realism. Usually human or animal figures are sculpted on a maquette basis, meaning the sculptures are small scale, usually 8″ to 16″ tall. When creating figures which are hollow, I begin by teaching students how to marver a hollow torso. Using a dowel, the child pierces a coil of clay then rolls it along the table, thinning the walls of the cylinder by rotating the dowel. Once the torso is hollowed, the arms are rolled out and attached using a ball and socket method. The torso is depressed at the shoulder, then scored and slipped. The legs are set into the cavity of the torso in the same manner. The head and neck are also morticed into the shoulders of the torso.

This bas-relief was created by a visually impaired girl of eighteen. Note the meticulous glazing of each element which was accomplished with the greatest effort and care.

This figure, created by a multiply handicapped boy, recalls the abstract expressionistic figures of Peter Volkus.

This ensemble of figurines was created by a group of gifted fifth graders. Using modeling tools, facial features were created without actually touching the clay with their hands. The pen created unusual eyeballs, the wooden stick, interesting eye sockets, the curved stick, smiling mouths. Emphasis is placed upon the expression of feeling as well as a sense of interrelationship and communication between figures.

180

Facial features are the most difficult aspect of the human figure to render. I encourage students to let the tools do the work for them—by pressing different forms into the clay, the features are automatically created. Pen points, for example, make excellent eye sockets with pupils. The tip of a small spoon creates a smiling mouth. Two thumbs depressed together create the recesses for the eyes, the ridge for the nose and forehead, all in one motion.

In sculpting figures, I emphasize making groups so that each model interacts in some way with the other. Therefore, I might encourage a student to create two farm horses to work together, or a man and his dog playing together. In this way I can promote sculptural skill in concert with social interaction, appropriate behavior and intimacy between peers, as well as other therapeutic issues. The figure is the ideal medium for working toward objectives which encompass the dual goals of therapeutic art education.

Students can often work with portraiture using the same figure modeling techniques. Although completely blind, one girl became quite expert at creating works that bear striking resemblances to their subjects. The method of sculpting a head can vary. Often, a solid block of clay is sculpted to a point of almost completion. Next, while in a leather-hard state, the entire piece is sawed in half with a wire, and hollowed out with a loop tool, leaving a ½″ thick wall. The piece is next reassembled using the slip score technique, and then the final details are added.

Although I have used this technique with success, I favor an alternative method which is more akin to maskmaking. First, a ball of clay is pinched as if forming a pot. Then, newspaper is crumpled up and taped together in the shape of a half-oval. The pinched pot is then draped over this paper form. The features are then added. Once the features are created, another clay form can be used to create the back of the head. After each piece firms up, the halves can be assembled with slip, keeping the paper inside as an armature that will eventually burn out in the firing process. (The

back of the head may also be left off to make a mask-like relief. Masks of this type are usually nonfunctional but can assume powerful imagery once mounted on the wall.)

Once the three-dimensional head has been completed, shoulders for the figure can be created using a larger paper form with a slab collar for the neck. After this portion is stiffened, the entire head can be secured in place and the features refined. The blind young woman mentioned above always painted her sculptures with realistic colors. The finished piece is interesting in that the eyes are modelled not as positive features but as sunken and sightless recesses. In any case, this nineteen-year-old was able to use this technique with great facility and expressiveness. Her sense of self-concept and esteem were enhanced by the skills she developed. Emotional issues were also routinely explored: her racial concerns, and her sensory deprivation, as well as the normal tribulations of pre-adolescent narcissism. Her attention to each cosmetic detail seemed to relate to her imperfect sense of object relations and wish fulfillment. Often she equated how she appeared in the sculpture with how she actually appeared to others.

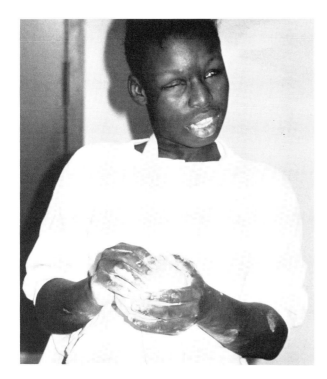

This young woman begins forming her ceramic head sculptures by expertly pinching out a clay ball. Although she is blind, her forms are consistently perfectly symmetrical and of even thickness: the result of years of practice.

Despite her inability to see, this student thought it quite natural to paint her sculpture in lifelike colors. The teacher assisted in this process by mixing the proper values and by masking off areas to create boundaries in which to paint.

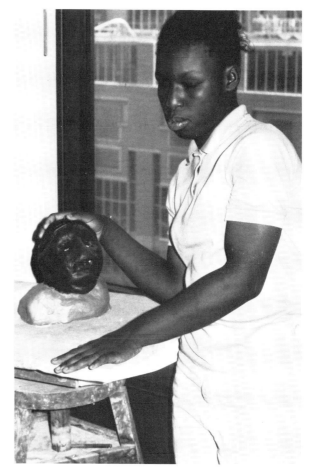

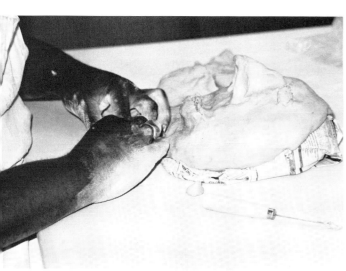

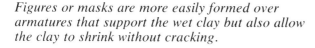

Figures or masks are more easily formed over armatures that support the wet clay but also allow the clay to shrink without cracking.

182   Deficits in object relations and self-concept often appear in the figures of handicapped students. Distortions of body image are common and will often require an assessment regarding the need for therapeutic intervention. For instance, one young man in my class created striking ceramic portraits but always sculpted electrical contacts on the forehead and neck similar to Frankenstein's monster. In response, I would discuss with him the symbolic function and aesthetic impact of these features, in an attempt to firm up his disturbed body image. My attempts at shoring up reality-testing in this student were largely ineffective. He took great joy in giving his figures fantastic capabilities and would not entertain the suggestion of rendering them simply normal. Given his determination, I eventually backed down and allowed his artistic license free rein despite its symptomatic nature.

In another case, a young man with multiple handicaps began to obsess over a racially motivated clubbing in New York City. He assailed the white man (he was black himself) as a hatemonger who was determined to exterminate all black people. He spontaneously created a figure in a posture of outrage with the arms outstretched clutching the murder weapon. It was never clear whether this figure depicted the murderer or represented the victim who holds up the weapon for the world to see. This piece allowed a measure of cathartic discharge for this relatively vulnerable and powerless individual, regardless of its raw and disturbing content.

In both of the above cases, I made no attempt to overtly neutralize the figures. While each child was supported toward making the figures structurally sound and integrated, I allowed their emotions a free rein. Although the raw content falls short of sublimation, the cathartic experience of creating the artwork allowed for the venting of powerful emotions which could not be symbolized through other more appropriate means.

Another figure self-portrait created by a young man with severe emotional problems.

An emotionally handicapped, visually impaired young man was able to portray figures that expressed great emotion. The figure holds a weapon purportedly used in a racial hate crime. He holds it out for the world to see the "error of their ways."

ADAPTING POTTERY TECHNIQUES

Students also respond well to creating recognizable, utilitarian objects that can be used, given away or even sold. (For more than one student the prime motivation for learning clay processes has been the possibility of selling his or her work. Often, the emotionally handicapped and economically disadvantaged will participate for this reason.) Adapting the pottery making process for the special needs child requires more than a teacher's casual familiarity with the process. The technology must be thoroughly understood before the medium and techniques can be scaled to the child's level of functioning or physical handicap without sacrificing aesthetic or functional integrity.

Hand building
The first experiences with clay are akin to play. Young or low-functioning children should experience the plasticity and other playful properties of clay in activities that are stimulating and fun. Behaviors such as self-stimulation can be incorporated into the first clay activities. This will lessen tactile resistance and engage the child's eye and hand coordination. For instance, the teacher may accommodate rocking or hand flashing behaviors by rolling out coils and dangling them before the child's eyes. Coils can be suspended above students' heads, then dropped, using various sound effects to encourage multi-sensory tracking. To interact with the child's hands, coils can be woven between the fingers or wrapped around the wrists as bracelets. Loops can be fabricated which are reminiscent of a ring stacking toy.

All of these activities which encourage the child to pick up the clay and manipulate it in any way that is safe or pleasureful are aimed at engaging the low-functioning child's attention without necessitating active participation. The first sessions can be merely a passive playtime that serves to excite the student's senses and curiosity, without pressure or expectation. After the child displays a readiness and willingness to touch and manipulate the clay, the instructor can begin teaching one of

Two sections of extruded coiled cylinders were used to create this birdbath, which sports a slump mold bowl. This method is useful for making large, slightly concave forms with minimal skill.

the clay forming techniques. These techniques are designed to reach a very low-functioning child without sacrificing or compromising aesthetic integrity. They can be easily scaled upward to meet the needs of the most advanced student potter.

The actual teaching of hand-building projects can be structured in a task-analysis format that breaks the procedure down into simple, highly definable tasks. Each element can be learned as an independent project, with the child attempting to master each step as he or she moves through the sequence. Whether the student uses the potter's wheel, slab or coil methods, the end product usually takes the shape of a hollow-built cylinder, a form considered central to most pottery or sculpture projects.

184

Slab-building

Another hand-building project easily adaptable to the handicapped child is the slab method. This process is probably the most stable handbuilt form, and therefore the most appropriate, for special needs children. Slab-building provides unlimited possibilities for sculptural experimentation, while also being excellent for functional pottery forms. Below is a task-analysis description for creating a slab-built clay cylinder.

1. On a table top construct a simple jig of two strips of wood ⅜″ thick, laid parallel at a width determined by the desired height of the cylinder.

2. Place a 2″ slice of clay between the strips and pound flat.

3. Using the rolling pin, the child rolls out a slab of clay, making sure the ends of the pin ride on the strips of wood. As the child rolls, the clay assumes the thickness of the strips, resulting in an even ¾″ slab.

4. Place a cardboard tube wrapped in paper on the slab on its side. Cut the slab to the proper length using the strips as guides.

5. Wrap the clay slab tightly around the form, welding the seam with the thumb crosswise to secure the cylinder around the form.

6. Smooth over the seam, using a concave metal rib with the stroke running the length of the cylinder.

7. Put the piece aside until a base can be rolled out, again using the strips as thickness guides. Cut the base to a rough circle and then place upon the banding wheel.

8. Place the clay cylinder upon the base. Trim the base to within ¼″ of the cylinder. Bring the excess up around the cylinder, then smooth with a right angled rib.

9. Roll the cylinder gently on its side on the canvas to refine its form and disengage it slightly from the cardboard cylinder.

10. Placed upright, withdraw the cardboard form, leaving the paper inside still in contact with the clay cylinder. Remove the paper later when the piece becomes firm.

The resulting clay cylinder can be adapted to a purpose or simply decorated. The basic, sturdy form of the cylinder can be easily altered in both sculptural and functional terms, thus expanding its aesthetic possibilities. The height can be extended to create vases or different sized canister sets. The width can be adapted to create planters, jars or ashtrays. By placing contrasting colored clays under the slab before it is fully rolled, one can create spontaneous, inlaid patterns of either realistic or abstract imagery. While still attached to the form, the clay cylinder can be gently rolled over templates made of pierced metal or plastic, in different geometric or free-form designs. The resulting surface will reflect the templates in bas-relief. Using abnormally thick slabs, the child can paddle the cylinder, creating a freely organic form that still retains a basically cylindrical shape. The dexterous student can apply a design by piercing the clay wall using a fettling knife, creating positive and negative shapes as in stained glass or a lantern. Lids, handles and knobs can all be added during the leather-hard stage. Small plaster molds of leaves, faces, animals or flowers can be pressed in clay and then attached to the cylinder to add an element of recognizable imagery and sculptural content to the piece. All of these operations are within the grasp of the most mentally or physically impaired students, provided that the instructor is flexible and somewhat ingenious at adapting the project to the student's needs.

If an embellishment is to be applied, the form should remain to give support when molding. In this case, the applique is a leaf, created from a small plaster press mold (and later trimmed by the teacher).

The finished piece was fired to stoneware without glaze and used as an ivy planter.

Coiling

One of the most popular methods of hand building is the coil method. Most art teachers are familiar with this method, although they may not be aware of the modifications necessary for students with special needs. The most important modification is the use of a supporting form. For example, a tube is often needed around which a child can wrap the clay coils without collapsing or distorting the piece. Wh ther made from cardboard or other materials—I have a supply of donated war surplus artillery shell containers for this purpose—it is vital that the form be fitted with a paper sleeve so that the clay will not stick to it. Once the cylinder is built up to sufficient height, the tube can be pulled out. The paper can be left to burn out in the kiln or be torn out after the piece reaches a firm, leather-hard stage.

When coils are rolled out by hand (using the palm only), there should be a rhythmic, even pressure. Apart from the standard horizontal cylindrical format, students can improvise by placing coils in patterns such as spirals, verticals or free form shapes. Coils can be left exposed on the outside, only the interior of the piece being welded for strength. The scale of pieces can be manipulated by increasing the size of the forms and thickness of the coils. Different colored clays can be introduced to create a marbleized or blended effect. Coils can also be placed into molds made of plaster and then welded together. When removed after the piece has hardened, the resulting clay piece will conform exactly to the form of the exterior mold.

In many situations, handicapped children cannot sustain their attention long enough to handle the many repetitions needed to hand-build with many coils. They may become fatigued or bored. It may be advisable, then, to simplify the coil rolling process by using a clay extruder. These manually operated machines force the clay through a small orifice, extruding a compressed, perfectly round coil of any circumference or length desired. Interchangeable dies can be used, allowing for unlimited forms to be extruded. By dispensing with the

These clay pieces are examples of pottery construction methods. The coil piece demonstrates how coils can be arranged differently as well as how they can be welded together. The square slab piece shows how to "lay in" coils to strengthen and reinforce the walls.

chore of rolling out countless coils, the student can divert his or her energies toward the creative and experimental aspects of coil-built pottery making.

The Potter's Wheel

More than any other ceramic process, using the potter's wheel inspires continued amazement and awe in young ceramics students. Seeing a shapeless ball of clay miraculously transformed into an infinite variety of forms, the child almost always is prompted to try his or her hand at this process. Yet of all the clay forming techniques, throwing on the wheel demands the most practice and technical skill. To adapt the potter's wheel and throwing process to meet the handicapped child's needs poses a formidable challenge to the art specialist.

The process of centering the clay on the wheel is an exceedingly difficult operation for the special needs child to master. The concept of centering alone can be incomprehensible, the physical coordination difficult and the physical exertion prohibitive. It might be advisable to purchase or fabricate a centering jig or arm. This device is a simple aluminum bar with a bicycle grip at its end. It is fitted with a metal plate which makes contact with the clay. By moving the arm up and down, the child has the leverage to exert considerable and constant force that essentially brings the clay under control. As the child adjusts the angle of the metal plate, a beehive form emerges that eventually becomes centered and ready for opening.

During the opening stage it is imperative that the child brace his or her elbows against the body. This will compensate for wrist weakness and will provide a degree of stability. By using relatively powerful back muscles, the child can exert considerable force and stability upon the piece. To open, the child may first need to drill the piece using a loop tool, since the thumbs or fingers may be too weak to muster such precise, intense pressure. Once the piece is sufficiently carved open, allow the child to use either the knuckles, fist or side of the hand to bring up the cylinder walls. Splints can be devised from tongue depressors or popsicle sticks to keep the fingers rigid and together. Rubber bands can also be pressed into service to bind several fingers together to use as one. Once the cylinder has been pulled to where the walls are ½″ thick, the piece can be considered acceptable for firing. Excessive lightness or thinness is not a desirable trait in the wheel work of a handicapped student. Maintaining thick walls, lip and foot will contribute to the overall strength and durability of the piece, as will using an aged, well-grogged clay body.

Throwing can also be accomplished by individuals without functional use of their limbs by using the wheel as a lathe. First the teacher must secure the clay to the wheel head and center it, since this is unquestionably impossible for those with quadriplegia. The child works the spinning ball of clay using tools fastened to a head stylus (a helmet fitted with a metal rod). A loop tool can be used to carve inside the clay ball. Using a rib laid up against the exterior walls the student can form a straight, clean profile. A contrasting colored slip clay or engobe can be applied using a brush mounted in the stylus. Once the liquid clay is applied, a cutting or sgraffito tool can be mounted so as to cut through the slip in a series of revolving lines and scratches. With practice, a cerebral palsied child in my class was able to become quite skilled at turning clay pots and decorating them using the sgraffito method.

At one time this cerebral palsied child needed splints to help his weak fingers in fine motor skills. Eventually his grip strengthened until adaptive devices were no longer needed.

Two lathe-formed, wheel-made pots were created by a quadriplegic girl using only a head stylus. The coil-made piece shown in the middle was also made by a paralyzed child.

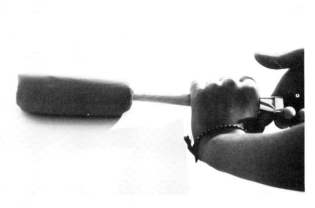

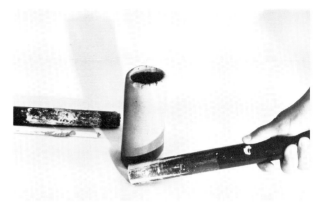

The dowel method allows students to create narrow cylinders which are seamless and already have a base. The student plunges a tapered wooden dowel into a coil, then places it on its side for marvering.

This completed cylinder was made with these three different-sized dowels.

Marvering is the rolling of the dowel back and forth to increase the size of the interior of the clay coil. Once the hole is enlarged, the next size dowel is put in place.

This student is finishing off the cylinder by placing a coil upon the lip, creating a sculptural element to the piece.

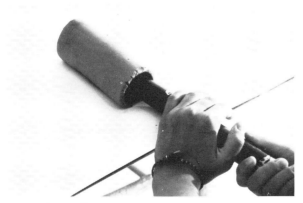

Once the walls are about ⅜ of an inch thick, the marvering is completed.

The Dowel or Marvering Method
Surprisingly, the most durable and aesthetically pleasing ceramic forms are often those which the child touches or models least. Often ceramic pieces suffer from being overworked, much in the same way as paintings. The more the student pushes, squeezes, adds on or carves away, the weaker or more distorted the piece becomes. Frequently the result is a lost piece and a frustrated and disappointed child. The dowel or marvering methods allows the child to quickly and easily create a sturdy, aesthetically pleasing ceramic cylinder without any seams or joints. The process dispenses with the laborious welding, slipping, scoring, smoothing and worrying over cracks during

the drying or firing process. Instead, cylinders can be formed quickly and easily, allowing the student to get on to the real task at hand—artistically embellishing and decorating the form.

To create a seamless cylinder, one need only procure a set of dowels or tool handles of different sizes. I use the handle of an artist's paintbrush for the smallest tool, since its tapered end allows easy penetration into the clay. The largest size is usually a broom handle sawed off to about 16″ in length.

A 3″ or 4″ thick coil of clay is rolled out on a canvas surface, approximately equal in length to the intended height of the finished cylinder. A tapered dowel or brush handle is pierced into the center of one end of the coil and pushed almost to the other end. This step often requires the assistance of the teacher to ensure a centered hole. The child then grasps the exposed end of the dowel and rolls or marvers it back and forth on the edge of the table's surface. As the hole enlarges, the child takes the dowel out and inserts the next larger size, gradually increasing the diameter of interior space. Once the cylinder is thin enough to fire yet strong enough to support itself vertically, it can be raised up and the last dowel removed. (If the clay sticks to the dowel, this means the dowel has been used too many times and has absorbed too much moisture or that the clay was too wet and sticky to begin with.)

One can create simple but elegant forms with this method by finishing the cylinder with a coil or other embellishments. A severely cerebral palsied child formed and decorated a vase using large dowels. The base is torn (which often occurs), yet the spontaneous and lively surface decoration carries the piece nicely. In a more advanced vein, a partially paralyzed college freshman combined doweled bases with slab upper bodies and delicately thrown bottle tops to create simple yet dynamic ceramic forms. Since he was too weak to throw conventionally sized forms, the small knobs allowed this student the moral victory of using the wheel to make viable ceramics through a process more within his motor capacity.

This piece has strong form and bold decoration. The piece was flattened after marvering, then fired in a raku kiln.

These marvered bottle forms were created by a young man who had recovered from Guillain-Barré syndrome, in which a portion of the nerves and muscles are paralyzed. Due to weakness in his fingers and hands he could only throw the smallest of forms, such as the knob atop the bottle. The middle layer is textured slab and the base is marvered.

Sling or Slump Molds

Interesting relief forms can be created using a simple canvas mold. A basic clay slab can be rolled onto a piece of unprimed canvas, and its shape determined by a cardboard or masonite rectangular form placed atop the slab. The child traces the form with a kitchen knife, cutting out the slab in the process. Once cut and trimmed, the slab and canvas can be placed atop a large cylinder such as a wastebasket or garbage can. Draped over the top, the weight of the slab causes the canvas to depress slightly, creating a natural platter or plate shape. Touching the center of the slab slightly will increase the slight convexity should the canvas not give. Once the slab is draped over the can, I encourage the children to slip their fingers underneath the edges to distort or slightly model portions of the form to give it a sculptural quality. A splash of silver raku glaze can impart a relatively sophisticated, highly aesthetic quality. To create this piece, the child need possess few skills other than using a rolling pin and the ability to create a few simple embellishments to finish the piece nicely.

This sling mold platter was made by another paralyzed student. A piece of canvas was draped over a pail, then the embellished slab was laid on. The weight of the slab drops the canvas enough to create a slightly concave platter form. Raku fired.

ALTERNATIVE CERAMIC PROCESSES

As often as possible, I attempt to incorporate aspects of ceramic history into students' studio work. The history of ceramics is a fascinating area for all children to experience. I often begin with the paleolithic cave paintings and prehistoric sculptures and reliefs of animals. Children delight in recreating these pieces, especially when they are given background stories on hunting magic and myth. Several of my lowest-functioning children have spontaneously created figures akin to those discovered in prehistoric sites. The works share identical elements of clay medium, hand modelling and firing—only their creation was separated by thousands of years!

Egyptian paste is another medium in which ceramic studio work can be related to art history. This clay is self-glazing and is workable only on a small scale. A Down syndrome boy created delicate animal forms using Egyptian paste. Plaster press molds can also be used to create Egyptian-like pieces which can later be transformed into jewelry of brilliant turquoise and scarlet hues, or placed upon slip-cast spheres.

The lids of these two cast jars have been cut into the hollow globe. Small press-molded ceramic frogs were then applied as decorative knobs. In this technique, slip-cast molds can be used in expressive ways.

Primitive techniques of pit-firing in sawdust or dung can also be carried out in the proper setting, where smoke is not a health or safety concern. I have conducted workshops in which children dug their own clay, created vessels using old baskets as forms and later fired their ware in a pit covered with horse manure. A similar technique involves using a gas kiln. Hearing-impaired students placed a pot in a sagger, which is a vessel which will contain the sawdust during the gas firing. During the firing the sawdust burned to ash, dramatically blackening all or parts of the pieces. Following their study of the art of Southwest potters, the hands-on experience of recovering their ware from the ash-filled sagger was truly exhilarating for students.

Raku methods can also be used, but only with advanced, relatively intact students. While this traditional Japanese technique is among the most exciting, removing the red-hot pots from the burning kiln can be very dangerous. I have conducted workshops, however, where the liability was reduced by having access to professional equipment and students who were mature and physically capable of handling this intense technique.

GLAZING AND DECORATION

A ceramic studio can become quickly filled with buckets of glazes, stains, engobes and other materials, creating a chaotic mess which can overwhelm even the most organized instructor. Simplify the glazing process, making it more manageable and orderly, especially for small programs by purchasing sets of underglazes in water-color pans for use when a student is painting a small-scale picture on his piece. Colors can be mixed and applied with different concentrations of water and pigment just as with watercolor, achieving similar results. For pots or larger sculptures, use dry, commercial coloring stains. These go a long way when mixed with water (usually in a blender) and can also be applied using a watercolor technique. For glazing, purchase one or two clear

Egyptian paste is pressed into a small plaster mold. This self-glazing clay is excellent for small decorative works or ceramic jewelry. This young man works with great concentration and skill with this sometimes difficult medium.

This middle school student is lifting a sawdust-fired vessel from its sagger. He became skilled at manipulating the sawdust to control the black and white values that result from the reduction atmosphere.

192 glazes in five gallon buckets. Should a child be painting a polychrome landscape or figure, the entire piece can then be encased in a glossy jacket of clear glaze. The effects are similar to the vibrant colors which emerge when a colorful stone is wetted. Commercial stains can also be added to the clear glaze with a blender to create colored glazes. Brushing on glaze often smudges delicate underglaze drawing or painting. Using a bucket of glaze allows children to dip their pieces and achieve a clean, even coating of glaze. (Students must be trained to wipe the bases of their pots, insuring that no glaze comes in contact with the kiln shelf. The teacher should always check the work to insure the pieces are ready for firing.)

FIRING

The usual firing process involves an electric kiln, which is relatively safe and effortless to use. This type of kiln should be fitted with an automatic shut-off and a timer as a convenience and as a safety factor. After initial experiments with different firing schedules and temperatures, excellent results can be routinely achieved with an electric kiln.

It is important to consider that in the therapeutic setting, children often have a great deal invested in their ceramic pieces. Thus, it is imperative that pieces make it through the fire, as this may have a direct effect upon therapeutic effectiveness of the clay experience. To have a piece explode or break up during the firing often becomes an unwelcomed metaphor for the child's own emotional or physical experience. Clay explodes because of several preventable reasons. Moisture is the most common cause, followed by uneven or excessive thickness, trapped pockets of air, or foreign bodies, such as plaster, in the clay.

It is the teacher's responsibility when working with young or emotionally handicapped students to insure that the work is dry, well-fabricated and hollow, so that it stands a good chance of surviving the firing. After every session, I check over each piece—tugging a cup's handle or a figure's arm—to insure that slip has been used in the fabrication. I check for sufficient hollowness and, in many instances, spend time refining the insides of a piece, excavating enough clay to maintain a ½″ to ⅝″ thickness. In some instances I have allowed certain handicapped children to sculpt or make pots from a solid block of clay which I then hollowed out.

Firing should be unhurried. The kiln's lid should be left cracked open and the elements turned on low overnight before proceeding with the regular firing schedule, especially if these are sculpted figures or heavily worked pots which are thickwalled and require a long time for moisture to evaporate. The slower the fire, the less cracking or shattering will occur.

Should accidents occur (and they sometimes do despite our efforts), I will attempt to repair broken ware if I feel that the piece is of great emotional or therapeutic importance, or if it represents a substantial investment in time or student effort. In such cases, I use epoxy to cement tight-fitting pieces back together and silicone caulk to adhere larger sections or to fill in gaps. Should a pot crack apart which does not represent a great emotional investment by the student, I reiterate that breakage is a normal part of the pottery process— that pots should be made in a spontaneous, casual way without preciousness. Works should be made in series, so that if one fails there will be three or four others to round out a set. Making pots should mirror the rhythms of living; creation should be a robust and contemplative process which accepts and even welcomes unexpected effects.

Unaccustomed to spontaneous art activity, this welding student found fabricating art forms an enjoyable side to his vocational training in a school for the deaf.

ADAPTATIONS

chapter 11

Dealing with Behavior

Given sufficient stress, deprivation or physical trauma, any child or adult is capable for a period of time, of becoming emotionally unstable. These factors often interact in varying degrees of severity and complexity, resulting in reactions of anger, frustration, fear, apathy and a range of other negative behaviors. In some cases the factors are short-lived and the associated emotions are of a transient nature. However, extended periods of physical or mental trauma, or an impoverished environment may leave the child permanently emotionally scarred. In either case, the behaviors resulting from emotional instability may have a profound effect upon the child's performance in the artroom. They not only impact upon an individual's ability to attend to tasks, concentrate, learn skills and freely express him or herself, but extend also into areas of socialization and the society of the classroom.

Peers and staff alike are deeply affected by children whose conduct is disordered or disturbed. Thus, dealing with emotions and the resultant behaviors sometimes must become a priority in therapeutic art education. Before techniques of self-expression can be adequately addressed, there must be a relatively ordered and secure atmosphere within the studio. Disruptions, vandalism and other acting-out behaviors subvert such an atmosphere, diminishing productivity and the overall effectiveness of the program. However, in dealing with disruptive or counter productive behaviors it is not enough to simply suppress or punish them.

We must understand the sources and the circumstances of such behaviors in order to deal with them with empathy and effectiveness.

BEHAVIOR: DRIVE THEORY

A child must be capable of handling his needs, desires and emotions in order for his behavior to remain free of neurotic symptoms and be socially acceptable. However, as Freud (1950) first pointed out, this is no simple task, since man is in a constant struggle to maintain the balance between providing instinctual gratification (so that neurotic symptoms are minimized) and meeting social expectations and demands. As Kramer points out, the dilemma is inescapable and has resulted in a fundamental cleavage in man's psychic organization: the primeval id versus the regulating, reality-appraising ego.

In animals, this balance is achieved by the regulation of needs and desires through instinct. An animal will automatically seek from its environment the things that are necessary for its survival. This faculty of instinct has been shown dramatically by Lorenz (1966) who described a captive-bred starling who was accustomed to receiving food from a dish. This bird would fly up and carry out the motions of capturing flying insects although the prey was nonexistent. It had never seen another bird hunt insects, yet it was programmed by instinct to carry out this behavior.

Insight into behavioral incidents can sometimes be facilitated through the use of "process drawings."

I was getting nervus then i askd mr H´ for a TimeOut

Lorenz described the cycle by which animals deal with instinctual energies in terms of damming and discharging. Instinctual energy mounts up until it is discharged in a consummatory act (feeding, sexual satisfaction etc.). After climaxing and discharging, the cycle begins again. As an animal or human interacts with the environment in search of need-gratification, behaviors are manifested which reflect the quantity and quality of instinctual discharge. Has there been enough food? Was it edible? Did it have foreign tastes? What about the timing of the meal? A child will respond differently to the same stimuli, depending upon the circumstances. Consider the example of a child who has just had her favorite dessert and is presented with another—her desire for gratification will be completely different, despite the identical stimulus.

Although animals and humans share in the damming/discharging phenomenon described by Lorenz and Freud, there is a fundamental difference. Humans have evolved beyond the automatic regulation of drives and depend upon the effective functioning of their intellect and consciousness. Although we are equally driven by need and desire, it is through these higher processes that we mediate and decide through what medium or act the drives will gain expression. This expression is shaped by social factors that are characteristic of one's culture. Most social learning theorists, such as Bandura (1977), emphasize the extent to which behavior is mediated by the processes of identification and modeling the behaviors of others. Iden-

tification with the aggressor is a frequently cited example: a child may emulate behaviors of more powerful or predatory individuals as a means of warding off feelings of vulnerability and powerlessness. This mechanism is often found in poor, inner-city cultures, where it is a function of survival to act with aggression, regardless of whether it is innately part of one's nature.

The role of art education therapy in addressing such behavior is two-fold. First, to assist in developing the child's ego capacities—including reality testing and appraisal—in order to hold primitive impulses in abeyance through self-control and constructive channeling. By providing healthy and creative outlets for the discharge of drive energy, we increase the child's capacity for sublimation and continued motivation.

Second, a child requires an environment that is conducive to making positive attachments and that promotes identification with positive role models. This entails structuring of classroom environments that promote fruitful social relationships and social responsibility. Bernhard (1988) advocates an "evolutionary perspective" in education that places a high priority on balancing the child's need for personal identity and self-satisfaction with the social needs of the group. Neill (1960) advocated similar ideas by devising a learning community that compensated for negative experiences in the home or school environments by presenting children with more healthful models of social functioning.

A certain by-product of the search for personal satisfaction and group relating is emotional or affective expression. Nathan (1969) sees emotions as aiding in the satisfaction of desire and supplementing the energy and motivation needed to satisfy one's needs. Emotions are also a kind of barometer by which one can gauge one's success in gratifying the desires. It is these shades of facial, verbal, artistic and other expressions which communicate the quality of life, through the medium of emotion.

EMOTIONS

Emotions are mysterious, intangible forces which affect every facet of a child's life. Although intense affect sometimes indicates that regulatory mechanisms have broken down and are symptoms of deep-seated conflict or turmoil, a child should be fully entitled to his or her emotions. They are a unique part of the self and a vital ingredient of the creative process. For the teacher to ignore or deny them is to deprive a child of something which is intrinsically personal and individual. Emotions reflect basic truths about the individual, such as, an angry, violent child who is forced to live under squalid, dangerous conditions. Aggression in this case could be considered a reasonable reaction which assists in the individual's survival in a hostile environment (Lorenz 1971). Viewed from this

perspective, how can we fault or penalize the child for emotions caused by a situation which is essentially beyond his or her control?

My approach to dealing with a child's emotions centers upon this belief that children have a right to feel the way they do, since they can rarely be held responsible for the conditions which bring about their emotional responses. Therefore, if a child is angry or fearful or bored, I take these reactions very seriously and attempt to empathize. Maintaining an empathic stance, however, does not mean that I am permissive or encourage a child to act out. Accepting a picture with violent content, for instance, is far different from allowing a child to punch his neighbor. Accommodating a child's emotional state must be distinguished from giving license to inappropriate or dangerous behavior. Just as a child should be free to harbor a thought or a feeling, so he or she must be responsible enough so that these emotions do not result in acts which infringe upon the freedoms of those around them.

Children must learn the limits of appropriate behavior. Regardless of whether they are retarded, emotionally disturbed or physically handicapped, all children need to recognize appropriate ways to express their emotions. They must learn to gauge the limits to which a teacher can be empathetic and to recognize under what circumstances they will be held responsible for their behavior.

How, then, can teachers remain empathic yet also maintain limits on behavior? There are two popular approaches which are applied both in the regular and special education settings. These approaches emphasize either the suppression of symptoms and behavior, which means that empathy becomes a low priority, or they emphasize a more therapeutic stance, which accommodates symptoms to a greater extent. In the educational sphere it is the behavioral approach which is more widely accepted and implemented—but not without its problems.

BEHAVIORAL VERSUS EMPATHIC APPROACHES

Problems with Behavior Modification

In special education settings, where behaviors often are more extreme than in the regular classroom, behavior modification techniques are often used. As devised by Skinner (1971), operant conditioning seeks to elicit behaviors which are desirable, which in this case means those which are conducive to learning, socialization and the preservation of an orderly environment. This is accomplished by offering a child contingencies which usually take the form of rewards or punishments. In most classroom settings punishment or "aversive conditioning" is a last resort for such intractable problems as self-injurious or assaultive behavior. A far more popular approach is the reward system, with the contingencies being pleasurable and positive in nature. They may range from a verbal pat on the back or extra privileges, to a token system where every privilege is purchased by the student, using tokens awarded for proper behavior.

Clements (1984) has put forth the most reasonable program of positive contingencies based upon the privileges model. He suggests rewards such as listening to the radio (with earplugs), choosing a new seat, having access to special or advanced media, techniques or audiovisual materials. Other privileges focus upon assisting the teacher in such activities as decorating the artroom, opening mail, straightening supplies, taking attendance, etc. Implementing contingencies is seen by Clements to be an art in itself. The type of reward, its obviousness to the other children, its frequency, the timing of application, all affect the end results. Clements also emphasizes the structure of the contingency—whether it should be expected or a surprise. He concurs with Skinner that a surprise reward is a more effective motivator than when the child knows beforehand exactly for what reward he or she is working. He also stresses that such a system does not emphasize the fear of privileges taken away, but rather the joy and surprise of special privileges bestowed. Ultimately, Clements sees the art teacher as fulfilling the role of "contingency manager" when dealing with behavior. Shaping responses, he concludes, demands adjusting the environment in finely tuned ways.

This type of approach is certainly more empathic and humanistic than the mechanical form of operant conditioning originally conceived by Skinner. Used judiciously, it is most effective with children who have difficulties delaying gratification or processing their actions, such as hyperactive or mentally retarded children. The conditioning assists the child in shutting out extraneous stimuli and helps to maintain focus upon the desired goals. Even in cases of extreme behavior the token system may be resorted to so that the child focuses his or her efforts on working through a project of even the briefest duration knowing that a tangible reward is forthcoming (Hewett 1974).

Despite the apparent effectiveness of behavioral conditioning techniques, they are not without their ethical or technical problems. To begin with, conditioning coaxes (or essentially bribes) an individual into conformity. Emotions which fuel the behavior are essentially ignored. The dynamics of the conflict which affect a behavior are never truly addressed; only outward appearance of the behavior may superficially change for the better. I say the change is superficial because in many cases children revert back to their old form if the consistency of the behavior program is compromised. Children are rarely successfully weaned from a behavior modification program and often regress when the situation changes—a new teacher, graduation, etc.

In cases where a behavior has been successfully "extinguished," symptoms often pop up again in different guises. Often this substitution of symptoms is even more troublesome than the original behavior. To cite an extreme example of this: a mentally retarded child was punished whenever he engaged in extreme self-stimulatory behavior. He was shot in the face with a water-filled spray bottle whenever his hand-waving or rocking escalated to exclude all other classroom activities. While this punishment initially did decrease the self-stimulation, other behaviors, such as handbiting and scratching, emerged. The teacher and therapists who administered these punishments found themselves wishing for the former, less harmful habit. Another problem was that the child eventually began to tolerate the spraying, so that greater frequency and velocity was needed to maintain its punishing effect. Eventually vinegar was mixed with the water to make the procedure even more noxious. Behavioral conditioning, especially aversive techniques, may become a war of wills between the child and staff. Children, regardless of their intellectual capabilities, often have indomitable spirits which are not easily crushed. I have often locked horns with children who, by force of their will, can endure and outlast even the most persistent punishments.

On the other hand, reward can be equally problematic in resolving a behavior. Even the lowest-functioning child can recognize that bribery is an ethically low form of human interaction. Buying favors from children does little to earn their trust or respect. Few enduring relationships can be built upon placing candy in a child's mouth. Weaning the child away from food reinforcers or tokens is often an impossible task as children become increasingly dependent upon them. Even bestowing privileges has its problems. Often this type of reward is also subject to an escalation phenomenon; the child comes to expect more frequent and increasingly generous freedoms. The limits of these privileges are often tested while the art educator attempts to manage the child's escalating appetite for special attention.

Trouble may also come when children are rewarded by allowing them to assist the teacher. Other students are often suspicious of children who win favors from their teachers and consider them "teacher's pets." All too often students take their resentment out on anyone who receives preferential attention. As Clements accurately points out, managing the range of new problems that arise through such procedures is often a balancing act which is demanding and difficult to negotiate.

Behavior modification, as Skinner conceived it, is a brilliant and effective means of changing behavior. In cases where the procedures are followed with absolute consistency, results can be dramatic despite the problems I have discussed. Yet, because it ignores or suppresses an individual's emotions, I feel behavior modification is too dehumanizing for use with children unless unusual circumstances warrant such drastic action, such as a low-functioning child who engages in life-threatening actions such as head-banging or physical assault on others. However, it should be noted that few institutions have the resources to carry out such a long term, exacting program. Instead, they carry out watered-down, inconsistently administered programs which serve only as a poor and ineffective substitute for Skinner's classic technique.

In behavioral modification programs that are reasonable and relatively successful, such as those described by Clements, effectiveness hinges upon the administrator's capacity to be sensitive and caring to the child's needs. Although Clements' program mostly depends upon positive contingencies, he acknowledges the difficulties in gauging frequency, timing, structure and other applications of this approach.

**Problems with the
Psychodynamic Approach**
A purely psychodynamic approach to dealing with behavior also has its limitations, particularly in the art education setting. The classroom must be considered a kind of micro-society where responsibilities, expectations and limitations must coexist with individual needs and freedoms for the good of the populace. Because the art educator is charged with creating and maintaining a secure and productive environment, the responsibility falls upon his or her shoulders for enforcing these parameters of behavior.

The concept of empathy in traditional psychotherapy demands a kind of unconditional acceptance of the individual. This includes a degree of permissiveness and a relaxation of inhibitions. According to psychoanalytic theory, these two factors are a requisite for the relinquishing of stultifying defenses so that previously repressed (and potentially disturbing) affect can be processed and confronted (Naumburg 1973). The psychotherapeutic situation also calls for an atmosphere that is free of judgment, so that feelings of shame or guilt are not aroused to inhibit the therapeutic process. The therapist and the patient must be willing to commit to an extended period of time, so that rapport and trust can be firmly established. Maintaining empathy may also encourage the patient to develop an intense attachment to the therapist. Because of this attachment, the patient may demand an exorbitant amount of attention. For an art teacher who must preside over and teach groups of children, sustaining such an exclusive and intimate relationship over an extended period of time with one or more students is at best logistically difficult and ethically inappropriate.

There are other problems with therapy which make it, in its traditional form, inappropriate to the artroom. Most problematic is accepting the breadth of a child's symptoms, particularly when they are acting out in ways contrary to what is appropriate to the classroom. Stirring up a child's suppressed thoughts and feelings, whether intentionally or not, carries enormous responsibility, especially when the child is oblivious to the material that has been dredged up from his or her unconscious. Without insight into the underlying causes of his or her feelings, the child essentially floats weightlessly in a kind of limbo—affected by unseen unconscious conflicts yet without a clue as to how to deal with them. It is at this point that the child needs support and guidance so that his or her often delicate nature is not overwhelmed by such powerful emotions. This support and guidance is something the teacher is frequently unable to provide due to lack of time and lack of training. What, then, is an appropriate tack to take when the art process has stirred up the child's unconscious and he or she is confronting disturbing ideas and feelings often for the first time? One answer lies in the inherent therapeutic powers of the art process itself.

ACTING OUT SYMBOLICALLY

In attempting to reconcile therapeutic and behavioral approaches one may point to the art process as a medium through which emotions can be exercised with both relative impunity and the possibility of gaining true insight. So long as a child can control his or her impulses sufficiently to handle the medium and tools safely, he or she should be free to express deep-seated concerns symbolically through the art imagery regardless of how graphic and disturbing the images might become.

Ordinarily art teachers may discourage or forbid the creation of aggressive or sexually provocative images in the artroom. Compared to the art therapy setting, the limitations on expression have been traditionally much narrower in the classroom. However, under certain circumstances such material can be reasonably tolerated in the art education setting. For instance, the child who knowingly creates a graphically violent or sexual image in order to gain attention and shock others is, in a sense, abusing the freedom of expression, since it infringes upon the rights of others not to be subjected to foul or disturbing stimulations. Such acting out is out of place in both the art education and art therapy setting. However, the child who is unconsciously processing ideas, feelings and experiences of a disturbing nature and inadvertently allows these concerns to filter through in the artwork should be accommodated with a degree of empathic acceptance. While it may be difficult to distinguish between premeditated and innocent expressions, with sufficient experience, the experienced teacher can usually discriminate between the two intentions. Observing the child's behavior during the art process and measuring the child's affect and verbalizations often indicates whether such expressions are naive or purely attention-getting devices.

The theory behind accepting provocative artwork is less a question of demonstrating sympathy for a child's problems, than assisting him or her to work them out. Here we return to the concept of sublimation, where the need to act upon emotions and impulses is mollified in the form of a vicarious experience and the pleasure in creating a symbolic equivalent. In sublimation, impulses such as rage and lust can be exercised and redirected until they are to some degree, neutralized. In this way, the art expression becomes the first step in actually mastering behaviors, by virtue of working through emotions instead of simply acting upon them or—the other extreme—oppressing them.

THE AUXILIARY EGO

Children who display emotional or behavioral problems are usually initially unable to sublimate through the art process because their ego is still in the formative stage of development. The art produced by such children is often given over to displacements in the form of chaotic discharge, aborted attempts, stifling rigidity or stereotypy, all of which represent infantile defense mechanisms. These mechanisms include autistic reactions, regression, perserveration or the fight–flight responses that often trigger acting-out behaviors. The more adaptive defenses such as identification with positive role models, rationalization, intellectualization and sublimation are often beyond the reach of these children.

The lack of adaptive defenses requires that some compensatory system be put in place to support the child toward more advanced functioning. To foster self-control and decision-making processes that are lacking in the impulsive child, Kramer, among others, offers the concept of "auxiliary ego"—a technique whereby the teacher serves as a model of ego functioning for the child by planning or providing the conditions under which the creative process can take place and be pleasurable. The auxiliary ego may substitute knowledge and deliberate acts in any area where the individual is unable to function fully, thus modifying methods according to the child's needs (Wilson 1979). The auxiliary ego functions of the art educator may include supplying demonstrations, extra energy, patience, control, reasoning, or support in any area where the child's own resources are wanting. In

some cases the art educator may enlist the services of a peer to act as a role model, to assist with skills or merely to act as a moral support. (This use of a peer should be monitored carefully so as not to pressure either child into a relationship that is counterproductive.)

MEASURED STATEMENTS

While the art process itself can often provide a medium for venting or rechannelling emotions, the art educator is equally dependent upon verbal responses he or she gives when dealing with behavior. Such responses are referred to as being "measured," meaning that the art educator chooses his or her words with care when applying them as an intervention. The intervention is often couched in casual or even humorous terms and does not appear premeditated or practiced, yet a serious message is communicated to the individual in terms which do not arouse the attention of peers.

Although measured statements are commonly used by many educators, it was Clements (1984) who developed a tripartite reference for verbally intervening with misbehaving children. This sequence for reinforcement involves couching verbal responses in different "persons"—*I, It, You*. The *I* sequence connects the student's feelings to their behavioral and artistic achievement by expressing the teacher's own feelings. Thus, the art teacher might comment, "I am really pleased how you handled it when Johnny spilled paint near your picture," or "I want you to know that I noticed how quiet you were today," etc. Clements explains that the *I* always precedes *it* or *you*, because it conveys respect for the student by expressing concern as a prelude to judging a situation.

Clements emphasizes the *it* and *you* part of the sequence, since it specifically addresses the particulars of an event in a concrete way. It assists the child by interpreting his behavior back to him. By saying "You are really concentrating on your own work today," or "You certainly are improving your ability to share materials," the teacher provides the child with an articulated and constructive idea of what has transpired and how it was handled. Reinterpreting or mirroring back a behavior can enable behavior disordered children to experience it and learn further from it. Since these children often act before they think, such useful narrations increase their self-awareness and subsequently improve behavior.

TESTING THE LIMITS OF BEHAVIOR

Empathy can be abused, manipulated and tested to its limits, as children attempt to measure the teacher's ability to handle a situation. In response to these testing behaviors, the teacher must be prepared to delineate the limits of empathic acceptance and be able to communicate these limits to the children in clear and consistent terms. This essentially is a rule-making policy; the teacher explains what he or she will accept and what he or she will reject. These expectations may differ among children, yet there must be a shared bottom line which the teacher enforces with absolute consistency. One such fundamental expectation is *that no child, regardless of physical or emotional state, is allowed to compromise the art experience of his or her peers.* This idea supports my tenet concerning the freedom to possess and express an emotion as long as it does not constitute an infringement. This one rule, as simple as it is, can effectively serve as the basis for a behavioral program which children of all levels can to some extent comprehend and adhere to. For instance, a child might have low self-esteem and thus may often crumple up her artwork and throw it in the garbage. While I will do all I can to rescue aborted or overworked pieces and encourage a child to work the piece to completion, should she decide to ultimately trash it, this is her perogative. However, should this same child allow her feelings to spill over to the work of her peers, this I will not tolerate. In a similar vein, should a child become upset at some-

thing, he might kick a trash can or pound his table in rage. Given the expectations of the particular child, this also might be accepted as an alternative to punching a peer or staff member. In both scenarios, the children have been allowed to express their emotions without seriously compromising (albeit just barely) the experience of others.

REMAINING NON-PUNITIVE

Once a child transgresses the limits we have established, what actions do we take? It is important that empathy remain a guiding principle in our dealings with children with behavior problems. Especially when dealing with the physically or mentally handicapped, we must also take steps to ensure the liberties of others. It is at this point where we may borrow some strategies from behavior modification, while making sure, however, that an empathic stance is maintained.

One method is removing the child from the conflict, and relocating him or her to an environment better suited to his or her needs. Ordinarily, depriving a child of participation is considered a punitive, disciplinary measure. In this case, however, it is important to recognize that it is the child who is defining the disciplinary and educational needs. Thus, an admonishment such as "You are bad, therefore you will be punished by sitting in a corner" would not be appropriate. Instead, I would attempt to narrate back to the child how his or her actions have dictated a change in the program. Instead of making a value judgment as to the "bad" character of the child, I would simply state the obvious: that for whatever reason, things have the child sufficiently rattled so that he or she cannot handle the materials safely just now, or cannot interact with peers today, although tomorrow may be another story. The child should be told that special modifications must be made for now in order to accommodate his or her behavior.

CONSEQUENCES OF ACTING OUT

Consequences to acting out might entail a variety of interventions. For minor infractions the tack might be a discreet semiprivate discussion during class or a conference after school. It might mean assigning a different work space away from arousing peers, or it may require modifications in the art project. For example, if wood-cutting gouges are being used and a child is not controlling them properly, he or she should be given less-dangerous tools such as rasps or stamps to complete the project.

When dealing with behavior problems I keep in mind the concept of least restricted environment. I try to maintain a normalized and democratic atmosphere, where restrictions are minimized until the children demonstrate a need for a tighter rein. As soon as an individual compromises this arrangement, restrictions begin. For instance, an habitual talker might be placed in a group with the reminder before class that you are purposefully allowing him the freedom to be in a social situation. The implied message of course is to not abuse this freedom. Should he begin to overstep his limitations I might demonstratively put my finger to my lips. Should this not work, a momentary stare might impress him, or a wordless visit to his table followed by a comment concerning his lack of productivity. Should he keep it up, the next step is relocation, followed by outright ostracism. If need be, I am prepared as a last resort to have the chronic talker stationed in an enclosed or partitioned carrel where work is solitary and devoid of interaction.

This progression of consequences begins with the least restrictions and works upward depending upon the choices the child makes. It is fascinating at times to observe a hyperkinetic or conduct-disordered child who may initiate a relocation sequence even without my directing or cuing her. Sensing their lack of control and the detrimental effect upon the class, students will occasionally move out of the group on their own to a more controlled or restricted situation, returning when they feel adequately composed and ready to deal with the stimulation that comes from group interaction. While the usual situation demands a verbal cue to set this process in motion, children do themselves become skilled at recognizing these circumstances and sometimes take the initiative.

In some instances, a momentary loss of control can escalate to a full-scale blow-up. Quarrelling, misusing materials or equipment or oppositional behavior can all sometimes be defused by immediate relocation. In milder instances, such as prolonged giggling or arguments, brief removal from the stimulus—a momentary trip to the water fountain, for example—is all that's needed. Possibly the plants can use watering. Anything that can cool down errant emotions and put the situation into perspective is a useful preventive consequence.

Once an argument or tantrum has reached blow-up proportions, I will send the child to a predetermined "processing" area. The least punitive of these areas will be relaxation-oriented, a place where an upset or frustrated child can calm down and process her emotions before she ends up in greater trouble. A relaxation area might comprise a partitioned area of the studio, where a soft chair, a plant and simple art materials are set up so that participation can continue during this time for regaining composure.

A more punitive version processing area is the "time-out" area, where more serious infractions are dealt with. Assaults, profanity, sexual promiscuity, tantrums, vandalism or severe oppositional behavior may warrant removing the child to an area which is devoid of comfort or stimulation. Time-out is most effective when an entire room can be allotted for this purpose. It should be empty and windowless with subdued lighting, yet well-ventilated. (Closets will not do for this purpose!) With behavior-disturbed populations the time-out room should be padded with foam mats, so as to absorb a tantrum without risking injury to the child. Deprived of stimulation, insulated by shock-absorbing walls, the recalcitrant child is free to act out until his or her energies wane. Often it is a combination of fatigue and boredom which prompts the child to cool off so that he or she may again rejoin the class. In this situation it is helpful to have a two-way mirror or spy hole, since the child must be constantly monitored (as per state law) without compromising the minimal-stimulation concept. It is the child who must decide when confinement is to end, by demonstrating the willingness and capacity to handle a less restrictive environment.

IMPORTANCE OF REFLECTION

The intention in removing a child from the regular environment is to provide a period of respite during which the child has the opportunity to reflect upon the chain of events which landed him or her in confinement. If a child is verbally or at least intellectually capable of reviewing the incident alone or with the support of the teacher, then the respite period becomes an opportunity for insight. Just as reflection is a crucial aspect in the art appreciation and criticism process, it is also vital for the child in terms of understanding and changing behavior.

Reflection can be accomplished in several ways, depending upon the setting. In situations where the child has just been removed from a conflict, I approach the child verbally as soon as he or she is calm enough to hold a conversation. Instead of accusing or berating, I inquire "What happened?" "Why," "How do you feel about it?" "How do you think the others feel?" "What steps could you have taken to avoid such a confrontation?" "What could I, the teacher have done to help you?" and so on. Because I will most likely not be able to spend an extended period of time during the class period, I might arrange for the student to come back after school to discuss the incident. More often I might request that the child continue to process the incident by doing a series of drawings. While in most cases aesthetic quality is strived for, more often than not these "behavior" pieces will remain schematic and unembellished. They demonstrate a pictographic quality; unadorned yet

This young man elected to take his aggressions out on the padded wall before he lost control of his behavior. For emotionally handicapped students, such safety valves are an indispensable part of the behavior program.

Processing an issue may take place away from the bustle of the workspace, in an area devoted to relaxation and reflection.

Working out an incident through drawing can help a child explore the circumstances and consequences of his or her actions. In this drawing, a hearing impaired young man was able to process both internal and external aspects of feelings that led to destructive behavior.

In this drawing, a young man works through a phase of placing blame and rage before taking responsibility for his actions.

communicative images combined with written narrative.

A deaf child recounted to me how he was provoked by a peer, lost control and assaulted him, forcing me to restrain him. In this particular case, little insight was gained during the reflective process as evidenced by the fact that he continued to blame the peer (who had not provoked him). He also saw my restraining him as an unnecessary punitive action (which it was not in light of the fact that he persisted in attacking the other child). However, in another instance, an emotionally handicapped child processed his punishment by a dorm counselor for abusing his furniture by acknowledging the counselor's anger as being warranted in light of his inappropriate behavior. His reflection gave way to a degree of acceptance and conciliation which might not have occurred had he been simply punished without the opportunity and guidance to process the incident.

In this drawing, a young man who was prone to biting when his temper exploded alludes to his dangerous behavior. It is not clear, however, whether he is expressing a warning to others that he is still potentially dangerous or that he is expressing repentance for a forbidden and grossly inappropriate act.

This young man portrayed his attempt to explain his destructive behavior to a dorm supervisor. He quite accurately registers the grim responses of the adult as he frantically attempted to rationalize his actions.

RESTRAINT

A child who loses control to the point of endangering himself, peers or staff may have to be restrained. Restraint in this context does not mean physical punishment nor does it necessarily mean being straight-jacketed. It is usually an act of immobilization, whereby the child is forced to sit or lay quietly until ready to remain composed.

In most cases, restraint is accomplished with the help of other staff members. Unless a child is young or of a slight build, it may be imprudent to tackle even a ten- or twelve-year-old who is out of control. In settings where outbursts are a possibility or even a daily occurrence, some form of code or alarm arrangement is usually set up by the institution. When the code is called, help is dispatched quickly and the situation dealt with in drill-like precision. (In such cases, the child is usually taken to the floor while his or her arms are immobilized. You must exercise extreme caution to protect yourself during this maneuver, especially taking care to keep your head to the side of the child's so that he or she cannot head-butt you, catching you in the nose, teeth or tongue.) Once the child has been immobilized, several staff members are usually needed to hold down the child as well as to speak soothingly, assuring him or her that they will loosen their grasp as soon as they see the readiness to remain in control. Once the child stops struggling and begins to relax, a period in the time-out room is a standard follow-up to such an episode. (The decision to restrain a child should only be made following then institution's guidelines as well as statutes regarding corporal punishment. In most states, even a hand on a child's shoulder constitutes corporal intervention. Therefore, to be legally protected, staff members must adhere to institutional policy and the institution should stand ready to defend the staff's actions should they be challenged.)

REESTABLISHING RAPPORT

After a child has acted out or spent time in the time-out areas, it is important that the teacher reestablish a positive relationship. It must be emphasized that the exile was purely a matter of reacting to the child's acts (regardless of whether it was an unconscious or conscious decision), and not a result of the teacher's anger or ill-feeling toward the child. An important part of the rapport process is to clear the air and impress upon the child that he or she now has a clean slate. This must be communicated in a subtle manner in ways that do not invite a reoccurrence of the behavior. Without apologizing or making light of the behavior, the teacher can provide a fresh start by allowing the child to do something around the studio which is gratifying. Passing out materials or feeding the fish are activities which serve as a subtle communication that all is back to normal without grudges or antagonism. Care must be taken, however, not to send the child conflicting signals. For children who have difficulties understanding rules and measuring the affective responses of staff, confusion can aggravate an already difficult situation. The teacher must handle reapproachment with keen awareness and sensitivity in order for it to be effective.

SPECIAL PROBLEMS WITH PSYCHOTIC AND AUTISTIC BEHAVIOR

Autistic behavior is often profoundly disturbed and often impossible to change. The causes are rooted in severe cogenital and emotional handicapping conditions, such as blindness (Fraiberg 1977), brain damage or other somatic damage (Rimland 1969), sensory deprivation (Delacota 1972) or familial mistreatment (Bettelheim 1972). These factors in combination may aggravate each other in subtle yet devastating ways. Children who display autistic behavior are often completely inaccessible to our interventions. They exhibit a kind of patho-

logical shyness; stimulation from the environment is shut out and normal life activities are an impossibility.

These distorted reactions to stimuli are often severe enough so that a child may be considered, for example, clinically deaf or impervious to pain. Often autistic children are completely self-absorbed, such as the child who spins a penny for hours on end or simply stares out one particular window. What is particularly apparent in these children is their avoidance of interaction with people. Even family members may be regarded as threats and are treated as if they do not exist. Autistic children reject interactions with their environment or with people on the grounds that it is simply too painful (both physically and emotionally). It is not known how autistic children process their surroundings. For all we know, the world is an incomprehensible, alien and awful place beset with constant noxious stimuli which the autistic child cannot decipher or endure.

In special education programs, the teacher's mission is to break through the autistic shell and replace self-stimulation with more adaptive behavior. The response to such an intrusion is invariably one of anxiety and in severe cases panic and rage reactions may occur. When the autistic behavior is suppressed and the child is inadequately prepared to cope with the teacher's version of reality, hypoactivity often gives way to extra-sensitive reactions. The problem is no longer lack of arousal, but that every reaction is potentially explosive. For example, when a child is forced to sit near the clock he or she has avoided, (because its ticking is perceived as a raucous din or a variation of Chinese water torture), the child no longer is able to remain self-absorbed. Panic or rage are the response to this insufferable stimuli. Autistic children frequently view other people as unpredictable and threatening; this is particularly the case with their autistic, severely disturbed peers. Should a child be forced to share a worktable with a peer, the reaction will no longer be one of passivity, but rather a fight or flight reaction (Tinbergen 1983).

Needless to say, dealing with such disturbed behavior requires special sensitivity and adaptation. The key is to minimize the provocational aspects of the art education process. Decreasing stimulation and confrontation in the art experience allows the autistic child the time to become accustomed to the artroom and its participants. An effective way of luring the child into the activity is to mirror his or her behavior in a form which translates into an art activity. For example, a child who will only arrange a set of blocks in a certain order may benefit by having the teacher engage in the same activity nearby. By observing how the teacher modulates the structures in different combinations of forms, the child is prompted to take a chance and vary her or his own construction. This type of parallel play has long been used in dealing with shy creatures such as chimpanzees and gorillas (Fossey 1983). Their behaviors are met by cautious coexistence, and mimicking which then slowly progresses in complexity and in the degree of interaction between participants.

Progress in parallel activities should be invariably slow and unhurried, giving the autistic child sufficient opportunity to adjust and coexist with his or her companions. As the autistic child displays increased tolerance for stimuli, the teacher can increase the stimulation and raise expectations for performance. This is, however, a painfully slow, often tedious process, with redundant repetition of activity being required to build the child's sense of security and familiarity. Undoubtedly, many of the activities we introduce to the autistic child are perceived as alien, even assaultive, acts. Great care must be taken to create an atmosphere of predictability and safety in order to lure the autistic child from his or her isolation. Despite such sensitive interventions, however, regression often occurs and must be expected and anticipated. During these periods of emotional instability and skill loss, the child must be supported without being pressed too hard to maintain productivity. Expectations should be adjusted so as to not further aggravate the child's already tenuous hold on reality. Often, these regressive periods will recede as mysteriously as they emerge, allowing the child to regain a degree of tolerance and participation.

SELF-STIMULATION

Children who have suffered sensory deprivations due to physical trauma or environmental impoverishment often engage in self-stimulating behavior. Mental retardation, brain damage, blindness, autism and multiple handicaps affect the amount and kind of stimulation the child receives from the environment. Individuals who are in institutions may also be deprived of exploring and interacting with their surroundings; their behavioral repertoire becomes impoverished, eccentric or even bizarre. These behaviors most often include rocking, hand waving or flashing, and echolalia (the repeating of words, songs or advertisements out of context). In more severe forms, head banging, teeth grinding and masturbation may be present. Self-stimulation can inhibit the engagement of other, more productive behaviors and, thus, is a problem worthy of our attention.

It is important to point out that everyone engages in some form of self-stimulating behavior, especially if deprived of adequate environmental stimulation. The commuter who spends long periods of time in traffic, the prisoner in solitary confinement, even the graduate student who must endure hours in the lecture hall may begin to self-stimulate. Self-stimulation such as bouncing a knee rapidly, twirling one's hair, tapping a pencil are all behaviors whose primary functions are to release energy and to derive a primitive form of pleasure.

When we view the autistic child repeatedly spinning his penny or the blind child gently rocking her head, we should keep in mind that those who dance at the local night club are essentially deriving the same pleasures through repetitive movements. However, what must be distinguished is that the child is locked into one or more repetitive or bizarre behaviors which exclude other activities necessary for education or even therapy. There are several strategies for working with the self-stimulatory child. The most prevalent in the education setting is behavior modification, where a child is either rewarded with food or privileges or punished for his or her actions. Depending upon the intensity and duration of the behavior, the strategy might be as light as a gentle reminder to "Keep hands nice," or in severe self-abusive cases, restraint or physical punishment may be used. While much self-stimulatory behavior will persist despite the most empathic or punitive approaches, it can be decreased to the extent that other activities can be introduced which will vie for the child's attention and participation.

In therapeutic art education, the approach is one of accommodation balanced by limit setting. In keeping with a philosophy which accepts idiosyncracy with tolerance, I will not ordinarily suppress a case of self-stimulation unless it is dangerous or socially inappropriate. Instead, I attempt to redirect and expand the behavior into forms which at once accommodate the child's right of expression while also making it more appropriate and productive. For instance, a child who is visually impaired might self-stimulate using the play of light through various lenses such as traffic reflectors, headlights, windows, eyeglasses or glassware. One could admonish the child for obsessing over this stimulus or, as an alternative, harness this fascination with reflection and refraction as part of the art experience. Kaleidoscopes, stained plastics, colored acetate, light projections can all serve to satisfy the child's hunger for visual stimulation in ways that open a new channel for its expression. For children who habitually rock back and forth, I have used music as a means of controlling behavior. By playing music during a break in the art activity, or preferably at the end of the session, the children are given the opportunity to beat time to an appropriate stimulus instead of being purely obsessional in their movements. With music at the close of the session, the children can look forward to an activity which enlivens cleanup time and adds a measure of celebration to the end of class. By allowing music only at the end, the teacher encourages the child to hold back the impulse to self-stimulate until it is sanctioned.

Children whose self-stimulation is more severe and health threatening can also be dealt with by re-

directing their self-abusive impulses through the art process. My own research experience has documented how a child who would head bang was able to eventually mollify his need to self-abuse by redirecting his aggression through robust activity with clay (Henley 1986). With my support and guidance, he was taught to use coils, rolling pins and wooden mallets to judiciously strike the clay, thus enabling him to lessen the frequency and intensity of his head-banging behavior.

RITUALISTIC AND COMPULSIVE BEHAVIORS

When children are under great stress and are forced to bind their anxiety so that they are not constantly acting out, (and thus pay the consequences) they may resort to ritualistic or compulsive behaviors. These are exceedingly primitive behaviors which involve aspects of self-stimulation, perseveration and repetition. For instance, an emotionally disturbed boy I worked with would habitually feel the entire frame of the artroom door before he entered. Another boy would smell the railings leading to the studio in a bizarre ritual which took up to ten minutes. In a less eccentric vein, a learning disabled girl of seven insisted upon being the sink monitor so that she could arrange and rearrange the brush stand, soap pads and sponges until it was, in her eyes, "perfect." Some children develop hand washing compulsion, frequently interrupting their work to scrub their hands even when using a relative clean medium such as crayon or colored pencil.

Because compulsivity and ritualism are exceedingly rigid, driven behaviors, they are difficult to break. These neurotic behaviors signify deep conflicts within the child which can only be addressed through medication and long-term psychotherapy. However, the art teacher can help by empathizing with the child while also encouraging self-control. Often, simply forbidding the hand washing or compulsive arranging will be met with fight or flight. I have seen intense tantrums and assaults from the gentlest children who evidently felt they had no other option but to defend their need to obsess. Others will simply panic, often running away in desperation to carry out the behavior in private.

The most effective straightforward approach is to allow a child to carry out the ritual so long as it remains socially appropriate and does not overly infringe upon productivity. While allowing the behavior a modicum of expression, the teacher can aim toward a gradual lessening of the intensity and duration of the behavior. Although such modifications will often be resisted, transitions can occur, given unhurried and subtle interventions which satisfy the compulsion or ritual yet seek to expand it with greater diversity. Thus, the brush-arranging sink monitor should be allowed to carry out this activity because it is appropriate and productive. However, attempts should be made to diminish the driven nature of the activity by encouraging her to move on to straightening paper piles or other materials. This at least adds a degree of flexibility to her compulsion. Eventually one would hope she might begin to alternate sink monitoring or paper straightening with some substitute activity unrelated to compulsive arranging.

In some instances, a child's obsession centers not on an object or an activity but another person. In one case I observed, a mildly retarded boy focused on a classmate, constantly asking about the individual, whether the two were still friends, whether they would eat lunch together, etc. This obsession escalated until the boy bit his friend in a frenzy of agitation and anxiety. In this case, I would have simply removed the other student from the obsessed child's group and thus lessened the stimulation available for obsessing. While the obsessed child undoubtedly would have reacted negatively to such a provocative move, eventually an out-of-sight, out-of-mind reaction probably would have occurred. This is not to say however, that some other object of obsession would not have taken that particular student's place; often some substitutive object or person will emerge to fill in the gap. However, given the options, the removal of the source of the obsession will sometimes re-

duce the child's anxiety and arousal levels, so that sufficient concentration can be directed back to continuing the art activity.

HYPERACTIVITY AND ATTENTION DEFICITS

Most teachers have encountered a child who is chronically distracted and whose hyperactivity often translates into disruptive behavior and poor productivity. In addition to short attention spans, children with ADHD also may have problems with coordination and auditory processing. The simplest activities of participating in the art program may be chaotic and overwhelming to such a child. The variables of the art studio environment with its colorful, dynamic materials and visual aids often present more stimulation than this type of child can assimilate. The informal setting, abstract nature of the activities, the bustle of activity can all interfere with the child's attention and increase agitation and confusion. Often this confusion leads to poor impulse control and acting-out behavior as stress and frustration builds to intolerable levels.

This is one of the instances when a behavior modification approach to structuring the art process is most effective and appropriate. Because of the inability of these children to focus on complex or rapidly changing situations, the art experience must be broken down using a task-analysis format. This format can be adapted to virtually every component of the program, from how to find and take a seat, to how to operate a pair of scissors and how to share a work space. Each operation must be viewed as a project in itself, the child should receive an acknowledgement for applying him- or herself effectively, as well as deal with consequences if his or her performance is inappropriate.

The example of finding a seat is one which we ordinarily take for granted and do not assign great significance to. Yet, for a child with neurological dysfunction, entering the artroom, negotiating the maze of tables, supplies and equipment without becoming distracted, competing with peers for a seat, then sitting down without incident can be an exhausting experience for both child and staff. Thus, the teacher may not be able to simply give a general direction; the task must be broken down into precise steps, using demonstration and other cues. Thus, the teacher might say, "Please go directly to this specific seat," then point or lead the child. Because these children often cannot differentiate figure/ground relationships or negotiate visually "busy" groupings of furniture, artroom tools and decorations, the environment may need to be simplified. Discrete, partitioned areas may need to be provided so that a sense of security and order is maintained. Seating carrels are useful for placing children in a controlled mini-environment while keeping them in close proximity to the other members of the class. Because distractible children are so susceptible to distorted perceptions, they may not be able to monitor their bodily movements. What one may interpret as an aggressive action may be a case of poor self-awareness or coordination. In these cases, the carrel environment can allow the child to develop a sense of limits while developing awareness and attention.

MOOD SWINGS

Several years ago I began working with a ten-year-old boy who suffered from severe mood swings which resulted in disruptive and even assaultive behavior in school. He had been given the usual workups with the school psychologist, psychiatric social worker and learning-disability consultant, none of whom could arrive at a consensus of what was prompting this child's extreme changes in disposition. At times his behavior lost control to the extent that he was put on home instruction. Evidently at home his outbursts were manageable, yet he still exhibited mood swings which his family considered simple eccentricity. After almost a year of home instruction, the child was diagnosed as

hypoglycemic. His mood swings and extreme behavior were due to low blood sugar. At home his parents had given him candy as a bribe to calm down. Once a regimen of high-sugar snacks, such as grapes or raisins, was instituted, his behavior leveled out and he was able to rejoin his mainstream class.

In one case I encountered, involving an eight-year-old boy, extensive tests yielded little information regarding his hyperactive behavior. Hyperthyroidism was at first suspected, then was discarded. Eventually the child was put on therapeutic dosages of the drug Ritalin, with miraculous results. The physicians were able to fine-tune the dosage so that the child could now concentrate, cooperate, take his time and get along better with his peers, without compromising his behavior in terms of drowsiness or depression. He was taken off the drug on weekends so that side effects such as the stunting of growth were minimized. Despite my suspiciousness and general resistance to medicating young children, I was simply astounded at the positive effects this medication had upon this child. Virtually overnight he was transformed from a contentious, frustrated and hyper-distracted child to a well-adjusted, happy individual with no apparent problems.

FEARFUL REACTIONS

Children who have suffered traumatic events are sometimes left with emotional scars in the form of phobic reactions. In psychological terms, phobias are considered irrational fears: a child is pathologically frightened by some place, person or situation. Such fears are usually debilitating for the individual; they may dictate how a child lives day-to-day life as he or she avoids the fearful situation at all costs.

Every so often such neurosis might be encountered in an intact child in the art education situation. However, the fearful reactions that are prevalent among special needs children are distinctly different from other neurotic phobias because the fears are grounded in reason. Given these children's physical and sensory disabilities, the environment can be a hostile, fearful place where safety cannot be taken for granted. For example, a mentally retarded child may not possess the deductive or abstract reasoning to appraise the danger of a given situation. A soldering or hot glue gun can be dangerously hot without flame, redness or visible radiation or heat. After being burned once, a reasonable reaction for such a child might be to retain a generalized fear of any tool or toy which resembles the soldering gun, based upon this one painful experience.

For cerebral palsied children who are confined to wheelchairs, a class pet such as a hamster or cricket might constitute an imagined physical threat. These defenseless, immobile children develop a heightened sense of vulnerability, realizing that any seemingly harmless creature can indeed cause bodily harm. This reaction may be generalized to a fear of all animals. Paralyzed children might share this hypersensitivity to both animate and inanimate things in the environment. Such a child realizes all too well that he cannot shield his face against falling objects. For example, he might fear the bookshelf above his bed or the dangling light fixture suspended from the ceiling. A fear of height may also be pronounced in such children. The paralyzed child who is used to the supine position may become frightened when she is put on a tilt table and raised to a vertical position as part of physical therapy. The height involved when standing can become an alien, terrifying experience. Blind children are another group which demonstrates an inability to take the environment for granted. A blind child might harbor a fear of doorways which can pose a dangerous, unpredictable threat as the door slams shut or unexpectedly swings against her.

I have also encountered deaf children who were fearful of normal hearing children. They believed, quite irrationally yet understandably, that normal hearing extends to actively listening in on someone's thoughts. Thus, they considered the hearing child a mind-reader and were intimidated and disturbed as a result. All of these examples point to the need for the art educator to become sensitized to the individual child, since such fearful reactions are personal idiosyncrasies which other children with similar disabilities may not share. Once sensitized to such reactions, the teacher can better modify the environment or take other steps to create a secure atmosphere in the artroom.

These modifications may be accomplished by engaging the fearful children with the sources of their fear in a sensitive, unhurried and systematic manner. For example, the fearful cerebral palsied child might choose one animal she is not afraid of, such as a fish. A fish bowl might be set up in order to desensitize the child. Later other related animals such as a frog or a newt might be added to the aquarium. In this way stimuli are introduced in a progression which raises the tolerance level and encourages more normal reactions to everyday stimulation. In the case just described, the fearful child developed a healthy interest in aquarium life and became quite knowledgeable and self-confident, and showed greater self-esteem. While a fear of squirrels and blue jays persisted, she took the first steps toward confronting and resolving these issues—all through normal classroom activities.

DEFEATISM AND DEPRESSION

Often children who are very capable art students react to their work with self-depreciation and a sense of worthlessness. Sometimes children will intentionally overwork or deface their pieces or simply crumple them into the wastebasket. They will defend these actions, despite the teacher's protestations, by saying "It wasn't any good in the first place." Among intact, mainstream children this may be a ploy by which the child is inappropriately seeking attention. In destroying or denouncing his or her work, the child is goading the teacher into exclaiming how wonderful it is. After repeated encounters with this maneuver, some teachers begin to ignore the behavior or take steps to discourage the child's attention-seeking and manipulative behavior.

Should this defeatism and depression be a constant pattern of behavior, however, it may suggest more than the usual preadolescent susceptibility to feelings of inferiority or low self-esteem. These behaviors may suggest serious depression, with anxiety being expressed in self-disparagement and a poor self-image. Should the child be sincerely reaching out to the teacher for support because of depression, or a serious lack of self-esteem, a more empathic approach is appropriate.

Whether a child is handicapped or gifted, one must be aware and sensitized to what the child is communicating regardless of how annoying or frustrating his or her methods. In one such instance where I dealt harshly with a chronic self-deprecator, he sank deeper into isolation and withdrawal. When I became aware of my misjudgment, he remained unresponsive to my attention. From then on I took a second look at these children and took their complaints of inferiority seriously. I learned that in denying the child the support he needed, I only confirmed to him his worthlessness. Since he looked up to me, such an inference was devastating and sent him reeling into even deeper depression. It is up to the teacher to assess when a child is sincerely despondent and in need of encouragement and support. Withdrawn behavior, flat or depressed affect, somatic complaints or lack of energy, as well as problems maintaining peer relationships may all suggest serious depression.

In order to support a depressed or withdrawn child the teacher must energetically and sincerely attempt to point out any strengths in evidence. One must boldly retrieve crumbled pieces, iron them if need be and demonstrate how the piece is worthy of rescue. Sometimes lines must be whited-out or muddied colors gessoed over. Skillful use of invisible or masking tape is also a must in situations where work was intentionally or mistakenly damaged. Damaged sculptures may require deft use of silicon gel or epoxy.

Stylistic or content changes are more difficult to effect. Auxiliary ego functions, such as drawing for the child, might be considered, as long as the work remains within the student's developmental level and style. Otherwise the teacher's intervention may intimidate the student and further aggravate the situation. For instance, one twelve-year-old, emotionally handicapped child in my class wanted to draw a cat. After repeated aborted attempts by the child, the student teacher attempted to help by drawing a cat as an example—only this rendering possessed art school sophistication and style. The child took one look at it and put her head between her arms in defeat. I hurriedly drew a cat in my patented sixth grade style, tapped her on the shoulder and aroused her interest one more time. She even allowed me to draw on her paper (although because of my "lack" of drawing skill—which she found curious—she needed to "improve" upon my linework). She went on to create a credible picture complete with the cat's scratching tree and pet mouse.

It is important when working with the defeatist child that the project's goals be within reach and do not inadvertently set the child up to fail. By the same token, goals must be placed high enough so that if he or she should falter, the child does not sense that he or she has failed at something easy and thus become even more despondent. By assessing individual needs and lending sincere ingenious support to rescue losing battles with the medium, defeated or depressed children can begin to battle their feelings of inferiority.

STRESS AND ANXIETY REACTIONS

Everyone, adult and child alike, must cope with situations in their lives which arouse stress and anxiety. Stress often begins on the first day of kindergarten, when the child must cope with the separation anxiety of leaving the mother, and often continues through the day of graduation, when the adolescent realizes he or she is entering a largely cold and competitive world. In most cases, the child can successfully work out these life stresses and become a well-adjusted kindergartner or a successful graduate. There are, however, those whose anxiety dominates their behavior. Their constant apprehension, tension, fear or nervousness manifests itself in impulsiveness, over-contentiousness, withdrawal, restlessness and various fearful reactions.

In the art education setting, I have encountered anxiety on an equal basis and in a wide range of guises among intact and special needs children alike. In some young children, anxiety reactions have resulted from parental overprotection; in class the child is overly concerned whether the light bulbs are too hot, or if the playground is safe or whether the custodian can be trusted. In some instances, pre-art motivation activities, such as discussions of current events, reading Grimm's fairy tales or discussing animal behavior have aroused feelings of apprehension and anxiety.

I have also encountered children who feel the weight of adult problems, including monetary or business worries, and concern over the physical health of parents. In some cases, the parents have tried to foster a precocious social awareness and maturity by inappropriately involving their children in their adult concerns. In such instances, the child's right to security, protection and to childhood bliss has been compromised, resulting in unnecessary burdening of the child before he or she possesses the maturity to cope.

Another form of parental or institutionally induced anxiety is an undue emphasis upon perfection. Incessant demands for perfect conduct, compliance, grades, athletic prowess may result in an increase in anxiety and its related effects. Often such demands are totally unrealistic, with the child being expected to achieve without the requisite ap-

titude or even interest in the activity. Sometimes a normally high-achieving child is expected to constantly excel and strive for even greater accomplishments. In one instance, a particularly talented hearing-impaired high school student was given a scholarship to attend a prestigious summer arts camp for normal hearing children. Despite her abundant skills, physical attractiveness and unusual maturity, she simply could not handle the pressures of constantly reading lips, interacting with only hearing peers and deciphering abstract art problems. She eventually left in mid-program with anxiety that bordered upon panic.

Another particularly contemporary problem is dealing with materially spoiled children whose parents are overly permissive or absentee. Because children naturally seek out limits in their behavior, they often become anxious when limits remain undefined. As Erich Fromm noted, even in adult life we sometimes tend to reject or escape from freedoms which are beset with danger or which burden us with decisions that bear enormous consequences. To instill an atmosphere of security and safety in the artroom, a stable framework of limits and expectations should be in place. Often what the teacher sees as troublesome behavior or acting out is nothing more than a child who is testing limits in order to reaffirm that firmness and security are consistent predictable features in the classroom.

chapter 12

Issues Relating to Creative Expression

Children's art offers the art educator an ideal window through which to glimpse the workings of a child's inner life. Visual representations of ideas, feelings, fantasies, perceptions and concerns may all filter through a single modest picture. The images will yield a wealth of information, should we be astute enough to realize what the child has communicated. It is the art teacher's responsibility to possess the knowledge and sensitivity to process this vital information. The art process and product offer the teacher an opportunity to affect positive changes in the child's behavior. By working toward the exploration and resolution of issues which surface during the art activity, changes in the child's emotions and behavior are possible.

Understanding a child's picture does not infer that the teacher must psychoanalyze, diagnose or assign symbolic connotations to the art images (Chapter 1). This practice of psychoanalysis is beyond the realm of the art educator. Projective techniques lie beyond the scope of the educator's mission and can be most destructive to both therapeutic goals and the art education process. Many professionals in art and special education also remain dubious of projective techniques which attempt to explain a child's inner dynamics or predict future behaviors. They voice their concern over the subjectivity of such interpretations. Often, they believe, projective assessments lead to stereotyping children and their problems. This

in turn can lead to easy rationalizations and self-fulfilling prophecies. There is also the danger that interpretations of artwork may reflect not the child's perceptions but adult symbolizations.

Once, as a member of an interdisciplinary team, I was asked to interpret a boy's artwork which I had not previously seen. The picture portrayed him undergoing some supernatural transformation from a meek and powerless runt into a character of omnipotent power. This character brandished a lightning bolt sword, slaying anyone who dared cross his path. Put on the spot, I remarked weakly that this child might be projecting his need to gain control over his environment, to impose his own egocentric will upon others using an elaborate fantasy to compensate for his own inadequacies. The team members all concurred with this seemingly reasonable interpretation. Upon returning home, I happened to make some remarks about this picture to which my eavesdropping son responded, "Oh, that's a popular T.V. cartoon show—in fact, it's a verbatim account of what occurs at the beginning of each program." Naturally, I felt hopelessly ignorant and embarrassed over what had occurred. A more prudent interpretation, given the inadequate information and my own vulnerable position at the team meeting, would have been that such a fantasy scene was for some reason a very powerful stimulus for this child. It served as a powerful motivator and evoked what was, for him, an im-

Issues of a personal nature may inadvertantly surface during the most innocent of art activities. This sixth grader's valentine to his mother reveals much about the state of this relationship.

portant image. With no other information to go on, (i.e., observations of behavior or case background), this represents the only responsible or reasonable analysis I could have made.

In art education, emphasis should be placed upon being a perceptive observer. Salient issues which the child is exploring in art will, more often than not, be overt and rich in elaboration. One only needs to function as a kind of receptacle, carefully looking and listening to discern the intentions of the artist. The content of children's art comprises mainly what they know, what they perceive and what they feel. These myriad memories, fantasies, emotions and ideas may or may not represent the handicapping condition, emotional illness or intellect.

My approach to assessing pathology in children's work is exceedingly cautious. In most cases, children in my program will not be singled out as being in need of therapeutic treatment on the basis of their being mentally retarded, blind, non-English-speaking or any other arbitrary condition. This implies that in approaching a special

needs child's artwork, we need to focus on any strengths in evidence, emphasizing where the child has surmounted his or her disability. Each child should be considered to be adapting and adjusting unless a combination of behavioral symptoms in concert with manifest problems in the artwork convinces us otherwise. This implies that the art teacher will usually work with a wide range of disabled populations without necessarily encountering psychopathology.

However, there are instances when a child (any child, not necessarily those with special needs) breaks down under the pressures of physical disability, emotional stress or environmental deprivation. Such a breakdown will inevitability show up in some form in the child's artwork. Regardless of whether the symptomatic image is the product of purely unconscious processes or of some degree of conscious deliberation, the art will convey some aspect of the child's state of mind. It may signify the nature of the problem, with regard to its state of consciousness, the defenses in use, and its prospects for resolution or insight. Often, emotionally laden material surges to the surface of the art imagery in graphic and powerful terms, expressing concerns which seldom filter through verbally. It is at this juncture that the teacher must remain keenly aware and poised for action. By recognizing problems at their onset, the teacher stands a better chance of intervening before an issue becomes a crisis.

In each of the following accounts, I will attempt to identify the significant aspects of the artwork and elucidate the steps taken to address the issues the child has raised. In describing these situations, I intend not to generalize or promote stereotypical views. Instead, I hope to give the reader a range of vicarious experiences, presenting graphic images created by students with a range of physical and emotional concerns. For the sake of brevity, the case accounts are abridged. They merely highlight the works as well as the steps taken to address each specific child with each specific issue.

DEALING WITH STEREOTYPES

In working with special populations, the teacher may encounter the following scenario: A group of six children are set up to work in a variety of dimensional media. Pastels, crayons, pencils and printmaking supplies are all set up in tantalizing array awaiting the children's choice in order to solve a design problem. After the teacher discusses possible themes, he or she may demonstrate the range of techniques and kinds of images that are possible to achieve with this medium. After exploring the medium, the children begin work on their own compositions. In surveying the works in progress however, the teacher becomes dismayed. The students' output comprises one name placard, several stick figures, a free-form scribble, a house with generic flowers and two attempts at rendering a GI Joe and a Garfield.

Although well drawn, cute TV characters such as this essentially glossed over the deep-seated anxieties simmering within this child.

If we suppose that the media and techniques were developmentally appropriate and the teacher presented them in a clear and lively way, to what do we attribute such meager results? The majority of these works cannot be considered true artistic creations, nor can they be considered fertile expressions of the students' imaginations. They are instead stereotypes. Lowenfeld (1982) defines *stereotypes* as repetitive and inflexible images that rely upon the conventions of mass culture rather than a healthy identification with one's own ideas, concerns and interests. Many children, especially those with special needs, will latch onto images they see in their culture and use them as prominent or prevalent subjects in their artwork. Using popular images can be a usual and healthy part of the development process. However, should these figures become overly repetitive and inflexible, they begin to dominate a child's iconography at the expense of other, more personal feelings and experiences. Stereotypical expression becomes an issue in art education when the child displays an over-reliance upon a limited range of subjects and thus precludes expansiveness and growth through the art process.

The causes of stereotypy fall roughly into two different categories. The first category sees the stereotype as representing an impoverishment or absence of sensory stimulation in the child's environment (Lowenfeld 1957). Poor and affluent children alike suffer deprivation of this kind. In our technological environment, television and other commercial media have largely replaced active, exuberant participation in the natural environment. Children are conditioned to expect ideas and experiences to be generated for them, since their own immature imaginations are no match for the special effects of the popular media. They are often overwhelmed by the sheer ingeniousness and volume of this media stimulation and are thus influenced by it in their art.

The other cause of stereotypy is associated with the more disturbed, emotionally handicapped student. In these cases, the child retreats into stereotypical expression due to some overriding emotional issue that he or she cannot face (Kramer 1971). Should the experiences be sufficiently traumatic, the child may not care to delve into either the past or present as a theme in art, thus avoiding deep-seated ideas and experiences by staying with the superficial, anonymous stereotype and ensuring that little evocative material will be stirred up during the art process.

INTERVENING WITH MEDIA STEREOTYPES

Regardless of the causes, whether it be sensory impoverishment or emotional conflict, stereotypy often involves images and themes borrowed from popular culture and commercial media. The most intractable and prevalent expression of stereotypy are the characters from cartoons, toys, films and advertisements. They can range in characterization from the saccharine sweet and cuddly to the demonic and violent. Once a child latches on to one of these figures, it can be especially difficult

to intervene in order to expand his or her visual repertoire. Especially with special needs children, instances of rigidity and resistance are often more prevalent than experimentation and diversity. In many cases the teacher must wean the child away from the security that the stereotype provides.

A degree of empathy and sensitivity must be exercised by the teacher to recognize stereotypy as an expression of vulnerability and insecurity on the part of the child. The teacher may begin demonstrating empathy by accepting the fact that the child has chosen this image, then begin resourcefully to motivate the student to extend his or her frame of reference. For instance, should a child insist upon involving a favorite cartoon character, I might begin by assuring the child that it was good that he or she could make that decision and is actively planning the work so independently. Instead of encouraging the child to actually copy or trace the character, however, I would provide a cutout illustration of that particular figure. (I keep an up-to-date collection of media figures on file, culled from advertisements, children's books and toy brochures.) I then ask the child where would he or she like to place the figure in his composition—in the sky? on a mountain top? in the water?—trying all the while to give that figure some kind of creative context. Once that is decided, the child is encouraged to create the surroundings for the character, including additional characters, and to depict the adventures that are occurring. An imaginative world is built up around the stereotype using the child's own imagination and ideas. The cutout becomes a catalyst, a point of departure from which the child can cautiously explore the environment while anchored to the object of his or her security. As the teacher helps extend the child's reference, in most cases the child will forget about the cutout altogether and move on to explore elements that are more personally fulfilling.

I discourage students from attempting to draw the stereotypical character itself for several important reasons. First and most obvious, I prefer the child's own original creations to the visually bland, superficially attractive media figures. These rarely contribute an aesthetic element to the child's art-work. Most importantly, however, such media figures are the products of adult minds and hands. These often deceptively simple, slick creations cannot easily be created by most children, since the skills required are beyond their developmental and artistic means. As much as the child obsesses over copying (or tracing) the figure accurately, the figure will rarely measure up to the original, commercial version. By attempting to recreate such a character, most children are essentially setting themselves up to fail, which in turn can lead to depleted self-esteem and decreased motivation. By manipulating the cutout figure, they are in effect let off the hook. The teacher has demonstrated an acceptance of the child's needs and vulnerability, yet at the same time, has given the child the means to use the uninspired media stereotype as a springboard for doing something really exciting.

EMOTIONAL CONSIDERATIONS OF STEREOTYPY

In most cases children are not fully invested in media figures, regardless of their surface appeal, since these are not the products of their own imaginations. It is the role of the teacher to assist the child in gaining this insight, first by demonstrating empathy, then by unobtrusively and resourcefully moving the child beyond mere copywork.

In some cases, however, children may become overly invested in their stereotype, due to some emotional problem that inhibits their capacity to draw upon their own experiences (Kramer 1971). Children with special needs are particularly at risk. They may become obsessed with and perseverate over media characters, and use them as a kind of defense that shields them from their emotional or physical trauma. Some mentally retarded children may not be able to make the distinction between fact and fantasy. One Down syndrome boy in a class I taught was obsessed with drawing the popular television character, the Hulk. He obsessively drew infantile versions of muscular, malevolent figures. This was not merely a case of identifica-

tion with an omnipotent character, which many normal children find irresistible. In this case, the child's defective and immature object relations led him to assume that anyone at any time could mysteriously transform themselves into a monstrous, seething beast. Complicating matters further was the fact that the television character and I were both named David. The boy transferred this association and in doing so, regarded me with fear and awe. Despite my reassurances, he lived in expectation that at any moment I would turn green and burst out of my clothes. Despite months of consistently kind and gentle interactions with this child, I felt that he continued to harbor the illusion.

Children with severe emotional handicaps may also confuse reality and fantasy concerning film or media characters. Popular horror films, certain rock bands and other cults can stimulate these children sufficiently so that they also over-identify. Some art programs for the emotionally handicapped will not accept stereotypical work that contains symbols, logos or depictions from these media, since these are seen as prompting negative reactions of fear, anger, anxiety and acting-out behavior. In my own program, such material is also discouraged, not only for its provocative nature, but because it is rigid, inflexible, anti-aesthetic and not growth-oriented. Sometimes, however, it is necessary to make exceptions on an individual basis. For example, one emotionally disturbed boy I taught was obsessed with the movie character Jason, a ghoul-like fiend who routinely butchered the other characters. I concluded that drawing Jason was an act of exorcism for this child—by reconvening this image over and over he hoped to purge him from his thinking. Thus, in accepting this image, my intention was to assist this child to somehow neutralize this monstrous character, to render it relatively harmless and lessen the intensity of the obsession. I intervened by first accepting the character, then by giving it a reality-oriented context. The child was encouraged to place the actor who played Jason someplace outside the movie's character. He responded by ingeniously creating the movie set, complete with director, cameramen and stage props. In doing this, the

child was able to relegate the character to a more benign setting, one that disarmed the nightmarish theme and rendered it as it should be: a dramatic production of fiction and fantasy. Through an intervention such as this, the media stereotype becomes less omnipotent and, one hopes, less a figure with which to identify. Attention can then be given to embellishing and elaborating ideas in an expansive direction.

Children who are attempting to repress disturbing issues that gnaw at them unconsciously often revert to stereotypes. One such boy of thirteen was able to draw cartoon and movie figures with outstanding skill. He received much positive attention for this from both peers and staff and prided himself upon his achievements. As well-drawn as these figures were, however, they told us nothing of the conflicts that were simmering within. For several months this student was praised for his efforts, to which he would smile and nod his head, as if saying, "Keep your distance and everything will remain pleasant." It was not until he arrived in the artroom one day in a state of rage that this

As his denial was pierced, this boy's artwork began to give his fears form through his art. Here he is depicting a recurrent nightmare in which things slither across an empty room, then inexplicably explode and drip down the walls.

facade began to crumble. He had pushed and injured a classmate and was being punished for his actions. As he began to work on a drawing involving a group of animals (which looked more like stuffed animals) in a zoo setting, he suddenly crumpled the paper and turned away extremely upset. At this point, I intervened and questioned him quietly about the incident for which he was being punished. It seemed that the other boy had told on him for leaving his bed that night (it was a residential school) and climbing in with another boy. The action was not sexual in nature; he had been awakened by recurring nightmares. I then asked if drawing the dream might help him get it out of his system, to which he agreed. He began with only a hazy recollection of images, but following a dialogue with me, he succeeded in piecing together the dream with astonishing clarity.

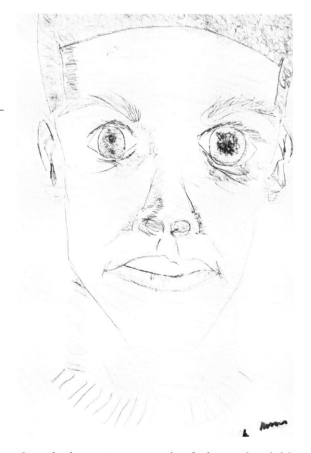

Once he began to process his feelings, the child's art became more energized and probing. This sensitive portrait was one of the many fine drawings completed after his cathartic dream pictures.

This session proved to be a pivotal one, since it offered the child an opportunity to displace his anxiety and obtain a measure of cathartic relief. In subsequent sessions he was able to put aside his stereotypic expressions and work in a more aesthetic and therapeutically useful mode. He was no longer compelled to constantly repress his emotions; instead he began to cautiously explore and approach the resolution of these conflicts.

In this case, the boy's capacity to muster sufficient ego strength to abandon his stereotypes suggested that sublimation was being approached. As he was able to contain his anxiety and channel it through more dynamic imagery, his art became more expansive and less dependent upon defense mechanisms. With the emotional issues being more frequently and effectively addressed, we were able to place a greater emphasis on art education and

aesthetic objectives. Eventually, after much time and patience, his emotional state began to mirror the gains in his art development. He became increasingly stable and resilient. He began to explore all kinds of issues and themes, especially self-portraiture. In one such penetrating study, he looked long and hard at himself, expressing his sensitivity, vulnerability and drafting skills in a loose, bold style (Henley 1989).

In some instances, where emotional disturbances render a child incapable of doing anything else, he or she may be actually encouraged to create a media character. One boy constantly drew himself catapulting and flying about, seemingly at the mercy of a bizarre kind of machine. In order to disarm this possibly dangerous delusion, I intervened by asking him what kind of people can actually fly about, hoping he might answer circus performers or gymnasts. He responded finally, after much confusion, that Spiderman can accomplish such a feat. I concluded that working within the metaphor of Spiderman was preferable to allowing a delusion to continue that might at some-time be dangerously acted upon. He was encouraged to depict Spiderman doing his flying act and thus to recognize the fact that flying is something outside the realm of human experience, something only experienced vicariously through fantasy. In this instance, based upon the individual needs of the child, I concluded that the stereotype was the lesser of two evils.

PERSEVERATION

Children will sometimes repeat a particular image which is not based upon media characters, stereotypes or cultural symbols. These images are created with a compulsive and obsessional tenacity that bespeaks of defensive, displacement activity. While many mature, intact artists such as Warhol, Johns and Oldenburg repeat images to an obsessive degree, they retain sufficient self-control and decision-making skills to alter or change their work should they wish. Using repetition of an im-

Sometimes stereotypes actually constitute favorable progress. Because this psychotic boy harbored delusions about flying, I encouraged him to depict only figures from cartoons or stories who soar as part of a fantasy.

This autistic boy felt that people were routinely ejected, catapulted and shot through the air by machines. This dangerous delusion became the first presenting problem to be addressed.

age as an extension of design theory, they are able to create an intense visual impact in their art. Most children who perseverate lack the ego strength to make conscious decisions to alter, explore and actively expand the images in their art. Their obsessions lock them into one mode from which they are unable to break free.

Perseveration may echo deep-seated infantile needs for security, consistency and reassurance that stem from the primal relationship with the mother who is responsible for gratifying these needs. A child who perseverates may be attempting to reclaim these unmet needs symbolically. Through repetition, the child may be attempting to work through or resolve some important incident, object, person or other issue that has a compelling significance. Some special needs children tend to react to these issues by obsessing over them. Perseveration becomes a common vehicle for express-

ing their concerns through their behavior and their art. Although perseveration is almost certainly pleasureful and reassuring for the child, it usually represents an aesthetic and expressive dead end in the child's creative and mental growth.

In cases where repetition is purely compulsive, the teacher must work toward freeing up the artistic style by means of cautious, non-confrontational interventions which appreciate what perseveration signifies for the special needs child. Art teachers should bear in mind Robbins' axiom (1987) that although we cannot take away their insecurities and anxieties through our interventions, we can provide a psychologically safe space which encourages children to take new risks by abandoning stereotypes. This safe environment reflects the rapprochement stage of development during which the child will not explore unless he or she is confident in the maternal object's attentiveness and accessability. As the art educator supports this process, he or she allows the child to experience such confidence which in turn promotes the maturation process.

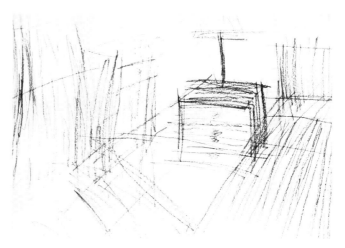

Perseveration usually suggests the incapacity to expand one's expression or behavior. The multiply handicapped boy of ten obsessed over interior spaces that were usually devoid of human presence.

Perseveration in artwork can take many forms. The varied forms are often amazing in their ingenuity and persistence. They are often created over extended periods of time, despite the best interventions. Not all perseveration is narrowly focused repetition that exhibits poor aesthetic sensibility and impoverished expressiveness. There are students who can use repetition in an obsessive, yet graphically powerful way. In such a case, the incessant use of one image or one style becomes an effective design device which may reconcile the element of perseveration. Indeed, it is a particularly sticky area for the teacher when a child's artistic style is at once perseverative and aesthetically interesting. Perseveration can be an active and effective element in artwork. Should the fact that a child is handicapped preclude him or her from using repetition as a stylistic device?

One multiply handicapped child I work with perseverates strictly upon buildings in various stages of construction and interior rooms. He has always worked in his kinesthetic, scribbling style, using architectural elements as the basis for his work. His prolific output is outstanding. It is not unusual for him to create fifty drawings per week in art class, within two ninety-minute periods.

Although this student's work was stylistically highly developed, it remained locked into autistic isolation. Human figures were conspicuously absent. Despite his impaired object relations, however, this boy eventually developed a rapport with his art teachers and art therapy interns, which in turn led to cautious exploration of human figures in his architectural interiors. His first introduction of human figures in his work was through televised images or pictures adorning the walls. In this ingenious manner, this child's perseveration with non-living objects slowly began to expand, based on a secure relationship with his instructors. As these people began to be increasingly part of his artistic life, they eventually attained life in his art.

Children with special needs will often stay with images, themes or ideas, that stem from their physical or emotional problems. It is up to the teacher to make the crucial decision whether the

This same ten-year-old began to cautiously populate his drawings with semi-animate humans in the form of televised images or portraits which hang on the wall.

perseveration requires intervention or should simply be allowed to be expressed. In the hands of a gifted artist, repetition is one of the most powerful graphic devices available in the visual vocabulary. Simply because it is a style which is often used by children with special needs, it should not be immediately perceived as something deficient or negative. However, as a barometer for motivational and artistic growth, perseveration is a displacement vehicle for anxiety. It rarely possesses the dynamicism and expansiveness one would associate with sublimation and fully formed expression.

DENIAL

Denial is one of the more primitive reactions that is often unconsciously used by emotionally handicapped children to defend against trauma. Through denial, the child creates an often impenetrable wall between the self and the source of the anxiety. Such a reaction may be dangerously delusional when the child rigidly and desperately adheres to some false premise in order to ward off an unwelcomed truth.

One young man with multiple handicaps ordinarily created artwork relatively unaffected by his physical handicap. His work was characterized by modes of transportation such as planes and ships, drawn in an accurate and neutral style. Toward the end of his senior year, however, the specter of graduation loomed over him, precipitating a crisis. What would he do with his life? A sheltered workshop was an unappetizing vocation for such a hardworking, perceptive young man. Disturbingly, his art began to run parallel to his emotional upheaval, with increasing references to himself in executive positions which virtually denied his handicap. In later pictures his delusions became ever more grandiose with portraits of himself as an airline pilot. These drawings were also supported by an equally unrealizable verbal claims: that, indeed, these were positions that were completely attainable as far as he was concerned. Only the most gentle discussion and probing allowed the staff to penetrate this pathetic fantasy. This constant support and reassuring approach allowed the boy to begin to accept his limitations. In one of his later works, it was clear that he was still displacing the conflict with elements of denial, yet he seemed to be processing his situation. While he still imagines himself in the cockpit of a airliner, he concedes that a sighted copilot must accompany him. This insight was followed by others, until eventually he would demonstrate at least a reluctant acceptance of his limitations without abandoning his hope for a brighter future.

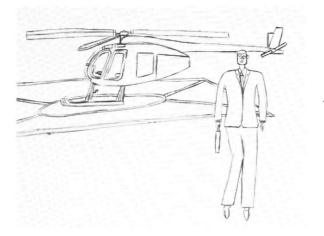

Denial is among the most primitive and dangerous of defense mechanisms. This young deaf/blind man unrealistically imagined himself becoming a jet-set executive. Numerous drawings of him in glamorous settings were created based on this delusional theme.

Eventually, this blind man began to acknowledge that he needed the assistance of a sighted person. Here he depicts himself in the cockpit with a sighted co-pilot, a first indication that his denial is giving way to a more realistic assessment of his handicap.

SEXUAL ISSUES IN ARTWORK

Gender Confusion

Preadolescence is a phase in child development when children are exploring their sexuality. As adolescents go through a myriad of somatic and psychological changes, they sometimes lack a coherent sense of self. As they strive to meet all the expectations set for them during this period, they may not possess the ego strength to cope—thus, they react in different ways. Often they will latch on to stereotypes which act as sexual role models. Or, they may regress into states of confusion which are reflected in their art in distorted, omitted or over-emphasized anatomical details. In any event, the art of latent or preadolescent students is often sexually charged and stands as an apt barometer to show how effectively the child is coping with this time of hormonal and social turmoil.

Ordinarily, when a student is asked during an art assignment to create a picture of a person, they will draw someone of their own gender. Should there be unresolved conflicts concerning their sexuality, they may draw the opposite sex, or distorted figures who possess characteristics of both sexes. Such expression may not be any cause for alarm or warrant any intervention beyond the teacher's support and understanding. However, should a child exhibit aberrant behaviors, such as inappropriate promiscuity, pornographic obsessions or a sustained silliness over the subject, then our attention might be turned to the issue. Addressing the issue does not infer, however, that the child should receive sex counseling while in the artroom. Interventions can be devised that center around the art process and serve to bolster self-identification, esteem and confidence as well as strengthening boundaries between self and others, all with the ultimate goal of addressing the sexual confusion. This process usually moves forward if and when the child can form a positive identification with healthy adults and peers.

For example, when a withdrawn, yet angry young man, who had in the past been punished for isolated incidents of aggressive and sexual behavior, was asked to draw a person, he responded with an opposite-sexed mermaid. According to Norse mythology the mermaid is a nurturing, love-inspired figure. This rendition, however, suggested a witch-like creature, whose malevolent face, hardened breasts and stunted hands are chilling in their effect. The entire composition perched precariously on a knife-like line of transparent water.

This emotionally handicapped boy rendered even the most nurturing sensual figures as malevolent and witch-like. He often drew these half-woman, half-mythical creatures instead of the usual gender identification pictures of sports heroes or other male role models which are the common subject for teenage boys.

Later, this same boy drew another gruesome figure which supposedly depicted one of his peers drawn in caricature. The monstrous features of this figure suggest displacement of sadistic sexual and violent impulses. More alarming, however, is the dual treatment of the gender: both male and female genitalia are prominent in both the nose and crotch, while overt femininity is portrayed in the pocketbook and Lord Fauntleroy suit.

As a teacher, my response to each of these two works was markedly different. The mermaid was drawn privately, without the expectation that it would be exhibited. The student begrudgingly showed it to me; he seemed embarrassed and a little disgusted over its content. I accepted this piece tentatively and explained that I had some suggestions that might strengthen the piece aesthetically, then I left it at that. However, my response to the caricature was much less accepting. Because it was an inappropriate forum for acting out (since it was based upon ridicule), I immediately confiscated it, remarking, "I don't think you can handle drawing the human figure today." He offered no resistance, but he took my meaning accurately and probably felt relieved that no punishment was forthcoming.

In trying to address this situation, I later asked this student whether there was anyone in his life, past or present, about whom he felt positive. After a prolonged silence in which he seemed to be taking inventory, he remarked that there was one person, a coach in a community basketball program who had taken an interest in him. I then asked him to describe this coach's qualities and how he might somehow be able to emulate them. I encouraged him to draw this image, so that he was better able to visualize and subsequently incorporate some of these qualities. The coach was drawn in action, with appropriate features, affect and body image. While somewhat stiff and heavy in line, the drawing nonetheless served as an excellent point of departure for working in a style that was more sexually neutral. The next step was to encourage the young man to depict himself working under the tutelage of this coach, which in effect cemented the

identification between them in a positive, productive and more enjoyable way. By moving this student in a direction that promoted a healthy identification and emotional investment in a role model, both behavior and artwork benefited. While the first pieces were permeated with the confusion and intense feeling indicative of displacement, the student's final figures indicated sublimation. As this boy developed a healthy identification, his art became increasingly neutral, yet retained the forceful elements suggestive of sublimation.

The same young man created this monstrous creature which exhibits male and female attributes.

Responding to a request to draw someone who had a positive effect upon him, this student drew his basketball coach. His rendering of the coach helped him in emphasizing the positive male role models in his life.

Drawing Nudes

On an art festival field trip to a local university, female middle school students were touring the studio facilities when they happened upon a life-drawing class that was using a nude model. Excitedly, they marveled over how the college students sat impassively with a mature woman disrobed before them. They formed a consensus that they would like to try this in their own life-drawing classes. In response, I asked them whether they too could maintain the seriousness and self-control needed to deal with such a stimulating topic. This motivational strategy challenged the children to rise to the occasion. They assured me that they could handle the project. I first supplied the students with magazine cutouts of abstract compositions using male and female forms. I issued the female-oriented images and told the class that if they could get through this exercise, they could then switch genders if they preferred. Although these fourteen-year-olds were painfully preadolescent, and highly sensitive to sexual issues, they were able to remain neutral and attentive during this project. Since they considered maturity to be a highly regarded peer value, only a few students acted out over the nudes. Although they exercised excellent self-control, they also maintained a sense of humor, making a few well-meaning jokes which I tolerated in order to keep the pressure and intensity at a low ebb. In the process, these students were challenged to experience the human body in abstract and aesthetic terms rather than as an object of sexual arousal. Andrew Wyeth's "Helga" nudes subsequently became great favorites with this class as a source of art history motivation. Since Wyeth painted his nudes with a kind of clinical detachment, it tended to neutralize some of the overt sexual connotation. Thus, material of this kind might be chosen for its ability to keep sexual stimulation to a minimum, while emphasizing design elements and gestural sensitivity of the nude figure.

It took exceedingly firm control of the students to insure that arousal was minimized. While such repression in the form of threats of discontinuing

After studying Wyeth's Helga nudes, this middle school girl painted many nude studies without silliness or even embarrassment.

the activity may appear to stifle the opportunity to work through and thus sublimate this material, it was necessary if the project was to be appropriate for this population. In this age group, the sublimation of highly charged subject matter may be an unreasonable goal.

Sexual Inhibition

Occasionally the teacher may encounter a student who is physically mature but whose artwork minimizes or neglects sexuality to an unusual degree. While in many cases the teacher may not take issue with the student's need to repress sexual fantasies or impulses, there are cases when such repres-

Some special needs children are intensely inhibited by sexual issues. Without stirring up these feelings, the teacher can attempt to promote normal social interactions between genders. These two comic strips by a gifted, hearing impaired girl explore these issues in a humorous way, thus lessening the anxiety they might produce.

sion inhibits a student from exercising full creative authority. A human figure does exhibit sexual and gender characteristics and for a student to deny them on a consistent basis may warrant intervention. Great care and sensitivity must be taken in such a situation so as not to inappropriately or irresponsibly stir up feelings in the child that he or she is not ready to deal with.

One such case involved a young woman of sixteen who was a gifted cartoon artist. Her rendering of the human figure was consistently androgynous, even when departing from the comic strip format. Her figures were whimsically drawn cartoon figures involving aliens, animals, toys or other sexless creatures. Most of her female figures were usually sexless, with a few depicted in the latency stage, as prepubescent girls still attached to

dolls or pets. While such immaturity could well be accommodated in behavioral or even social terms, it had a disturbing and somewhat stifling affect upon this student's artistic ability, especially in light of her formidable skills.

As a beginning intervention to address this issue, I suggested that the student teacher encourage this student to draw some girls from teen magazines. (These figures were at once sensual and feminine, yet were innocently portrayed and not overtly sexual.) Over a period of months, this student was given more mature, yet equally neutral magazines, such as *Redbook*. She was encouraged to draw exactly what she saw in the form and style of the illustrator. In this exercise the student teacher attempted to move this student gently through the developmental milestones beyond that of sexual denial. Concentrating on figurative work had a positive effect upon her capacity to begin to explore sexual issues securely and appropriately. Her art similarly benefited by exhibiting greater exuberance and affective intensity which was socially age-appropriate.

Obsession, Distortion and Object Loss

An emotionally handicapped girl of twelve had been creating numerous landscapes, still lifes and figurative studies, all rendered in a naive and somewhat stereotypical style. During the school year, her teacher became pregnant. During this period, the child's work became obsessed with gestation and fetal development, to the point of excluding all other subject matter. These strangely distorted figures were created for a period of four weeks, during which time, she explored the sequences of pregnancy in a static, perseverative manner. I was not so concerned about the symbolic nature of this obsession. It might have been fuelled by the loss of an important person in her life, or possibly she was trying to reconcile physiological processes that were both obscure and threatening. No one can be sure how this near-psychotic child perceived the business of procreation, fetal development and childbirth. As someone who had defective object relations—as evidenced in her difficulties in testing and maintaining an accurate sense of reality—it is possible that she thought anyone could, at any moment, become magically impregnated. More than once she pointedly asked whether she, or even I, had a baby growing inside.

To dispel this confusion and attempt to neutralize what was becoming an overriding issue for this student, I suggested a number of approaches to her artwork. After one of her poorly differentiated figures was drawn, I assisted her in placing it in a comprehensible, reality-oriented context. Thus, an isolated, distorted figure was placed at the doctor's office for a check-up, or sitting at home with a husband, or on a visit to her classroom to show off the new baby. All of these contexts reinforced the idea that procreation was a normal physiological process engaged in by adults who would be happy to share the joy of their newborn. It was not a magical, insidious occurrence wrapped in physical violation, malignancy or abandonment. By grounding her ideas in an emotionally neutral and rational context, this girl was able to advance her object relations to the extent that her artwork

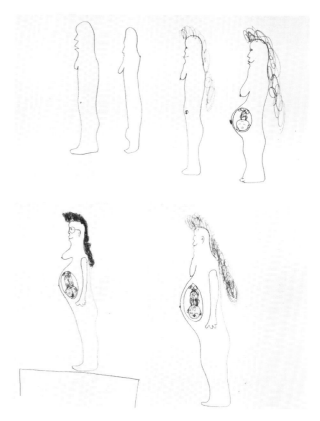

This autistic girl became obsessed with procreation and fetal development after her pregnant teacher took a pregnancy leave from school. She became delusional and imagined that she too was pregnant through countless images that depict the different stages of pregnancy.

could once again move forward without the obsession that had arrested her progress. Her artwork falls short of sublimation, given the delicate state of her ego and its capacity to appraise the reality of a situation. Despite her psychological immaturity, however, the child was able to address the issue sufficiently so that it was no longer a major source of anxiety. Therefore, we might regard her work as being indicative of precursory sublimative activity, given its sense of problem solving, self-control and straightforward treatment of what was once loaded subject matter.

Using Kramer's Third Hand technique, the pregnancy obsession was addressed by assisting this girl in devising symbolic resolutions to her disturbing ideas.

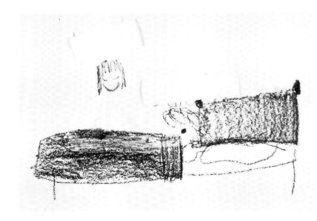

This disturbing picture portrayed the purported seduction of this ten-year-old autistic child by her babysitter. It was found later to be a fabricated story despite its realistic depiction.

Child Abuse

One of the more painful and upsetting issues to deal with as a teacher is the incidence of child abuse. Sexual, physical and mental harassment by adult relatives, siblings, and even teachers is an all-too-common occurrence, and evidence of abuse will surface occasionally in the art of the abused child. While the teacher cannot ascertain the occurrence of abuse simply on the grounds of the artwork, there may be changes in the child's behavior or indications of physical injury that suggest abuse.

It is very important to realize that although a child may be producing artwork that is suggestive of sexual or physical harassment, it may be wholly fantasy. Discriminating between a child's rich and active fantasy life and real experiences can be a slippery problem at best (as Freud discovered when he developed—and later revised—his seduction theory). The teacher must exercise extreme caution in even bringing up suspicions with administrators. However, should a teacher be confronted with overt references to sexual abuse, it is his or her responsibility to alert those administrators who are responsible for initiating the proper course of action.

In one case I encountered, a ten-year-old girl with prior emotional problems graphically portrayed images of herself being molested by a teenage babysitter. She drew the sitter standing over her in bed in a direct reference to being seduced. In another piece, she drew the two scratching each other in bed. I became alarmed when these works became increasingly graphic and realistic in their narrative. They seemed too well-embellished with too many details to be solely fantasy material. After alerting my supervisor, I was asked to write up my impressions of the case, especially with regard to whether the artwork was a manifestation of fantasy or the grim recollections of actual fact. Ultimately it was up to the administration to follow through, with my role being one of objective yet responsive concern.

In another example, the seduction was already an established fact. This six-year-old girl had been abused since the age of three and though she was now mainstreamed in a regular classroom, she still was extremely fragile emotionally. She would usually work in a normal, productive fashion with the class, but on occasion would regress to seriously disturbed behavior. What was so fascinating about this case is that the child was able to anticipate these periods of regression and would communicate this via her artwork. It was one of the few cases in my experience where a child so young, and so emotionally at risk, was able to muster sufficient control and insight, to give an artistic early warning of an approaching period of regression. In the last incident she drew a small house which floated aimlessly through the air, belching smoke from every window. This child never made overt sexual reference to her abuse (although she was well aware of it and could articulate it verbally with a psychotherapist). As her art teacher, I did nothing to stir up memories or elicit sexual material during our sessions. Yet this image of a house overwhelmed by a sky of grey smoke clouds recurred in this child's work like a tenacious night terror.

This was a case where I hesitated to intervene to modify the image, since the child was exceedingly adamant about leaving it unchanged. It was as though she needed this avenue of cathartic release, and, once created, the anguish accompanying this image was dispelled, allowing her to return to her other studio work without obsessing over this one, upsetting image.

For some children, relating to others at home, school or in public constitutes a threatening, upsetting experience. Because these students are reluctant to interact with people, their art constitutes a vital release of expression as well as communication. Individuals with autism, conduct disorders, social pathology and psychosis can give constructive form to their ideas and feelings through the art process without being harassed or confronted. Indeed, many of these children take refuge in their art for precisely this reason. It is important for the art teacher to recognize these interpersonal problems as they surface in the artwork so that he or she can better anticipate and hopefully address them through the appropriate art educational or therapeutic interventions.

AUTISTIC WITHDRAWAL

Whether caused by neurological damage or emotional trauma, autism remains a most profound interpersonal dysfunction. Autistic individuals may have an aversion to their teachers, therapists and peers, as well as their parents and siblings. Why these children react with such profound intolerance and repugnance toward others remains speculation. Regardless of autism's enigmatic nature, autistic pictorial expression may manifest itself in clearly discernable, sometimes powerful terms. Such strong autistic expression challenges the teacher to respond in ways that cultivate the artistic expression while also attempting to mollify the extent of the child's isolation and fear.

In severest cases, an autistic child may function on a level equal to a low-functioning, mentally retarded child. Given the extent of the developmental arrest, the child will probably not be able to work in a representational style. In these cases, the artwork is similar to that of the mentally retarded, with random semi-controlled configurations being elicited after much teacher effort. Such creations are often obsessional, self-stimulatory or perseverative and are symptomatic of primitive and infantile defense mechanisms. Often the images created by autistic students allude to their incapacity to accept or thrive upon maternal care. They compensate by focusing all their attention on inanimate objects which are invested with the affect usually reserved for family or friends. This obsession provides the autistic individual with the sameness, predictability and control that is not forthcoming in interactions with people. Such a preoccupation can carry over into the child's thought processes to the extent that one autistic young man once casually told me, "I was made in

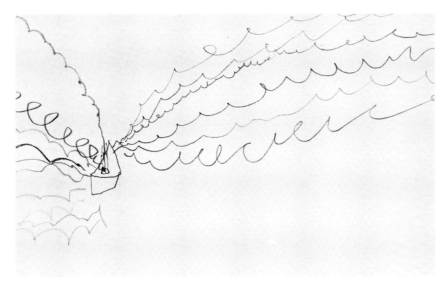

This sexually abused child portrays her house as always "burning down, killing everyone inside." Such portrayals provided cathartic release for pent-up emotions.

This high school senior often drew upon her memories of being sexually molested, recalling even the times when such abuse occurred. Given the disturbing content of these works, they were used during sessions with the school social worker.

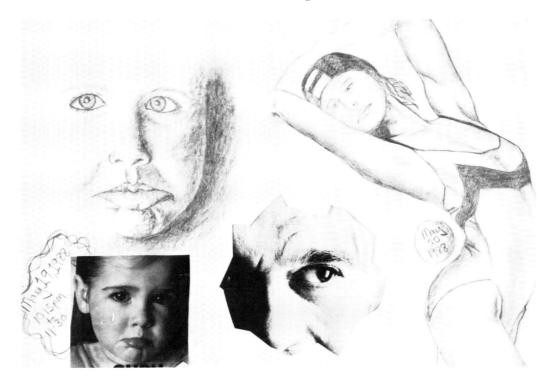

a factory you know, I'm really a machine." Such an acknowledgment testifies to the lengths to which the mind will delude itself so as to avoid a painful reality. This pattern is most evident at the upper end of the developmental scale, where it is not uncommon to see representational artwork from the hands of autistic individuals who possess intact or near-normal intelligence. In these works the most conspicuous element is an absence of human forms and interactions (Bettleheim 1972).

One young man's work was dominated by a proliferation of mechanical objects. Such a choice of subject matter was not arbitrary or casual; this young man of twenty took refuge in the world of electronic gadgetry—both in his art and in his interests outside of the studio. Over the course of two years of art therapy, this autistic artist graduated from machinery to human figures who interestingly, retained an object-like mechanical quality. His use of metaphor in this piece is significant, as he evokes a sense of body armour in which he can survey the world while remaining impervious to the eyes of others. This young man eventually did begin to humanize his human figures after consistent, long term art therapy on an individual and small-group basis. The pivotal factor in this process was his ability to feel accepted by me and to feel secure in the studio environment. Once he was able to make this crucial attachment and thus form a therapeutic alliance, he was able to translate this newly formed relationship into his art. Eventually his alliance allowed him to move developmentally away from me as a quasi-maternal figure, so as to see himself for the first time as a truly individualized entity. In his final work before graduation, he created his first and last self-portrait. Shunning even the indirect confrontation of looking into a mirror, he methodically felt his own body and face, then, reconstructed his impressions in a graduation context. This culminating piece effectively conveys a many-faceted metaphor based upon a rite of passage, as the artist finds himself mastering developmental milestones which had remained unmet from infancy. Graduation from

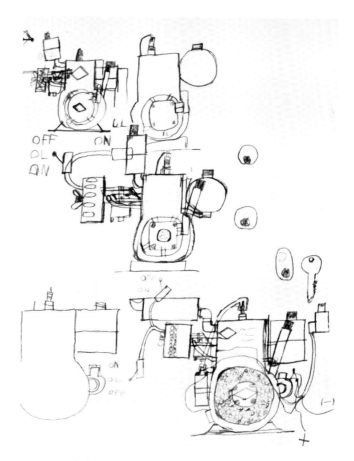

Autistic children often omit any reference to people in their behavior and artwork. In his art this gifted boy obsessed about mechanical objects with prolific and proficient facility.

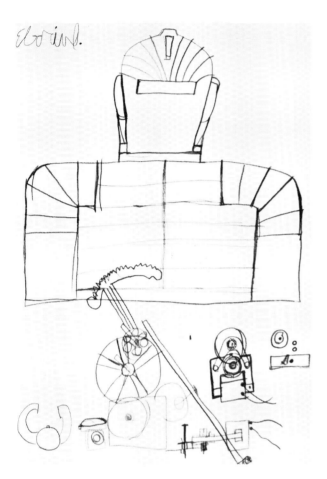

One of this gifted, autistic boy's first figures re-ferred directly to his autistic shell, which pro-tects him from anxiety-provoking interactions with people. Note the armored figure who is face-less, uncommunicative and otherworldly.

After several years of art education therapy this autistic boy finally began to render figures. In his last piece before graduation, he depicts himself in cap and gown, ready to enter a frightening, alien world.

school seemed to coincide with the achievement of object constancy, as he gained the startling realiza-tion that he certifiably existed as a person. The portrait attests to a sense of self-discovery as the figure peers out at the viewer with a shocked and somewhat pained expression. The prospect of ac-tually confronting this new person was indeed an alien and unsettling experience. This metaphor was carried through in its most literal form, for during the graduation ceremony I was amazed to see that this portrait accompanied him up to the podium as he collected his diploma.

Poor differentiation of self-boundaries marks this bizarre figure study by a young man with symbiotic psychosis. This rare disorder is characterized by a pathological attachment to the mother. The two figures appear to be merging or mirror images of each other.

A psychotic delusional system with uniquely elaborated elements convey the depth of paranoia and hallucinations that plagued this student's emotional life.

Problem with Symbiotic Ties and Separation

Separation reactions which assume severe forms may result in symbiotic psychosis (Mahler 1968). One such case involved a Down syndrome young man whose relationship to his mother and sister was so enmeshed that his figurative imagery was consistently in a state of merging. One of his pictures depicted the two figures literally tied in a symbiotic union, with each face mirroring the other. Throughout this young man's art therapy program, focus was on facilitating separation and building self-concept and a sense of empowerment that was not so dependent upon the females in his family. This was, however, an excruciatingly slow process. Caution was not only required when addressing the issue with the student, but also when working with the family. Understandably, they sheltered their retarded child in such a way that successful separation was thwarted until they understood that such coddling was destructive to the boy's emotional development.

Psychosis

Although psychotic children are rarely mainstreamed in public schools, the art educator and particularly the art therapist will encounter them in therapeutic day schools or hospital settings. Art educational interventions can assist in grounding a child's thought and feeling systems through the support and motivation process. However, delving into delusional systems requires expertise in unconscious processes that may be beyond the scope of therapeutic art education.

THE CHRONICALLY ANGRY CHILD

For whatever reason, some children possess a constant, indefatigable amount of anger which often simmers until some precipitating event causes it to explode. Children most severely afflicted are unlikely to produce much of anything in the artroom. There might be much scribbling, paint smearing, clay pounding or other forms of aggressive/regressive displacement during the sessions, but these activities will usually preclude the possibility of creating a product. Even if such an angry child is able to integrate sufficiently so as to manipulate the medium in a meaningful and productive way, a new set of problems may present themselves. Because the aggressive child is struggling to maintain control of his or her impulses, the artwork is likely to be tightly defended. Stereotypes often appear in the work, as the pendulum swings from the impulsive to the constricted. Overcoming such defenses is, of course, tricky at best, since the teacher is attempting to defuse a kind of time bomb—one false move and the constrictedness unwinds with terrific force. It becomes imperative that the teacher view the artwork with genuine interest, support and empathy, so that the child can feel sufficiently secure to loosen up artistic style without loosening self-control. Here again, defensive stereotypes, cartoons, media figures and written narratives can all be expected until the child demonstrates the readiness to put some affect into his or her art. The teacher must remain poised to applaud this occasion, especially if it is accompanied by reasonably appropriate behavior. It is during these episodes where intense affect is balanced with self-control that sublimation becomes a possibility.

One twenty-year-old young woman drew a stereotypical stick figure with an intensely aggressive quality. This figure was preceded by a highly agitated regressive circular scribbling that literally embossed the paper by virtue of the pen's pressure. This piece functioned as a viable alternative to aggressive release. In subsequent sessions, this young woman tirelessly scribbled out these intense

Overcome with rage, this chronically angry child invests her stick figure with uncommon intensity of feeling. Finally she broke down during the sketch and reverted back to aggressive infantile scribbling.

little figures, displacing vasts amounts of assaultive affect. While she never got past this act of displacement, it did have the direct effect of lessening her seriously disturbed behavior—a considerable enough achievement in light of her handicaps.

Along the same lines, another young man—who was mentally retarded as well as emotionally handicapped—consistently drew one style of stick figure. These figures were depicted floating in large flocks, their fingers outstretched in a ghostly fashion. Efforts to wean this eighteen-year-old from the stereotype had proven ineffective. His explosive behavior was much feared at the school. A change came spontaneously, however, when the young man's mother failed to show up at his residential school for their weekly visit. Anticipating an incident of the worst kind, the staff put him in

After his mother missed her bi-monthly visitation, this mentally retarded boy was overcome with rage. After calming him down, I gave him a black scratch board upon which to vent his anger. The result is this powerful image.

The processing of issues can also be accomplished via art. This boy recounted his run-in with the principal by citing a mythical devil as the source of his problems.

I get mad when....

"supervised seclusion." Since it was his studio time-slot, I felt compelled to offer him materials despite the probability that he might lose his temper. Miraculously he picked up a pencil and, inverting it, began to aggressively scratch into black sgraffito paper using the metal ferule (after he bit off the eraser). In his first departure from his stereotypic style, the figure's body was dispensed with; its head now howled while sitting atop something akin to a chopping block. The urgency, pain and graphic intensity infused this work with a power unrivaled by the art this student made while in a calm state. Such a compelling and hauntingly beautiful image approaches sublimation, given its economy of means, evocative feeling and technical control. It is one of the few instances in my experience when such a low-functioning child had achieved this distinction.

POST-TRAUMATIC REACTIONS

It is not uncommon for school psychologists and counselors to use art as a means of working through reactions of fear, grief and other emotions when their students have experienced a traumatic event. By drawing about the incident, it is hoped that the children are given a measure of cathartic relief while they exercise the trauma and contain it within an external and selectively safe place. Their reliving of the event through symbolic means allows for the ventilation of feelings as well as the opportunity to exercise control and gain mastery over the situation.

Several years ago NASA's space shuttle Challenger blew up before the eyes of thousands of school children. This was a horrible enough experience for the normal child who is relatively emotionally stable and intellectually intact. For special needs children who may not be able to separate fact from fantasy, such a nightmarish disaster may assume enormous proportions. Such was the case when I was called in to attempt to allay the fears of several classes of normal and handicapped children who had witnessed the launch on television.

After the space shuttle's disastrous destruction, these boys drew upon their own experience of this traumatic event. In the first drawing, the approach is more emotional, while in the second, the intention is to "try again" and to "fix" the ship "so it never happens again."

Most were only too glad to draw this event. I began by allowing them to draw whatever came to mind concerning the exploding ship. For this purpose many used pastels and crayons to communicate the flash of fire and smoke against the brilliant blue, Florida sky. I then requested that they make a second drawing in which they imagined the shuttle in a redesigned "safe" version. The drawings that were elicited were beset with mechanical problems which I went around and assisted the students in repairing until most felt they had a serviceable shuttle ready for launch.

The objective, of course, was to first allow for the free expression of grief, shock and terror in the hopes that the children would benefit from such a release. The second exercise—which draws upon Kramer's method of the "Third Hand"—aimed at mollifying the children's fear, concentrating instead on how the shuttle will be made safer and again fly into space under less stressful and upsetting conditions.

A high school girl's depression is recounted in this picture of "a long, dark and scary hallway in which a figure crawls along in fright."

DEPRESSED REACTIONS

Eliciting artwork from children who are depressed can be an agonizing experience. Defeatism, apathy, anger, sadness can all diminish the urge to create. With the appropriate motivation, however, many children eventually respond, and in the process explore their emotions in quite poignant terms. For instance, a high school senior with major depression spent months hospitalized in a lethargic state. She made a positive identification with a female art therapist who recounted her own bout of depression. Inspired by this testimonial, the patient began to explore her own fears and sadness in shadowy charcoal drawings. By giving form to her feelings some release was possible. In one case, an already clinically depressed child of eleven was hospitalized during the separation of his parents which had left him devastated further. Indifferent, impenetrable, and hostile if pressed, he worked only begrudgingly until he saw an old *National Geographic* with a story on the climbing of Mt. Everest. In therapy, his therapist had evidently likened a depression to climbing out of a deep hole. In a flash of insight, he applied this idea to the assault on the great mountain in the Himalayas. Seizing the initiative, he attempted to draw himself engaged in this great undertaking.

While engaged in the task of illustrating the climb, he began to falter. As he painted the great brown mass of the mountain, he inadvertently painted over the tiny figure depicting himself. Thus, the meek, ineffectual child was already vanquished by the great mountain. I urged the boy to redraw the figure. Using the Kramer "Third Hand," together we reworked the climber, this time large enough to become a factor in the composition. Although he painted himself virtually swamped with brown, he managed to give the figure some contrast by painting over the shirt in yellow. He then painted a menacing patch of snow and ice under the figure's feet, remarking "Now I'll slip for sure." I countered by asking him whether there was anything we could do to save this climber from slipping. He then decided to

After he drew himself dangling off a mountain, I encouraged this depressed and suicidal child that a life line might help make his task of overcoming the climb safer.

paint in a lifeline from which he would be safely suspended. Although I saw this as a viable solution, the boy went on to paint in the most tenuous, blood-red, liquidy line imaginable—one that wouldn't hold anything safely. Again I intervened, helping him thicken the rope and thus assisting in giving his endeavor a chance of succeeding.

In the end both of us were exhausted, having painted and repainted this piece so that it served as a fitting, upbeat metaphor for his successful treatment of his depression. In this case, Kramer's

"Third Hand" interventions acted to unobtrusively support the child during the art process, enabling him to derive a measure of mastery and control through the successful outcome of his artwork. This was a case where both the child and the teacher knew what the stakes were in reaching this goal. Luckily in this instance, the victorious mountain climber served as a symbolic equivalent for the child's outlook on therapy.

chapter 13

Assessment

In attempting to evaluate the performance of the special needs child, two considerations must be undertaken. First, assessment tools must be developed that address all facets of the child's functioning, including motivation, skill development, behavior, aesthetic expressivity and affect. Secondly, while a child's exceptionality should be accommodated, there also must be some emphasis upon maintaining expectations of performance. Unless we prompt the child to participate, to control impulses and to reflect upon his or her work and behavior, little creative or mental growth can be expected. This is, of course, a sometimes conflicted process which pits the exceptionality of the child and the subjectivity of the artwork against some measure of normative comparison. This assessment may measure the student against individualized goals or peer-group objectives. Whichever, it provides a standard by which the teacher can gauge a student's movement in the program. The goals and objectives that are established in the different domains of functioning must somehow reflect the enormous complexity and the mystery of the art process. It is not enough to simply record which skill was mastered at what time or which colors can now be recognized. Exceptional children who never master areas such as color theory or motor skills such as scissor usage may go on to create interesting images. Some of the most remarkable paintings I have ever seen were created by a child who knew nothing of primary colors, perspective or other rules of composition. Yet his interior spaces with their incongruous color values

and the multiple uses of perspective imparted a vigor and boldness rarely seen in work done by an eleven-year-old.

Many practitioners continue to use Lowenfeld's Developmental Approach (1957) for assessing the child's stage of functioning. It is indeed pertinent and helpful to be able to identify at what stage a child is currently functioning, since it gives the teacher a point of reference. Such a point assists in planning strategy, so that we can assist the child to move through the developmental milestones toward greater maturation through the art process. However, does such a framework tell us anything further about the child and his or her art? We can assume, for example, that the mentally retarded Down syndrome child may remain mired in the preschematic stage of artistic development. Does this articulate anything about the richness and expressivity of his or her art? Does such a categorization indicate the formulation of unique and fresh solutions to a timeworn problem? What about the extent to which his self-concept and image have been enhanced through the successes gained through his or her art experiences? Seen in this context, the developmental approach popularized by Lowenfeld is limited to cognitive and maturational growth and may not have a bearing upon the nature or breadth of a child's artistic capacities.

On the other hand, a child may be skillful at creating images in what appears to be a highly evolved style, yet such precocity may be misleading. The famous autistic child savant Nadia, despite her precocity, was locked into a narrow sub-

Objectifying such intangibles as caustic humor, rebelliousness or absurdity is part of the challenge of determining the success of the art object. This precocious seventh grader made grading a particularly distasteful event.

ject matter that could be considered suffocatingly obsessive. Images of great draftsmanship were repeated without conventional indications of expansion or growth. A reasonable assessment in her case would focus more upon the static qualities of her work, rather than its sensational precocity. Severely disturbed, autistic, retarded and sensory-impaired children often perceive their environment in highly atypical ways. As a result, their impressions sometimes are projected through bizarre, eccentric, sometimes shocking images. Although these images reflect the child's disturbance or symptoms more than their facility as artists, does this discount the aesthetic viability of the artwork?

These questions are among the multitude that the teacher will encounter when attempting to assess artwork which may be disconcertingly bizarre or idiosyncratic. Assessment strategies must both accommodate and probe the dynamics of what the child is communicating through his or her art. Again, only by examining the different areas of a child's functioning can we gain insight into the child's art process and products. Without becom-

ing overly judgmental, sentimental or clinical, the teacher can assess a child's changes within the program through careful observation and detailed notation. Besides gaining insight into the child's dynamics, process notation can also evaluate instructional or therapeutic interventions for their appropriateness and effectiveness.

THE FIVE DOMAINS

The domains under consideration are: motivation, behavior, skill acquisition, aesthetic/expressivity and affect. By noting strengths and weaknesses in each of these areas, the teacher is able to isolate problems or exploit successes. Each domain provides specific information that can be plotted, gauged by graph or statistically analyzed. Although scientific rigor is expected in art education, it is vital that data be collected without sacrificing our humanistic values and traditions. Thus, the intent in these assessment tools is not to reduce the child to a list of characteristics or symptoms. The intention is to make the child come fully alive and to contribute increasingly effective and rational assessment strategies that benefit not the investigator but the child.

MOTIVATIONAL NOTATIONS

Child's Name: _____ Date: _____

Does the child display willingness and openness to participate?
Comment

enthusiastic, cooperative, compliant, interested, reticent, oppositional, withdrawn, resistant, resistant with eventual compliance.
Other _____
_____

Does the child initiate each step of the activity?
Comment

self-initiated, needs verbal motivation, needs physical demonstration, requests corrections on picture, needs prolonged attention.
Other _____
_____

What is the quality and level of task attention or concentration?
Comment

self-absorbed, intensive, compliant, perfunctory, distracted, distracted yet perservering, obsessive, obsessive yet productive, in need of redirection (number of cues _____ in _____ amount of time).
Other _____
_____

How long is interest sustained in the activity before necessitating a major change in medium, technique or theme?
Comment

No. of minutes:
120 90 60 40 20 15 10 5

Is the child able to devise theme, subject matter or appropriate solution to problem?
Comment

self-initiating, requires verbal motivation, requires audio-visual aides, other props or strategies _____.
Other _____
_____

Motivation

Without sufficient willingness to participate, a child may never advance toward gaining competency in skills or developing aesthetic awareness. Poor motivation can produce resistance, inhibition, withdrawal and acting-out behaviors. Therefore, it is crucial that the art teacher be attuned to the motivational status of the child and be skilled in applying those stimuli or strategies that best arouse a child's urge to create.

The checklist and narrative form (opposite) is designed to assess the nature and intensity of a child's motivation. It is set up for both quick notation and extensive narrative description of problems, successes and interventions. The structure of the form supports a least restrictive environment. Self-initiative, uninhibited participation, sustained interest and original elaboration of ideas receive the highest value. Should a child require additional stimulation or direction, these interventions are implemented in the most unobtrusive, least restricting way.

This motivational assessment can be adopted for different applications and populations. It can be used as an outline for a notation system, for writing narrative, for grading and for developing IEP (Individualized Education Plan) goals and objectives. The frequency of its use will also depend upon the reason for application.

The leading questions on this form can be answered in narrative form when used in grading. In question #1, a comment might be, "The child displays initiative and enthusiasm before most activities." If used in a more frequent application, such as weekly evaluations, simply encircling the closest descriptor might be all that is needed. Statistical data might be culled from this form by assigning numerical values to the different descriptors. One might create a scale which selects a few descriptors which would infer progress or regress. Thus, *enthusiastic* might be assigned a 5, *cooperative* a 4, *compliant* a 3, *reticent* a 2, and *resistant* a 1. In this way graphic representations of the child's motivation can be tallied and plotted as in the following model.

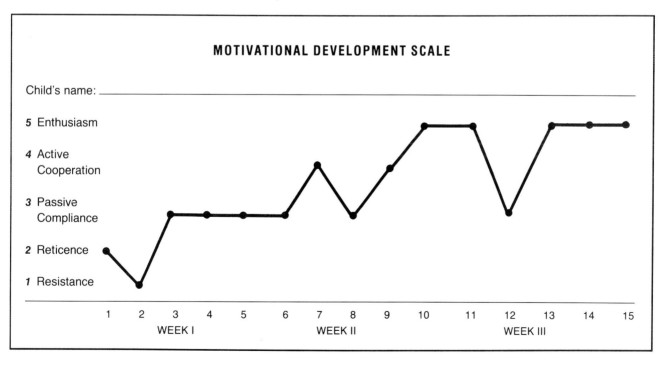

BEHAVIOR NOTATIONS

Name: _____ Date: _____

	SESSION				
	1	2	3	4	5
Behavior displayed upon entering studio	6	6	6	7	7
Behavior displayed during motivation and verbal instructions	6	6	7	7	8
Behavior displayed during material handouts	5	6	6	7	7
Behavior displayed sharing materials	6	6	7	3	7
Behavior displayed maintaining own workspace without transgressing	7	7	8	7	8
Behavior displayed during peer social interactions	7	7	7	7	7
Behavior displayed during reflection/criticism phase of session	5	5	7	7	7
Behavior displayed during cleanup procedures	5	5	5	6	7
Behavior displayed exiting art studio	N/A				

Please elaborate: *Student requires preventive cuing to maintain impulse control particularly during least-structured time during session.*

Numerical Code
8 Appropriate: Independent
7 Appropriate: Independent with cues
6 Appropriate: Requires monitoring & special structure
5 Disruptive: Isolated incident/cooperative after cues
4 Disruptive: Requires individual seating (rest of session)
3 Disruptive: Requires minimal stimulation area 10, 15, 20 minutes, rest of session
2 Disruptive: Requires time out 10, 15, 20, 30 minutes, rest of session
1 Disruptive: Requires removal from session

Behavior

The behavior of a child has far-reaching consequences in the art studio. A child who is well-adjusted, energetic, socially appropriate and cooperative has increased chances of having a successful art experience. Those who are withdrawn, listless, aggressive, oppositional or disruptive will most likely have a negative experience. Behavior becomes an issue most frequently when it interferes with peers and staff who are trying to maintain a pleasant, upbeat and cooperative atmosphere in the studio. Infringing upon another's right to learn and work constitutes a restrictive environment. Therefore, infractions of class rules, disruptions, or other acting-out behaviors, vandalism against artwork, tools and media, all conspire to destroy a positive creative environment. To a lesser degree, behaviors which have only personal consequences for a child's own performance are also at issue. The child who exhibits inhibited, distracted, frustrated, angry or indifferent behaviors will also display diminished productivity and social interactions. While such behaviors are less likely to be punished or acted upon by the teacher, they do warrant attention and intervention. These child/staff and child/peer interactions should at least be noted so that changes in social emotional adjustment can be tracked over the short and long term.

Behavior notations may be scaled and adapted in response to different situations. Obviously, if a child has been a consistently well-adapted and well-behaved individual, there may not be any reason to plot behavior. However should some precipitating stress factor change this, the teacher might be asked to monitor and document the child's changing needs in the classroom. This behavior notation system follows the sequence of least restrictive interventions. It plots how much freedom a child can manage in the classroom and how well he or she responds to the interventions or cues of the teacher.

Skill Acquisition

Because of the objective nature of the skill acquisition domain, teachers rely upon a comprehensive checklist which identifies a target skill and the extent to which the child has demonstrated competency. In most cases, the teacher will devise a checklist for each project, using the task-analysis format. This should be modified to reflect the chronological and mental age of the child, with consideration given to the social factors discussed in the section on structuring the art process. In devising a checklist to reflect an individual need it is important to note the child's current readiness levels. Beginning with the child's current levels of mastery, the teacher can then begin to formulate pertinent goals and objectives for each art process. Within this domain, attention is focused upon a child's cognitive problem-solving abilities, psychomotor and perceptual development, within both an educational and a developmental context.

The checklist provided is meant to be generic, without regard to age, functioning level or nature of a handicapping condition. These objectives are formulated to reflect the minimal competencies that are universally needed in order to make art. To adapt these objectives for specific populations, scaling and task-analysis will be necessary.

Aesthetic/Expressive Domain

Assessing the aesthetic worth of a child's art product, whether it be for the purpose of critiquing or giving a grade, continues to be controversial. On one hand, writers such as Wilson (1988) have set about to objectify aesthetic sensibility as tangible evidence of student performance. This process usually takes the form of evaluations that compare students with one another or criterion references that judge artworks against fixed standards. Such objectification has been criticized by some as not leaving sufficient room for the intangible, irrational or spiritual qualities of an aesthetic experience (Henley 1991). In response, a more subjective approach can be determined mainly by the instructor's own value system. Such a system often reflects preferences formed by academic or cultural influences.

SKILL NOTATIONS

Name: _____ Date: _____

Psychomotor Development

_6_ The child can grasp, release and coordinate tool or medium appropriately.

_6_ The child can apply tool or medium to appropriate area (i.e., brush to water, water to paint, etc.).

_5_ The child can apply appropriate quantity of medium (i.e., paint, paste, glaze) onto art object.

_3_ The child can apply marks, lines, forms and other elements into a controlled configuration.

_4_ The child can manipulate three-dimensional medium in basic shapes (i.e., clay, oils, spheres, cubes, pancakes).

_4_ The child can carry over basic tool manipulation in a variety of medium (i.e., scissors, ceramic loop tools).

_5_ The child can mix dry or liquid medium such as glaze, paint or plaster.

_2_ The child can manipulate basic process tools (i.e., proof press, potter's wheel, airbrush).

_2_ The child can use advanced process tools (bandsaw, wood cut chisels, razor knife).

Cognitive Development

_____ The child can comprehend basic verbal or demonstrated directions.

_____ The child can comprehend appropriate application of medium.

_____ The child can sequence medium in correct order (paint to water, to paper, back to paint).

_____ The child can begin to conceptualize figures in artwork (naming scribbles, schemas, etc.).

_____ The child can develop personally relevant themes or subject matter in a preconceived way.

_____ The child can begin to embellish themes and elaborate ideas.

_____ The child can begin to solve problems with original, creative solutions.

_____ The child can extend repertoire of imagery, themes and ideas beyond normal range including the human figure.

_____ The child can explore variations of tool usage, and medium in unexpected ways.

_____ The child can begin to combine two or more media in multi-media context.

_____ The child can be able to reflect upon art product through verbal or mental analysis.

Perceptual Development

_____ The child can perceive figure from ground.

_____ The child can depict awareness of scale and spatial relationships.

_____ The child can discriminate between colors.

_____ The child can depict classes or groupings of figures or objects.

_____ The child can depict time and sequence.

_____ The child can depict quantity.

_____ The child can perceive gestalt information (perceiving parts to be whole).

_____ The child can develop an environmental awareness of people, places and things.

_____ The child can depict figures with sexual characteristics and age factors.

_____ The child can depict a horizon line.

_____ The child can depict depth perception and perspective.

_____ The child can begin to render subject matter as he sees or perceives the object and no longer as he conceives or knows about the object.

_____ The child can render in accurate, representational terms.

_____ The child can conceptualize abstractions, nonobjective and other perceptual/cognitive art concepts.

My approach to assessment attempts to recognize both objective and subjective constructs. Art criticism with exceptional children can effectively make use of comparisons and references that attempt to articulate the possibilities of the present direction and future exploration. Criticism can be sensitively administered using careful, upbeat language. Attempts to find the positive attributes of each work are crucial to this process. Referencing can be made on a "personal best" basis, or in comparison with appropriately like-minded or like-styled peers, without framing the discussion in competitive terms. A critique can also be approached comparatively within the context of art historical or contemporary artists who are "kindred" spirits. These may take the form of artists or cultures who have worked in styles or genres that reflect the modernist sensibility that is often found in the work of many exceptional artists. For critique purposes, parallels with the art of Dubuffet, Klee, Miró, African masks, Mimbre pottery or Zen brushwork may speak with relevance to the exceptional child who uses similar devices of simplification, distortion, abstraction, etc.

An essential aspect of recognizing aesthetic quality in children's art is that of "elaboration." During the art process, every effort should be made to actualize the children's ideas, feelings and experiences so that their images can achieve an elaboration that fully forms the image. This infers that it is the teacher who must often take the responsibility for importing aesthetic quality in the art process itself. By carefully activating the imagination, offering tantalizing media and facilitating reflection over the artwork, the teacher acts as a guide to help illuminate the viability and importance of the work to the child—even in cases where such awareness remains indifferent or oblivious.

The following inventory outlines a range of aesthetic objectives that are pertinent to children with special needs. This list is meant as a point of departure from which to further elaborate and expand, given the art teacher's own circumstances.

Aesthetic/Expressive Skills

_____ The child will use elements of lines in configurations with varying widths and pressures.

_____ The child will vary the sizes, shapes and values of forms in composition.

_____ The child will develop a sense of balance in composition.

_____ The child will develop a sense of repetition as an element in composition.

_____ The child will develop a sense of emphasis as an element in composition.

_____ The child will develop a sense of movement as an element in composition.

_____ The child will develop a sense of rhythm as an element in composition.

_____ The child will begin to overlap, contrast and intersect forms.

_____ The child will begin to use negative space as well as positive space.

_____ The child will gain experience in working spontaneously and quickly (as in one-minute life drawing exercise).

_____ The child will gain experience in interpreting visual stimuli both imaginatively and accurately.

_____ The child will begin to interject unusual, incongruous, emboldened images in compositions that draw upon imagination, dreams, memories and experiences.

_____ The child will be able to depict a range of emotions, expressions and communications between human figures.

_____ The child will be exposed to a variety of age and functioning level appropriate art historical materials and reproductions.

_____ The child will be able to use such materials in terms of influence, motivation or technical inspiration for his or her own work.

_____ The child will extend his or her own limits of style technique and expressivity to break new ground regardless of the attractiveness or traditional aspects of the imagery.

PROCESS NOTES

Patient/Client: _____ Day and Date: _____ Time: _____ Media: _____

Context
group or individual; list all group members including art educator, therapist, supervisor, interns. Diagram of seating arrangement.

Significant note (brief)
—radical change from previous sessions
—first refusal to attend after very regular attendance
—first departure from stereotyped imagery
—lost control of media or behavior
—left transitional object (teddy bear) in a classroom
—significant group member missing

1. Observations of General Behavior (Patient/Client's response to session, art therapist, group)
   compliant   oriented to reality
   resistant   apparently hallucinating
   depressed   disruptive
   hostile   friendly
   related

2. During Session

   A. Patient/Client's Response:

   Response to Media:
   —afraid of it? Resistant?
   —rushes right in?
   —has difficulty selecting materials?
   —manipulates materials easily? Destructively?
   —has short attention span or long?
   —any physical problems (blurry vision, tremor)?

   Response to Art Therapist:
   —ignores you? seems frightened?
   —seeks you out for technical assistance? for ideas?
   —looks to you for approval?
   —behaves in a hostile or provocative manner?
   —if hostile or provocative, how does he or she respond to your interventions?
   —responds in a guarded or interested way to your interest in his or her artwork?

   Response to Other Patients:
   —does he or she acknowledge their existence?
   —initiate contact with other patients?
   —behave towards them or their art products in a critical, aggressive or helpful way?

   —does he or she respond to friendly overtures?
   —is he or she interested in others' artwork and what it might reflect about their problems?

   B. Therapist's Interventions and Response to Patient/Client
   —left an empty chair between self and patient
   —placed brightly colored chalks next to patient
   —handed patient a pencil
   —ignored patient
   —removed all paint and clay, leaving only drawing material
   —drew portrait of withdrawn patient
   —offered larger/smaller paper

   C. Pertinent Dialogue (patient/client's and therapist's)
   —repeated patient's name frequently to orient him or her
   —remained silent throughout session
   —responded to personal questions with detailed answers
   —noted the connection between past and present artwork

   Art Production

   A. Detailed description of artwork including sketch of the production
   —Structural and formal aspects: color
   —line quality: rigid, empty, confused, lyrical, fragmented, obsessive
   —developmental considerations
   —areas of conflict: erasures, omissions, shading
   —origin of ideas for content

   B. Patient/Client's verbal and affective response to art product(s)
   —described picture and contents with enthusiasm
   —commented on the apparent disorganization
   —was disturbed by the quality of the production
   —appeared to be pleased with effort
   —appears to have insight as to what artwork reflects about his or her inner life
   Note contradictions between overtly stated subject matter and the message conveyed by the work itself.

C. Therapist's response to art product(s)—verbal and affective
   —effusive praise
   —frightened by chaotic or aggressive content
   —jealous of patient/client's skill and talent
   —gently supportive

4. Art Therapist's Assessment

   A. Art production (outstanding deficits, capacities, deviations, visual motor functions.)

   B. Facets of personality (relate to artwork)
      —self-image (sexual identity, self-esteem, ego ideals)
      —perception of self in relation to others (peers, authority figures, family)
      —sense of reality (body image, distortion, depersonalization)
      —thought processes (memory, judgement, concrete-abstract thinking)
      —defenses
      —attitude (mood quality, activity level)
      —capacity for use of art therapy (ego gratification, ego maturation, learning, functioning, mastery through art)

5. Summary and Goals

   A. General tone of session

   B. Changes in patient/client's behavior, affect, art productions and interactions during session

   C. Changes compared with past sessions

   D. Goals:
      Short term (comments to note for next session)
      Long term

6. Briefly indicate therapist's reaction to patient/client and session
   —uncomfortable with highly charged art material
   —angry when patient withdrew
   —frustrated when nothing happened
   —frightened by patient's intimate questions or remarks
   —embarrassed by patient's intimate questions or remarks

Affective Domain

Art naturally stirs up and unleashes an artist's emotions, concerns, conflicts, joys and other affective responses. A child will experience and project through the art experience how he or she feels in terms of self-concept, self-image and self-esteem. Many handicapped children who are physically deformed, unattractive or bizarre in their mannerisms may be sufficiently self-conscious about themselves so that a strong emotional response is elicited in the artwork. Autistic, retarded, psychotic, physically handicapped and sensory-impaired children may possess a defective sense of self. They may experience themselves as incomplete, damaged, or even machinelike. Their appraisal of themselves may interfere with appropriate emotional responses which may become decidedly distorted, intense or bizarre. This affect may be further amplified during the art process. It is the nature of the art process to dredge up emotions as well as ideas, impulses, fantasies and instincts which are ordinarily repressed or otherwise held in check by the ego. Art has the propensity to arouse and loosen these controls so that a weakened or arrested ego may not be sufficiently fortified to hold such intense affect in check. The ego in this case, can be viewed as straining to contain the up-rush of previously contained affect (Naumberg 1973). Should a child not be able to hold up under the enormous pressures, affective regression might ensue, rendering the child autistic, psychotic, assaultive or otherwise disturbed.

It becomes a vital task of the art process to accommodate a child's emotional life. The art experience must allow for this discharge of pent-up emotions while also furnishing the impulse control and structure to redirect impulse toward creative and productive means. The teacher must see to it that the art process becomes a stabilizing force in children whose emotions may be in disarray.

The assessment procedure shown here, developed by Laurie Wilson and used for processing affective responses in the art studio, observes a child's interactions with self, others and the art medium. This process notation lends itself to a

PROCESS NOTE EXAMPLE

Student: *N.B.   11/12/   3:40–4:50pm   Easel Painting With Tempera*

Context

Group of twelve boys ages 12–13, mixed learning disabilities and behavior problems.

Significant note

N.B. had spent last period in time-out for threatening the teachers' aide.

1. *N.B. entered in agitated state, complaining about previous injustice. Vowed not to participate until he spoke to the principal. Initial resistance although was not actively disruptive.*

2A. Media

After 12 minutes started mixing tempera paint and after 20 minutes began to apply it to paper (on table—not using easel). Worked for 16 minutes until cleanup although continued to be distracted and agitated.

Response to Teacher

Refused initial attempts to be motivated. Charged that art therapist always "sides" with other teachers. Also maintained that he was angry from last session because the aprons had wet paint on them and admonished A.T. to keep them clean. Eventually participated but did not solicit A.T.'s approval or comments.

Response to Peers

Ignored all peers until cleanup at which time he verbally abused co-worker at sink for splashing the paint. (Although N.B. had turned the water on too high).

2B. Art Therapist's Interventions

Verbally motivated using N.B.'s work from last week as model. Allowed individual seating without use of easels. Gave encouragement and verbal support. No technical guidance given (N.B. simply played with colors).

2C. Pertinent Dialogue

At one point said, "I think I could work better with you if you weren't a teacher."—alluding to N.B.'s problems with authority figures.

3A. Art Production

Painting #1

3B. Verbal/Affective Responses

No verbal responses except to say it was an "experiment." Affectively, patient appeared to calm down after painting although became agitated again during cleanup.

3C. Art Therapist's Response

Remarked that next week perhaps he could find some "content" in the painting and outline any forms he found with pen and ink. N.B. offered a positive nod in response.

4. Assessment

N.B. used painting initially as a play/pre-art activity, mixing and pouring to create new hues. Once he applied the paint, he continued to allow the tempera to puddle and run to create new colors and abstract forms. This kinetic style enabled N.B. to work out need for regressed manipulative activity while also redirecting aggression and agitation through semichaotic discharge. Displacement defenses in evidence. Little concern over finished product although N.B. did stop working before colors became overworked and muddied.

5. Summary

A. *Tone of session was volatile. N.B. seemed liable to explode at any moment especially if frustrated.*

B. *N.B. appeared to be calmed and more concentrative as he engaged the materials.*

C. *Past sessions were more productive and advanced since N.B. was not upset.*

D. *Short term goal: To have N.B. rework painting to explore forms and emotions that were stirred during the art process.*

Long Term: To increase N.B.'s frustration tolerance, capacity to resolve conflict through reflection and to use the art process beyond displacement mechanisms.

narrative format due to its use of descriptors which describe subjective shades of meaning. It begins with notations on the child's initial emotional state, reactions to peers, teacher and environment and how the art process stirs up further responses (Wilson 1980).

As with the assessment forms for other domains, this example can be shortened, lengthened or otherwise adopted for specific purposes or specific populations. For example, one could convert observations of depressed affect to numerical values and create a chart similar to the one in the behavior assessment form. Although reducing a feeling to a number runs contrary to a humanistic approach, in some settings or situations, definitive data is required, particularly when state, school or governmental agencies are funding the program.

THE USE OF VIDEO IN ASSESSMENT

Although the equipment is relatively expensive, the video camera and recorder have become an increasingly common and useful tool in the educational/therapeutic milieu, particularly when special needs children are involved. Teaching staffs have realized the medium's potential as an instructional aid, an assessment tool and an art form in itself. It is an excellent means of documenting the many facets of the art program and can be used for funding purposes, inservice instruction for staff and student viewing pleasure.

Staff can benefit by reviewing footage of themselves instructing, interacting and coping with the problems that arise during instruction. The videotape can detect interventions that were mishandled, developmentally inappropriate, inconsistent or that further aggravated a classroom problem. Playback can change the sometimes wishful and inaccurate self-images that instructors develop of themselves (McNiff & Cook 1980). Breaking through such denial enables the art instructor to gain insight into the behavioral dynamics that can greatly affect the workings of the art program. It is almost impossible to always be cognizant of every

interaction during the art session while the instructor is preoccupied with working with the children. By reviewing tapes made over a series of art classes, the teacher can effectively step back from the program and accurately gauge the long-term effects of interventions upon the students.

Long-term videotaping gives the instructor a more global view of the program's impact. A major problem in working with children with special needs is discerning cumulative achievement, because such evidence emerges erratically and in such small increments. For instance, the instructor may be demoralized over a child's lack of progress or the inability to effect a positive change in a child's behavior. In reviewing the video footage, however, the instructor may realize that the child has, in fact, made significant strides over a period of time, although they were imperceptible on a daily basis.

The video camera can also record the effects of the studio environment upon individual or group behavior. The instructor can detect areas that breed conflict or excess socializing. He or she can observe the effects of the relaxation center upon an agitated child in seclusion. The effects of glare or reflection upon the visually impaired child can be recorded. Studio equipment, seating arrangements, motivational areas can all be assessed by analyzing videotape footage.

Children who habitually act out or disrupt the class are usually not aware of their actions. They will have trouble analyzing the events that provoked them. They cannot anticipate the reactions of others, and they may be too upset or confused to comprehend the disciplinary measures. Having the child review the episodes on tape allows the child to see him- or herself in action: How expressions turn ugly; how provocations are imagined or misunderstood and, hopefully, how self-defeating and counterproductive such incidents are. Especially for the child who is nonverbal or communication handicapped, the video image can cut through the language barrier and graphically convey the details of an otherwise incomprehensible situation.

Children with behavioral problems can also acquire increased self-regard through the practice of videotaping positive behaviors. This technique involves collecting and showing sequences where the child attended to task or related well to peers or staff. By viewing him- or herself in a positive light, the child may begin to realize that he or she does indeed possess some redeeming qualities: that there are instances when he or she is a pleasure to work and interact with. As children begin to identify and incorporate these positive images of themselves, they become their own best role models, literally fashioning newly adaptive behaviors using the video as a guide to change.

INDIVIDUALIZED EDUCATION PLAN

In some cases, the art educator will be required to participate in program development for children with special needs. The Education for All Handicapped Children Act (1975) insures that all children who have been identified as requiring special education be provided with an individualized education plan (IEP). This plan acts as documentation that the child is receiving individualized attention. It outlines both the instructional and behavioral and goals objectives which have been targeted as being reasonably achievable for the individual. The instructional objectives focus upon skill development with attention to the perceptual, cognitive and psychomotor domains. Behavioral objectives entail motivation, behaviors and affective responses. In formulating the IEP, the teacher will bring together the task-analysis format with the assessment procedures previously discussed. The child's need for remediation or areas of behavior that need work will form a baseline from which to develop rational goals.

It is a difficult task to present an example of a typical IEP because formats differ between states and institutions whose program approaches may be entirely different. In most programs in educational settings, the objectives will focus mainly upon skill development without consideration of

affect. Should this be the case, the teacher should modify the format to include all of the assessment domains or whichever areas are of pressing concern. Although educational settings must be accountable for the skills taught to a child, the case can be made that emotions impact upon behavior which, in turn, affects learning.

It is important that all phases of a child's performance be noted and considered as objectives in the IEP. Comprehensive planning and assessment not only benefits the child directly by pinpointing educational and therapeutic need, but also serves as a basis for research data and program evaluation. Because of the concrete, specific nature of the IEP format, the data is applicable to many forms of research. One can identify projects which are effective with certain populations. Stumbling blocks with certain media can be identified. Subtle changes in behavior can sometimes be more accurately ascertained by consulting the charts than by actual observation. In some cases, notations of art and artwork can sometimes furnish desperately needed input to multi-disciplinary teams whose assessment tools may rely upon language skills or I.Q. testing which do not effectively tap some children's potential. Most crucial to this assessment procedure is the ability to gauge the teacher's effectiveness in formulating and applying instructional strategies and therapeutic interventions. No longer can art programs rely solely upon subjective or anecdotal evaluations of children. Precise data must be clearly communicated which concretely demonstrate the needs of children and the steps taken toward addressing those needs—not only for the teacher's own edification, but also as a forum that insures accountability when requested by administrations for whom art programs are often a low priority.

Writing the IEP Goals and Objectives
In formulating an IEP, the first task is to clearly differentiate between a goal and an objective. Under Public Law 94-142, a *goal* is a statement that projects the desired improvement in a particular domain. It is generally long-term and broad in

scope, although it must be measurable, relevant to the child's problems and useful or applicable with realistic, achievable expectations. An *objective* is much more specific and entails the listing of discrete operations that must be mastered in order to reach the goal. Objectives must be observable and measurable in terms of results. The objectives are what define the individualized nature of the program; they recognize a child's strengths and weaknesses, both cognitively and behaviorally. Objectives may reflect the interventions used to address a problem, including motivational strategies.

The format for the IEP specifically directs the manner in which goals and objectives are to be written:

A. Order of priority
B. Areas for improvement (cognitive, affective, behavioral and physical)
C. How it will improve (through what subject area)
D. How much it will improve
E. How improvements will be measured (in terms of percentage or other criteria).

In order to explain the properties of goals and objectives, I have provided lists that outline how they may be worded, their scope and their individualized aspects. While these examples might be applicable to many types of children and institutions, they are not meant to be copied verbatum. They are a starting point from which the reader is encouraged to further develop specific goals and objectives for each child.

The following goals and objectives are divided into three domains—cognitive/motor functions, affect/motivation and behavior/social function. It is important to note the verbs that have been employed in writing both the goals and objectives. Given the broad nature of the goal itself, the verbs are similarly general—*develop, respond, identify, regulate,* etc. Objectives should be correlated to the goal in specific language which identifies what areas of improvement are desired and to what extent improvement is expected. Objectives usually use percentages as a criteria for change, although

without exact monitoring devices this is usually a subjective judgement on the part of the art teacher. Objectives are succinctly stated yet should also be descriptive. Verbs should be used which clarify the action taking place. Nebulous terms such as *create, make, stop* or *learn how to* are not effective. More descriptive terms such as *identify, transcribe, group, render, prepare, sequence, recognize, ignore* or *engage* are used for the sake of brevity and clarification.

In setting up the objectives, task-analysis format can be used for placing the tasks in sequential order, from the simple to the complex. In this way one can identify the furthest point to which the child has progressed and then use that point as the departure for the set of objectives in the next IEP. Note that despite the specificity of the following objectives, they can be broken down further should this be required. For instance, if a child's IEP focuses mainly upon instructional objectives, the areas of cognition domain can be gone into with greater depth, since the time and space usually devoted to affect or behavior might not be used if this is a stable, well-behaved student. Again, the specific needs of the child guide the IEP.

EXAMPLE GOALS AND OBJECTIVES

Cognitive/Motor Functions

Goal

The student will develop greater awareness of and competency over various media and techniques.

Through greater awareness of and competency over various media and techniques, the student will advance in the developmental milestones on an age appropriate basis.

Objectives

—to identify the sensory qualities of basic medium (i.e., smooth/rough, dark/light, etc) 50% over current levels.
—to group, sort or compose materials in configurations 50% over current levels.
—to modify materials by means of tearing, manipulating or cutting 20% over current levels.
—to sequence basic art operations 20% over current levels (i.e., brush to water, brush to paint, brush to paper, etc.).
—to manipulate basic fabrication medium (i.e., glue or paste) with 50% effectiveness over current levels.
—to demonstrate an awareness and/or appreciation of a finished product 15% over current levels.
—to recognize or identify basic design elements in finished artworks 10% over current levels.
—to recognize or identify basic design principles in finished artworks 10% over current levels.
—to increase the quantity of details in the art imagery by 25% over current levels.
—to increase the elaboration and embellishing of details in the art imagery 25% over current levels.
—to broaden the repertoire of themes and subject matter 20% over current levels.

Behavior/Socialization

Goal

The student will develop adaptive interpersonal behaviors. The student will demonstrate increased self-control and regulation of impulses appropriate to the mainstream setting.

Objectives

—To enter the classroom without disruption 20% over current levels.
—To distribute and share materials with peers appropriately 40% over current levels.
—To maintain individual and group work spaces without unwarranted mess 25% over current levels.

—To communicate with peers without unwarranted conflict 25% over current levels.
—To resolve conflicts without resorting to physical aggression 50% over current levels.
—To seek the instructor's mediation in inter-peer conflicts before resorting to verbal or physical abuse 50% over current levels.
—To assent to requests from instructor for a time-out sequence without opposition 75% over current levels.
—To interact with peers during the art activity 20% over current levels.
—To operate and maintain studio equipment safety 75% over current levels.
—To demonstrate increased assertiveness when interacting with peers 25% over current levels.
—To reflect upon and share ideas about peer artwork during art criticism periods without pejorative or punitive verbalization.

Affect/Motivation

Goal

The student will improve spontaneous participation in the art product, demonstrating increased positive affect during the art process and over the resulting art production.

Objectives

—To demonstrate a willingness to participate as evidenced by manipulation of materials and tools 20% over current levels.
—To initiate each step of the art activity with minimum verbal direction 10% over current levels.
—To demonstrate increased flexibility and expansiveness in the artwork as evidenced by a willingness to experiment with unfamiliar medium 20% over current levels.
—To accept the instructor's input and feedback without unreasonable resistance 10% over current levels.
—To demonstrate increased positive response to own artwork, should it be warranted, 20% over current levels.
—To concentrate upon artwork for a full 45 minutes without more than two verbal cues for refocusing.
—To attend to clean-up regimens for full 15 minutes without verbal support.
—To use the art process as a conduit for redirecting aggressive affect 20% over current levels.
—To manage anxiety in the beginning and end of class by 20% over current levels.
—To display increased self-confidence and self-worth by 10% over current levels.

SAMPLE IEP

School Year _____ Case: *Twelve year old Attention Deficit–Hyperactive Disorder; short attention span, poor sequencing, sometimes destructive to materials, tools. Intact intelligence.*

Level: *Middle School* Subject Area/Course Title: *Art Education/Therapy*

Present Education/Skill Development Status: *Commensurate with Third Grade, Schematic Stage*

Sources for determining present Educational/Skill Development Status: *Lowenfeld Developmental Scale.*

Strategies: *Short projects, task analysis with directive structure*

Mastery Key
1. Exposed to process
2. In process of learning
3. Mastered given assistance
4. Independent mastery

Date Started: _____ Date of Expected Completion: _____ Time/Periods Per Week __2__
Minutes Per Period __45__

Annual Goal	Objectives	Mastery Date ____
Cognitive/Motor: *To gain age appropriate competency with basic media and techniques.*	1. To master basic hand tools and their applications by 50% over current levels.	3
	2. To identify basic elements of design in own artwork by 25% over current levels.	3
	3. To identify six famous artworks and discuss their properties 20% over current levels.	2
	4. To increase the quantity of details in human figure drawing 20% over existing levels.	3
Affective/Motivation: *To develop adoptive behaviors and the capacity for reflection.*	1. To display increased self-confidence and self-worth 25% over current levels.	4
	2. To redirect anxiety and anger through verbal interaction and reflection 20% over current behaviors.	3
	3. To manage anxiety in the beginning and end of class when structure is lax by 20% over existing levels.	3
Behavior/Social: *To control impulsivity and aggressive discharge with peers.*	1. To demonstrate delayed gratification 20% over current levels.	2
	2. To maintain verbal dialogue in lieu of physical assaults when angered 50% over current levels.	2
	3. To demonstrate capacity for reflection after incidents 25% over current levels.	2

SAMPLE IEP

School Year _____ Case: _Twelve year old Learning Disabled. Hyperactive, short attention span, poor sequencing, sometimes destructive to materials, tools. Intact intelligence._

Level: _Middle School_ Subject Area/Course Title: _Art Education/Therapy_

Present Education/Skill Development Status: _Commensurate with Third Grade, Schematic Stage_

Sources for determining present Educational/Skill Development Status: _Lowenfeld Developmental Scale._

Strategies: _Short projects, task analysis with directive structure_

Mastery Key
1. Exposed to process
2. In process of learning
3. Mastered given assistance
4. Independent mastery

Date Started: _____ Date of Expected Completion: _____ Time/Periods Per Week ___2___
Minutes Per Period __45__

Annual Goal	Objectives	Mastery Date _____
Cognitive/Motor: _To gain age appropriate competency with basic media and techniques._	1. To master basic hand tools and their applications by 50% over current levels.	3
	2. To identify basic elements of design in own artwork by 25% over current levels.	3
	3. To identify six famous artworks and discuss their properties 20% over current levels.	2
	4. To increase the quantity of details in human figure drawing 20% over existing levels.	3
Affective/Motivation: _To develop adoptive behaviors and the capacity for reflection._	1. To display increased self-confidence and self-worth 25% over current levels.	4
	2. To redirect anxiety and anger through verbal interaction and reflection 20% over current behaviors.	3
	3. To manage anxiety in the beginning and end of class when structure is lax by 20% over existing levels.	3
Behavior/Social: _To control impulsivity and aggressive discharge with peers._	1. To demonstrate delayed gratification 20% over current levels.	2
	2. To maintain verbal dialogue in lieu of physical assaults when angered 50% over current levels.	2
	3. To demonstrate capacity for reflection after incidents 25% over current levels.	2

SAMPLE IEP

School Year _____ Case: _Eighteen year old paraplegic cerebral palsy. Intact intelligence, poor self-concept and_
confidence. Spasticity extreme. Hardworking.

Level: _____ Subject Area/Course Title: _Art Education/Therapy_

Present Education/Skill Development Status: _Conceptually at senior high level, motor function impaired_

Sources for determining present Educational/Skill Development Status: _Lowenfeld Developmental Scale._

Strategies: _Camouflaged projects, least-restrictive intervention, adaptation of tools and media_

Mastery Key
1. Exposed to process
2. In process of learning
3. Mastered given assistance
4. Independent mastery

Date Started: _____ Date of Expected Completion: _____ Time/Periods Per Week __2__
Minutes Per Period __60__

Annual Goal	Objectives	Mastery Date _____
Cognitive/Motor: _To gain motor coordination, competency over medium and technique, as well as art appreciation material related to the art activity._	1. _To operate adaptive potter's wheel with limited physical support 25% over current levels._ 2. _To demonstrate knowledge of historical pottery styles and techniques 85% over current levels._ 3. _To manipulate glaze materials, blender, spray airbrush with limited physical assistance 20% over current levels._ 4. _To design original container design reflective of historical style._	
Affective/Motivation: _To enhance self-confidence and self-worth through spontaneous and sustained participation._	1. _To decrease self-defeatist attitudes when encountering unfamiliar equipment and techniques by 40% over current levels._ 2. _To verbalize frustrations before they escalate into spastic fits 20% over current levels._ 3. _To recognize the body's signs of fatigue and rest for 10-minute periods during the project 25% over current levels._	
Behavior/Social: _To interact with peers and staff in an age-appropriate manner._	1. _To demonstrate increased awareness of verbal comments to females that may be sexually provocative 75% over current levels._ 2. _To choose responsibilities during group work which are within physical capabilities._ 3. _To improve responsibility during cleanup procedures 70% over current levels._	

chapter 14

Aesthetics and Criticism

In working with young artists, especially those with special needs, the issues of aesthetics and art criticism require careful consideration. In formulating an aesthetic which recognizes the creative potential of these individuals, one must identify those aspects of their work which are uniquely their own. Such identification may be difficult, since much of the teacher's work involves strategies for eliciting art by way of adaptive or remedial educational/therapeutic interventions. With support or guidance of this kind, it is inevitable that the stamp of the educator's aesthetic values will be brought to bear upon the often fragile artistic sensibilities of the child.

The focus in this chapter is upon those students who manage to create art spontaneously and freely. These children often create images which are relatively free of teacher influence or expectation. Often, they run contrary to the teacher's instructions or guidance, resulting in art which is antisocial, raw, regressive or otherwise disturbing in content or style. Such provocative imagery may, however, possess an inherent aesthetic sensibility and evocative power, despite the fact that its content reflects the artists' physical, mental or emotional problems. The images which emerge are often a study in paradoxes: They will exude both strength and forcefulness while revealing an underlying fragility. It is this interplay between original artistic vision and a debilitating condition which gives this art its unique aesthetic sensibility.

In a pilot study begun in 1984, I attempted to correlate the incidence of artistic giftedness between normal children and those with special needs (including those with the most severe disabling conditions, such as mental retardation). I found that in terms of originality of style, design sensibility and intensity of motivation, the incidence of giftedness was nine percent among both groups. While the giftedness took radically different forms, innate artistic drive and sensibility seemed unaffected by the individual's intelligence quotient or degree of emotional handicap (Henley 1987).

APPROACHING ART WITH SPECIAL NEEDS

Despite the finding that giftedness has been identified with approximately equal frequency in both intact and special needs groups, the critical perspective from which the work of each group is viewed is quite different. Ordinarily, the art of normal gifted individuals is seen as the product of an innate ability which, if nurtured by a supportive environment, will flourish and mature. The art of the special needs child, however, is usually approached from a clinical perspective—couched in terms of the disabling conditions. Art education or art therapy professionals are usually trained to evaluate the art of these individuals in a case study

The aesthetic of the exceptional child finds a kindred spirit in the art of such modernists as Paul Klee (left). The drawing to the right is by a young man with Down syndrome.

frame of reference. Deviations in performance or imagery are analyzed so that procedures aimed at treatment can be formulated. Rarely is the art of the special needs student allowed to stand on aesthetic merit alone, since the forces which appear to bring a freshness or idiosyncracy of style to the work are coincidently seen as being a product or symptom of the disabling condition. From this perspective, the art of the special needs child is seen as a matter of *compensation*. This implies that the art was created despite the artist's deficits, once they have suppressed or surmounted the forces which render them "abnormal." That these "disabling" forces may be a potential agent for enhancing the aesthetic impact of the art is usually not considered.

Assigning aesthetic worth to the images created by special needs students may put the art educator in an ethical and professional bind. For example, if a student's image might be compared aesthetically to the mode of figurative abstraction practiced by Klee, Dubuffet and others, we might respond to its inventive manipulation of design elements and its idiosyncratic abstraction of the figure. However, the same piece, when viewed as the work of a special needs student, might be regarded as developmentally arrested with a pathological body image in which the sexual parts are particularly distorted. The teacher may hesitate to assign aesthetic repleteness to such an image, since it is his or her mission to "improve" or "overcome" such expressions of impoverishment. The question, then, may be whether it is irresponsible to embrace the artistic expression while also being

260 charged with remediating the artist toward greater normalcy.

I believe that sensitivity and open-mindedness are needed when considering the aesthetic aspects of the art produced by special needs students. In formulating such an aesthetic, it is vital that the prejudices, expectations and demands of the so-called normal world give way to a recognition that there are other modes of perceiving and expressing which are equally viable.

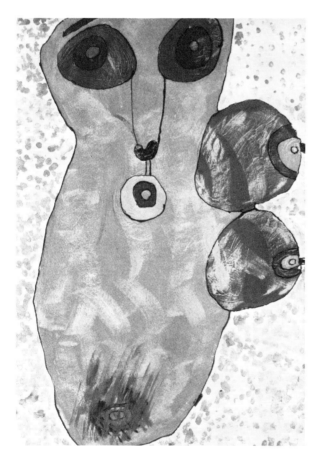

Although the style may be infantile or bizarre, this work by a European member of a cooperative art studio, is aesthetically modernistic.

TRANSCENDING CULTURAL BIAS

It is important to recognize that much of the art created by those with special needs is not born of suffering or deficiency. As Lowenfeld pointed out in his formulations of subjective and objective responses to conditions, an individual with gross abnormalities may often create with total control and creative fervor. In such cases, the same reservoir of sensory pleasure, conceptualization and emotional power fuels the intact or handicapped artist during the creative act. However, since the artist with special needs often perceives and expresses in atypical ways, his or her art will be strikingly different than that which is created by the intact artist. Thus, the art critic who is decidedly oriented to the norm may have difficulty identifying with images which are based upon distortion, perseveration, simplification and other devices favored by the special needs artist.

One must bear in mind, however, that the typical art critic is guided by the very subjective values and belief systems which are peculiar to this culture. The institutions which govern this system, particularly the education and mental health establishments, take a narrow view of what constitutes artistic accomplishment as well as psychological health.

The dominant Western psychic organization sees the development of a rational intellect or a functioning ego (depending upon if one is speaking educationally or psychologically) as the central apparatus from which all "normal" functioning flows. Many so-called third world or primitive cultures function quite effectively using magical or spiritual belief systems as the focus of their orientation to reality (Highwater 1981). Because the Western psyche is fundamentally pragmatic and analytical, any prolonged or direct submersion into irrationality implies grave risks. Those, who for some reason do lapse into what is perceived as psychic disorganization, sensory deprivation or inadequate intellectualization, are thus perceived as abnormal (Laing 1969).

It is this exclusively Western orientation to reality that may preempt our capacity to empathize with the special needs artist. Since most child art, and especially that produced by the psychotic, retarded or autistic may appear alien to the adult viewer, it discourages them from seeking to appreciate it. Like many in society who have difficulty in comprehending or identifying with nonconformity, art critics too often fail to overcome their cultural bias. They adhere to the Western method of assessing the artist's historical references, contemporary influences, as well as trying to read into the work the "personal story" of the artist. When references and influences are nowhere to be found and a personal story as we know it is not understood, it is natural for even insightful critics to shake their heads and see such work as evidence of a basic lack of talent or skill or as symptoms requiring treatment. This breakdown of empathic appreciation essentially deprives the art of special needs artists of aesthetic recognition.

Such a viewpoint is insensitive and narrow-minded. Art, by its very definition, should seek to expand its parameters and delve into the many recesses of the individual and social psyche. Art should be open-ended so that images or art forms which do not yield their meaning easily are not discounted simply due to ethnocentrism.

HISTORICAL BASIS FOR APPRECIATION OF ART BRUT

Throughout art history we know that critics have resisted art which subverts traditional values. For instance, because of Western ethnocentricity, the arts of Africa, Oceania and Pre-Columbian America were considered for years to be simply a curiosity —bizarre and mysterious artifacts of a "savage mind" (Rubin 1984). Early modern artists were first to acknowledge a so-called primitive aesthetic, using it as a jumping off point to launch the modernist movement. There was the inevitable rancor which followed, as critics assailed "ethnographic degenerative influences" in European art. However, this early resistance was ignored by the burgeoning modernists who saw the primitive aesthetic as a means of challenging the collective, institutional values of their culture. It additionally served to question the repressive, class conscious conventions of Victorian bourgeois society. The early moderns drew upon the art of schizophrenics and other mentally ill artists to inspire further explorations away from rational, linear thought. Breton, Rimbaud, Dali and others who associated with Dadaism and Surrealism celebrated the bizarre, incomprehensible images that were being collected throughout Europe's insane asylums. These dramatic art movements which explored the relationship between madness and genius served to shake the foundations of Western classic art, moving it toward a wholly new aesthetic experience (MacGregor 1989).

As the early modernists used the conceptual and aesthetic properties of primitive and schizophrenic art, the post-war generation was obligated to take it a step further. In the 1940's, Jean Dubuffet called for an aesthetic which denounced culture altogether. He called into question the need for art to communicate anything at all comprehensible. Dubuffet termed this "raw" or "pure" art, *L' Art Brut* (1986). Art Brut celebrated the "abnormality" of the artist. It embraced the art of psychotics, mystics, retardates and untrained peasants who remained ignorant or indifferent to cultural convention, preferring instead to create from pure, authentic impulses. Hallucinations, divine intervention or plain eccentricity superceded the cultural preoccupation with beauty, commercial success or social promotion.

Later in the 1960's the influence of "anti-artists," such as Warhol, demanded an equally unorthodox existential position. Art was seen as an extra-phenomenal object which must be examined without prior conceptual commitments. The art object should free the viewer for an experience which is unique—with its own set of relationships and no prior, generalized or imaginary transference of any kind expected or assumed (Leepa 1966). The viewer did not rely upon an identification or empathy with the artist's vision for an aesthetic experience. The viewer was left to battle out the existential experience and redefine those values and beliefs which transcend cultural identification, sentimentality and romanticism.

It is within this framework of early modernist primitivism (later existential Pop Art and Neo-Expressionism), as well as the radical formulations of Dubuffet, that the following special needs artists are presented. While these individuals are essentially ignorant of any of their historical antecedents, they can be viewed as offspring—born with the collective drive to create and thus give meaning to their world via their unique artistic visions.

THE CONTEMPORARY PRIMITIVE

Abstracted figures with primitive and modernist sensibilities characterize the art of many individuals with mental handicaps. Peter, a young man retarded by Down syndrome, works in a manner which recalls the figure sculptures of New Guinea and the masks of the Fang Tribe of West Africa, as well as Dubuffet's own childlike abstractions. Peter uses complex configurations of grids, geometric shapes and organic forms which appear to multiply and mutate the figures' internal and external forms. By exaggerating and repeating certain elements, Peter is able to create a remarkable range of abstracted figures.

Often the inner and outer space of the figures is chaotic, confused or otherwise poorly differentiated. It is probable that Peter's sense of object relations and self-awareness is quite fluid, prompting him to continually explore what is self and what is space in relation to self. Although this object confusion is symptomatic of emotional immaturity, the art seems not to suffer. In fact, sometimes the artist maintains remarkable control over his designs, enabling one to argue that a degree of conscious manipulation is functioning regardless of how regressed or bizarre it may be. Despite Peter's inability to communicate through his art, he wields a formidable graphic vocabulary; the line between control and symptom remains imperceptible.

This young man creates countless intricate figures which are reminiscent of African masks and Dubuffet's child-like figures.

Mask. Fang from Gabon, Africa. Painted wood. Verité collection, Paris.

Dubuffet's figure work was inspired by the abstractions created by children, psychiatric patients and other outsider artists. Collection of the Guggenheim Museum.

Two fantastic compositions that disintegrate into numerous figurative fragments.

Rapid strokes and multi-layered contrasting colors of wax crayons create this dynamic architectural study by a legally blind, deaf and autistic twelve-year-old.

The work of Jason, a legally blind twelve-year-old with congenital deafness, is patently abstract and expressionistic. He literally attacks a canvas or paper, slashing, scrubbing and layering pigments in an action style that makes any of the New York action school seem tame. His strong graphic sensibility is illustrated by the subtle sophistication of tonal contrasts and black architectural forms interacting with airy whites and complementary greys. The overpowering blocks of color are rhythmically embellished by repetitive line work which calls to mind Kline's calligraphic works and Motherwell's *Eulegy to the Spanish Republic* series. In color pencil his line work is equally furious, with strong rhythmic forms that convey the pace of the art process.

In some cases the preferred objects of abstraction are architectural rather than figurative. This image, created by a twelve-year-old deaf, legally blind, autistic child, combines distortion and repetition along with kinesthetic intensity.

Bold contrasts between the heavy wax line work and pale washes characterize this child's early paintings.

In one illustration, Rouault comes to mind, as a thick black band contours the figure, intensifying contrast and distorting figure/ground relationships. Viewed from a developmental perspective, perhaps Jason is straining to maintain a differentiation between inner and outer self-reality. Purely from an artistic viewpoint he is simply employing a design device which intensifies visual impact through an interplay of sharp contrasts and subtle ambiguities.

For other special needs artists, organic kinesthetic expression gives way to drafting which is more rigid, and hard-edged. Blocks and planes of flat color combine with rhythmic multi-angled perspectives to create a striking interplay of form and value. One such artist, Thomas, arrived at the School of the Art Institute of Chicago in a suit and tie and carrying a sheaf of hundreds of striking studies done in pencil and oil crayon. It seems that, having never attended school, Thomas stayed home and drew constantly, producing literally hundreds of these city vistas from his low-altitude perspective.

Jason's human figures are equally individualistic in style. Like other abstract expressionists, he uses the scribble to impart a suggestion of form through kinesthetic gesture. A loose yet precise flow of lines is used with terse economy. The slashing scribbles seem boldly indifferent, as if to confidently understate the artist's command of the figure—a device Gombrich (1960) termed the "et-cetera principle," whereby the scribble attempts to depict mass conceptually, leaving the viewer to fill in the "missing" elements.

After a year of therapeutic intervention, this child began to incorporate human figures into his compositions, although the drafting remains intensely kinesthetic and architectural.

The interplay between the grid designs of urban planning and flat, saturated blocks of color characterize the architectural works of this Down syndrome artist.

Viewed from afar in series, any recognizable imagery tends to dissolve into pure rhythm and color. In Thomas' work the deceptively solid forms of the city blocks, vegetation and water become one vast circulatory or vascular system, as forms pulsate through the grids. The extreme narrowness of the subject matter and the rigidity in the grid-like compositions perhaps alludes to the artist's need to evoke patterns of predictability, familiarity and order. The compulsivity and static quality that is often present in such a style is often seen as being suffocating. Yet these pictures are spared this by their lively animation and naive charm. The pulsing rhythms recall Mondrian's *Broadway Boogie Woogie*. Both artists depend upon the interplay of geometric form and color to create a sense of perspective, scale and vibrancy.

The pulse of urban life was also the source of fascination for a deaf/blind artist. Jeff was born hearing-impaired and legally blind, yet he managed to create vast cityscapes from memory without the benefit of photographs or other visual aids. In fact, I have never seen him use a ruler or straight-edge, even when composing hundreds of windows in perfectly aligned rows. Most of his compositions are composites of city scenes he has observed. Thus, skyscrapers are juxtaposed with elevated trains, bridges and trainways. Street levels are crossed by subterranean scenes of subways, stations and stairwells. Despite his preoccupation with vast scale, his images involve intimate and detailed scenarios of peoples' daily lives. In one of the tiny ¼″ square windows one might see an IV bottle and hose along with part of a hospital bed. In another, a house plant is partly obscured by a tattered curtain. On escalators, commuters trudge to their homebound trains while shoppers lug their bags and bundles. These intricate details animate Jeff's enormous cityscapes in an exciting way.

Jeff's long-range perspectives and the interplay

between the schematic blocks of architectural form and pastel color in these works are reminiscent of Thiebaud's paintings of downtown San Francisco. Yet because Jeff's medium of choice is exclusively the felt marker, his works don't have the lusciousness of Thiebaud's images. They are somewhat more childlike because of the flattened values which markers impart.

Jeff's initial drawings focused upon panoramic vistas of housing projects. Obsessed with drawing these enormous forms, then filling in countless windows, Jeff would become self-stimulatory during his drawing process.

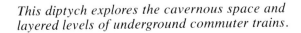
This diptych explores the cavernous space and layered levels of underground commuter trains.

Although Jeff continued to perseverate upon large-scale scenes, he eventually treated them on a more intimate and introspective basis.

These large-scale compositions demonstrate an intense need to obsess over the repetitive elements found in city scenes. The relentlessness with which Jeff dutifully records each window, each antenna, each pedestrian might point to the need to bind anxiety through perseveration. No one can predict what the response to the roar of the subway or the sight of the massive World Trade Center would have upon a young man sheltered both at home and at school. With severely damaged senses and distorted sensory processing, the stimulation might simultaneously excite and frighten such a child. By creating these images, he can perhaps gain a modicum of mastery and control over these overwhelming sensory forces while also partaking of the vicarious thrills such experiences afford. In any event, Jeff's extraordinary drawings are eloquent testimony to the compensatory abilities of one so severely impaired. While his work might suffer from repetition, color insensibility and stereotype, all this is compensated for by the sheer scope of its elements and the freshness of vision it celebrates.

A breakthrough came in Jeff's work when he began to explore different interior spaces. While his large scale, architectural works were schematic and cartoonish, his interiors appear more dynamic and mature. One figure explores a New York City subway station with its token booth, turnstiles and commuters caught in a midday lull. In this piece, only the agitated shading indicates the developmental immaturity of the artist. Yet the eccentric framing of the composition, with its doorway revealing a glimpse of the outside scenery, adds an element of sophistication to the work. The subway train in yet another figure also shows obsessive cross-hatching and scribbling, yet it is balanced by the uncluttered white of the sprung arches and vaulted ceilings. The delicate lines balance the visual busy-work, adding a sense of visual relief to the work.

In cases in which the artist's emotional handicaps affect his or her art more than organic retardation, realism is often achieved. Numerous cases of artistic giftedness have been documented with autistic individuals who work in a realistic, perceptive style (Selfe 1977, Henley 1989, Rimland 1978). The most celebrated case is the widely studied child, Nadia, who despite severe emotional and developmental deficits, was able to render figures with a representational skill that was considered absolutely fantastic. The verve and consummate draftsmanship of her figure studies reminded writers of such masters as da Vinci (Winner 1986), Daumier (Pariser 1981) and Delacroix (Gardner 1979). These comparisons become even more outlandish when one realizes that her horse studies were created from memory, without instruction or direction, at age six. During her period of "mature" artistic productivity, Nadia was without functional language, behaviorally autistic and unable or unwilling to accomplish the simplest preschool-level activity. Yet this child created images which defied the rules of developmental stages in art. The horses are drawn in dramatic motion, galloping with dust swirling, hoofs rendered in multi-

ple exposures, tails swishing in the wind. Her cockerel figures have a commanding presence, with arched necks, flared nostrils and eyes filled with expression. These drawings are not only stylistically mature, but also point out the artist's special needs, her vulnerability, sensitivity and isolation.

Nadia's most celebrated image makes use of disparate elements to change the composition. The disturbing interplay between the cartoonish rider, the snorting steed and bizarre head which dangles like so much baggage is characteristic of Nadia's style.

270

COGNITION AND AESTHETIC SENSIBILITY

To some aestheticians such "art criticism" may seem overblown, grandiose and romanticized. As postmodern critics continue to deride the naiveté of the modernist tradition, so might they consider comparisons between accomplished, celebrated artists and students with retardation or psychosis dangerously naive and misleading (Wilson 1989). Both cognitive and psychodynamic aestheticians have voiced their objections to the Art Brut of special needs individuals and offer persuasive agreements that warrant discussion.

Many cognitively oriented aestheticians profess an appreciation of child art, including the work of special needs children. They respond to the freshness of style and creative intensity which occurs in the strongest examples of this art. Although they are moved emotionally, they see the work as aesthetically limited (Pariser 1981, Winner 1984). The

Another of Nadia's horse and rider images astoundingly created at age 6.

crucial element in their view is *intentionality:* whether the child artist is as truly in control of his or her imagery as the serious adult artist (Kris 1952). The question is whether the abstractions, distortions and simplifications of the child are consciously employed or are simply by-products of naiveté or developmental immaturity. Winner (1982) argues that the artist must demonstrate the capacity for rational deliberation in planning, execution and reflection over his or her art productions. She cites Goodman, who uses the term "repleteness" to describe this ability. Goodman poses the aesthetic question, not in terms of "What is art?" but "When is it art?" In other words, Goodman contends that the elements in the work "count" aesthetically only if they are intentionally manipulated. A simplistic example of this would be the artist's thumbprint which is left on a print. Unless the artist can convince the viewer that this thumbprint is integral to the piece, it is seen as evidence of incompetence.

The art of children may at first glance be sophisticated and unique in artistic vision. However, at the root of this uniqueness may be kinesthetic activity which is only barely controlled by the child. The resulting image may not have any metaphorical significance in the adult sense and for this reason may not be considered an aesthetic communication.

In Peter's case, for example, the abstracting of the human figure would not be construed as high art by the cognitivist, since Peter is unable to draw *without* distorting. Nadia's art would be similarly disqualified because the child supposedly could not conceptualize the subjects of her drawings (Paine 1989). Pariser (1981) reminded the viewer that aesthetic effects do not always proceed from aesthetic causes. Gardner echoed this concern when he equated Nadia to a computer which calls up images from its memory without purpose or volition (1979). In the cognitive view, then, optical accuracy or stylistic originality without established concept formation precludes an aesthetic statement.

THE LIMITATIONS OF
THE COGNITIVE VIEW

The capacity to plan, execute and reflect over one's artistic efforts are fundamental to the making of art. Without some capacity for these faculties, the art would indeed be suspect and could be dismissed as serendipitous or a freakish accident. However, simply because the critic may not be able to understand how child artists plan or execute, this should not imply that such faculties are not in operation. In the case, for example, of autistic artists who are emotionally inhibited or averse to language, one can only guess at their planning or intentions. The mentally retarded artist is in a similar position, since he or she learns and grows at a different pace and often does not assimilate the information which the teacher is offering. Subsequently, the retarded artist's art may be devoid of "proper" imagery and he or she is often not up to task when explanations of the work are required.

In contrast, Dubuffet's sense of the aesthetic views such deficits as attributes. He argues that by remaining incommunicado as well as socially and educationally indifferent, the child artist may intensify the graphic density and originality of the work (Cardinal 1989). He assails the critic whose preoccupation with left brain abilities blinds him to the intuitive and sensory modes of creating which the art of special needs children often embody. As a form of nonverbal communication, such art serves a vital purpose: to discharge and express material which cannot be articulated through other modalities. The imagery of Art Brut often alludes to those shades of meaning which are not easily transcribed into verbal or intellectual modes. The same can be said of Edvard Munch's *The Scream* or Francis Bacon's *Heads* series. These images' power resides in their ambiguity and visceral quality; they essentially transcend rational discourse. Dubuffet's figures aspire to a state of childishness which recalls prelingual and preconceptual modes of thought. In twelfth-century Japan, Zen painters

rebelled against the tenets of Chinese painting and its incessant intellectualization and moralization. The monochromatic painters of the minimalist style, in particular, strained to purge themselves of the confining dictates of rational deliberation. They strove to approximate a state of egolessness, which powered their brushes to proceed with childlike directness and spontaneity (Hisamatsu 1974). The same sentiment can be seen in the Abstract Expressionist movement, as artists such as Kline, Gottleib and Motherwell embraced the sensual and gestural, spurning narrative forms of visual dialogue.

Critics throughout history have dismissed what they cannot analyze or quantify. For instance, early dealers in African art valued most those sculptures which were heavily influenced by or reminiscent of Western work. The more outlandish and daring work was largely ignored. When this art was collected and used as inspiration for modern experiments, its conceptual contexts were sometimes misunderstood. Some early modernists ascribed inaccurate symbolizations and made condescending inferences about the "noble savage" (Rubin 1984). Just as this ethnocentricity often blinded Western aestheticians to the fundamental truths of primitive art, so may we be misled in believing that the rational, linear thinking of Western intellectualization is superior to the vastly different thought processes of the special needs child. Despite the most exhaustive I.Q. and perceptual testing of Nadia, Selfe did not significantly advance our understanding of the art or art process of this autistic savant. The art and the artist remain an ineffable mystery which defies rational analysis.

Given these observations, many writers, even those with cognitive orientation, are cautious when it comes to equating intelligence and creative ability (Winner 1984). Cardinal (1989) has pointed to scores of outsider artists whose eccentric intellects fostered an art with elaborated systems of images not fixed in terms of linear logic. Susanne Langer (1953) has also supported the validity of non-discursive thinking processes which rely more upon the fluid manipulation of images and symbols. More recently, Howard Gardner presented the idea of multiple intelligences in which visual/spatial abilities are seen as discrete abilities which may function apart from other cognitive domains. Both Gardner (1987) and Winner (1984) conclude that the capacity to create art is not wholly dependent upon intact intelligence.

ART AS SYMPTOM

Just as the cognitivist points to deficits in intellect, psychodynamically-oriented aestheticians focus upon psychological deficits as adversely affecting the art product. Kramer (1971), Rimland (1978) and others assert that art which is born of pathology cannot aspire to aesthetic greatness. This includes work which contains opaque or unintelligible messages or symbols which cannot hope to move or inform the viewer. Kramer also decries art which is impulse-ridden, mindlessly emotional or affectively inhibited. For Kramer, art in the true sense of the word implies that while emotions will fuel the art process, they must also be integrated into the other domains. When the emotions serve both self-expression and communication, they can then serve as an analogue for a broad range of experiences, thus increasing aesthetic viability. The art of autistic individuals, because of its unintelligible nature or narrow content would consequently be disqualified from delivering a true aesthetic experience.

Kramer's argument with regard to art as a symptom focuses upon "freedom to change." Although intact artists have the freedom to purposefully create works which are distorted, simplified or childish, the limited capabilities of artists such as Nadia and Peter deny them that freedom. To the extent that they are enmeshed within their disability their artistic efforts are subordinated to their pathologies. As with the cognitive view, the psychodynamic aesthetician requires that the artist be in control—meaning that the artist be psychologically stable and have the capacity to expand and grow by controlling impulses and fantasies through defenses which are not neurotic, primitive or otherwise dysfunctional.

Rimland (1978), for example, considered Nadia's art to be symptomatic of an attention deficit disorder. Because she lacked an awareness or control over a broad spectrum of stimuli in her environment (i.e., household activities, family interactions, etc.), she was left instead to focus intensively upon a limited, highly condensed beam of stimuli. Her exclusion of "meaningful" stimuli resulted in concentration so narrow that her artistic skill simply became a showcase for her pathological symptoms. From this viewpoint, the question of aesthetic viability dies with the diagnosis of art as symptom.

THE LIMITATIONS OF THE PSYCHODYNAMIC VIEW

Psychodynamic aestheticians argue that, unless the artist is in full possession of his or her artistic abilities, including affect or emotion, aesthetic integrity will diminish. However, as I stated earlier in this chapter, emotional "health" is a relative distinction. Depending upon one's cultural orientation or personal tolerances, psychopathology can be interpreted in vastly different ways. Much has been written about the idiosyncratic nature of the artist's psyche. There is an inclination to romanticize the pathological aspects of the artist's affective temperament (especially schizoid, narcissistic or manic attributes) to such an unfortunate extent that the lay public might naively equate craziness with artistic inclination and talent. However erroneous it may be, such stereotypy has its roots in the fact that artists generally must draw upon and use potentially dangerous instinctual drives through the process of regression to incorporate powerful visions and drives which fuel and vitalize the art process. It is recognized that the process of dipping into such sources of artistic power are fraught with danger, given the psychic conflicts between the primary process id and the higher-functioning ego.

Most writers agree that the artist must possess sufficient ego strength to resist the gravitational pull which is exerted during the art process when primary process functioning is most stimulated. Once the artist taps into the primary process powers of imagination and visualization, as well as his or her sensory impressions and experiences, he or she must be able to reintegrate in order to apply such inspiration according to the demands of reality. Otherwise the image will never reach fruition. Without roots in reality, it will remain simply an idea or a figment of imagination.

"Regression in the service of the ego" as conceived by Ernst Kris (1952) describes a process whereby regression proceeds to the point of primary process inspiration, yet retains sufficient reality orientation so that a balance is struck between the two modes of functioning. Often the very conflict that is generated through maintaining this balance vitalizes the artist's work. In my view, Kris's theory is an excellent criteria for distinguishing whether an artist is sufficiently rooted in the reality of the ego to produce work of aesthetic value. The balance between the originality and intensity of the primary process on the one hand and on the other the capacity to use the medium and techniques effectively and to solve creative problems contributes heavily to an aesthetic experience. For instance, Peter's images are deeply rooted in the primary process, with distortions and condensations being dominant. Yet there must be sufficient ego control, since he was able to create products which evolve into new forms and configurations, and he was able to explore abstract figures in aesthetically viable ways. While Nadia was more constricted in terms of range of affective content and style, her art does reflect a highly skilled use of design elements. Her charged facial expressions are offset by the precision of her life drawing. Jeff's work is perhaps constricted in his stereotypic choice of materials (felt markers) and the repetitive nature of his design elements, yet his later works reveal some movement toward greater animation and less reliance upon rigid schemes.

There is no question that all these artists are affected by their cognitive and psychological limitations. None of them function independently, nor are they fully in command of their art. Yet, in my view, both the special needs and intact artist share characteristics. Both are emotionally vulnerable as they attempt to manage their creative drives. Both must attempt to coexist with an intense sensory acuity to visual and other stimuli. Powers of visualization may be so hyper-focused that both the artist's aesthetic and emotional equilibrium are affected.

It is accurate to say that all of the special needs artists reviewed display an intense motivation that borders upon a consuming obsession to create their art. They work essentially in isolation, oblivious to the demands of academic expectation or social protocol. Instead they focus whatever mental and physical capacities they possess exclusively upon their art. While much of their behavior runs contrary to what the art teacher might conceive as a model art student, one is reminded that such driven, single-minded intensity is a valued trait among seasoned artists. Indeed, artists have always immersed themselves in lifestyles which center around their work, which virtually require a degree of obsessiveness, preoccupation, eccentricity and an aversion to domestication. Biographies of Pollock, Rothko, Guston and others of the New York School describe an almost ascetic existence with hyperactivity, all-consuming studio sessions being offset by bouts of alcoholism and emotional despondency.

Elements of style such as repetition, compulsivity, distortion and stereotypy are routinely considered indications of pathology in the work of special needs artists. While this may be valid in some cases, it would be insensitive and irresponsible to dismiss the aesthetic use of such devices as being overwhelmingly pathological. Throughout art history, artists have developed their identity by assaulting the image of realism. Thus, just as Warhol

274   repeats, Seurat obsesses, Picasso distorts, Gottlieb simplifies and Guston stereotypes, so do many special needs artists employ the same stylistic devices. Despite the observation that Nadia's cockerels may initially seem frozen and void of meaningful context, there is an understated yet clear emotional charge in them. The cocks' eyes roll back, their pupils are masterfully positioned to convey a range of possible emotions—fear, confusion, paranoia, shock—all with remarkable subtlety and economy of means. The viewer is riveted to these "windows to the soul" and is held captive there, just as we are with Bacon's austere and incomprehensible heads. Admittedly, such an aesthetic experience is hardly an uplifting or light-hearted affair. Neither is it a casual one. One does stand, however, to gain in empathy and insight—one which allows a momentary "glimpse into a

world beyond our logic and our physical experience and thus allows us to commence briefly with those forces that are astir in all of us but to which we dare not respond." (Licht 1987).

CONCLUSION

The art process is indeed an idiosyncratic extension of an artist's personality. How do we hope to judge the autistic child who stares into the air for hours before committing a line to paper? Is this so different from a Francis Bacon standing embattled in his attic studio among the rubble and debris that form his paintings? Consider Henry Darger, the eighty-year-old bagman who used only the image of the pubescent Morton Salt girl as the basis of thousands of watercolor paintings. Is this not the

Shock, panic and fear clearly register in Nadia's superbly drawn cockerals. Age 6.

very same process which Warhol used to create critical acclaim as he manufactured similar images of Marilyn Monroe? In my view, it is the same impulse to pay homage to a powerful American icon.

To become a receptive viewer and appreciator of the art of special needs gifted individuals, one must be willing to suspend the preoccupation with rational analytical thought and perception which has so limited Western aesthetics. One must be able to become sufficiently open-minded and sensitive so that an appreciation of the unknown, the bizarre and the alien becomes less of a threat than an intrigue. We must acknowledge that there are other ways of seeing, feeling and expressing which may run contrary to the visual information which ordinarily informs a viewer during an aesthetic experience. Just as Warhol required viewers to suspend all that we knew about the Campbell's soup can in order for it to yield its latent secrets, so might the artist with special needs require a similar ontological stance.

In acknowledging our shortcomings in empathizing with or comprehending the art of the special needs population, particularly those with severe deficits, we are positioned to heed Dubuffet's plea for a critical perspective which bypasses the conventional rules of aesthetics. Dubuffet's Art Brut allows for an art which defers to the viewers' senses and intuition in order to appreciate those who are working in unconventional graphic symbol systems. Should we subscribe to such an expanded aesthetic, new and more meaningful descriptors are needed. For example, critics of Art Brut will describe the aesthetic experience in terms such as *magical, visceral, driven, unprecedented, primordial, imaginative* or *intense*. Such descriptors might contrast with the usual references, such as *beautiful, balanced, inspiring, informed, innovative* and so forth. In Art Brut emphasis upon technical and conceptual slickness is replaced by an indifference to the formal properties of the artwork, as well as to the informational needs of a viewing audience. Finally, Dubbefet insisted that psychopathology in both the art and the artist should not be seen in terms of impoverishment or liability, but as a creative resource from which something singular, spontaneous and truthful can emerge.

The public seems to have responded to this opportunity since interest in Art Brut has grown appreciably in the last fifteen years. Perhaps, gallery goers too have tired of the postmodernist sensationalism and conceptual overkill that is ubiquitous in the current gallery scene. In response, the public may have found the naivete of the art of special needs artists a refreshing aesthetic alternative. In Europe galleries and museums such as Art En Marge and Kunstler Aus Stetten are exhibiting the work of special needs artists—not as case curiosities but as work of artists who enjoy aesthetic parity with their intact peers. As the work of special needs artists moves out of the hallways and display cases of hospitals and schools and into mainstream galleries in the art community, one senses a significant shift in aesthetic awareness. Especially when one realizes that the curatorial emphasis has been on the aesthetic merit and not the individual's handicapping condition or bizarre behavior. Respected critics have also responded by writing catalog essays and articles which discuss this art without patronization or condescension (Cardinal 1989, Klager 1989).

With this increased exposure and public awareness have come improved opportunities for post school-age individuals to work in proper studio environments with quality media and equipment. There are studios that now exclusively accommodate special needs artists in an atelier atmosphere which is conducive to creating serious artwork. With a normal, pro-art environment, the special needs artist might continue to evolve in style and in adaptive behavior until the ideal balance is struck and aesthetic viability is enhanced.

Bibliography

Anderson, F. *Art for All the Children*. Springfield, IL: Charles Thomas, 1978.

Arnheim, R. "The Art of Psychotics." *The Arts in Psychotherapy*. Vol. 4., 1977.

Bandura, A. *Characteristics of Children's Behavior Disorders*. Columbus, OH: Merrill, 1977.

Barron, F. *Creativity and Psychological Health: Origins of Personality and Creative Freedom*. Princeton: Van Nostrand, 1963.

Baumiester, A. "Self-injurious Behavior." *International Review of Research in Mental Retardation*. New York: Academic Press, 1973.

Bernhard, G. *Primates in the Classroom: An Evolutionary Perspective on Children's Education*. Amherst, MA: The University Press, 1988.

Bettelheim, B. *The Empty Fortress*. Glencoe, IL: The Free Press, 1976.

Bloom, B. *Stability and Change in Human Characteristics*. New York: J. Wiley, 1964.

Brenner, C. *An Elementary Textbook of Psychoanalysis*. New York: Anchor Press, 1974.

Brofenbrenner, V. *Two Worlds of Childhood*. New York: Simon and Schuster, 1972.

Brothers, L. "A Biological Perspective on Empathy." *American Journal of Psychiatry*. Vol. 146 (1). January, 1989.

Bruner, J. *The Process of Education*. New York: Vintage Books, 1960.

Bryan, T. and Bryan, J. *Understanding Learning Disabilities*. Sherman Oaks, CA: Alfred, 1986.

Cameron, N. and Rychlak, J.F., *Personality Development and Psychopathology*. Boston: Houghton Mifflin, 1984.

Cane, F. *The Artist in Each of Us*. Revised Edition. Craftsbury Common, VT: Art Therapy Publications, 1983.

Carden, F. *Incidence of Psychopathology in Residentially Placed Hearing Impaired Children*. Unpublished Survey. Marie Katzenbach School for the Deaf, 1986.

Cardinal, R. "The Primitive Scratch," *Pictures at an Exhibition*. A. Gilroy and T. Dalley, Eds. London and New York: Tavistock/Routledge, 1989.

Clements, Claire B. and R.D., *Art and Mainstreaming: Art Instruction for Exceptional Children in Regular School Classes*. Springfield, IL: Charles Thomas, Inc., 1984.

Cruickshank, W.M. *Psychology of Exceptional Children and Youth*, Englewood Cliffs: Prentice Hall, 1955.

Dalton, M.M. "A Visual Survey of 5000 School Children." *Journal of Educational Research* 37, p. 81–94, 1963.

Delagato, A. *The Ultimate Stranger: The Autistic Child*. New York: MacMillan, 1972.

Dubuffet, J. *Asphyxiating Culture*. New York: Four Walls Eight Windows, 1986.

Erikson, E. *Identity: Youth and Crisis*. New York: Norton, 1986.

Ethnic Heritage and Language: Schools in America. American Folklife Center, Library of Congress, 1989.

Fossey, D. *Gorillas in the Mist*. Houghton-Mifflin: New York, 1983.

Fraiberg, S. *Insights from the Blind*. New York: Basic Books, 1977.

Freud, S. *Beyond the Pleasure Principle*, J. Strachey, Ed., New York: Norton Library, 1990.

Gardner, H. "Children's Art: Nadia's Challenge." *Psychology Today*, 1979.

—. *Frames of Mind: Theory of Multiple Intelligence*. New York: Basic Books, 1985.

Gombrich, E. *Art and Illusion: A Study in the Psychology of Pictorial Representation*. Princeton: Princeton University Press, 1960.

Guilford, J. *Creative Talents: Their Nature, Uses and Development*. London: Bearly Ltd., 1986.

Henley, D. "Affective Expression in Post Modern Art Education." *Art Education*, March, 1991.

—. "Art Therapy for the Hearing Impaired with Special Needs." *American Journal of Art Therapy*. Vol. 25, No. 3, Feb., 1987.

—. "Artistic Giftedness in the Multiply Handicapped." *Advances in Art Therapy*. H. Wadeson, ed. New York: John Wiley, 1989.

—. "Developing a Criteria for Artistic Giftedness: Balancing Cognitive, Affective and Creative Issues." Unpublished Thesis, 1986.

—. "Developing Object Relations Through the Use of Clay in Art Therapy." *American Journal of Art Therapy*, Vol. 29, No. 3, 1991.

—. "Emotional Handicaps in Low Functioning Children." *Arts in Psychotherapy*, Vol. 13, (1), 1986.

—. "Incidence of Artistic Giftedness in the Multiply Handicapped." *Advances in Art Therapy*. H. Wadeson, ed. 1989.

—. "Stereotypes in Children's Art: Art Therapeutic Interventions Using Lowenfeld's Motivational Techniques." *American Journal of Art Therapy*. Vol. 27, (4) 1989.

Hartman, H. "Notes on the Reality Principle." *The Psychoanalytic Study of the Child*. Vol. II, Ruth Eissler, et al., eds., 1956.

Hewett, F.M. *Educating Exceptional Learners*. Boston: Allyn and Bacon, 1974.

Highwater, J. *The Primal Mind: Vision and Reality in Indian America*. New York: Harper and Row, 1981.

Holt, John. *How Children Fail*. New York: Dell, 1988.

Hsiamatu, S. *Zen and the Fine Arts*. N.Y.: Harper and Row, 1974.

Ingram, C. *Education of the Slow Learning Child*. New York: MacMillan and Company, 1960.

Itard, I. *Wild Boy of Aveyron*. New York: Appleton-Century-Crofts, 1962.

Jackson, Phillip. *Life in Classrooms*. New York: Teachers College Press, 1990.

Kanner, L. *Child Psychiatry*. 4th ed. Springfield, IL: Charles Thomas, 1972.

Kepes, G. *Language of Vision*. Chicago: Paul Theobald and Co., 1944.

Kirk, S. and Gallagher, J. *Educating Exceptional Children*. Sixth Edition. Boston: Houghton Mifflin, 1989.

Klager, M. *Phenommenon Kinderszeichung*. Abbildungen, Geb. Padagogischen Verlag, 1989.

Kramer, Edith. *Art as Therapy with Children*. New York: Schocken, 1971.

Kramer, Edith. *Childhood and Art Therapy*. New York: Schocken, 1979.

Kramer, Edith. "The Art Therapist's Third Hand." *American Journal of Art Therapy*. Vol. 24, 1986.

Kris, E. *Psychoanalytic Explorations in Art*. N.Y.: International University Press, 1952.

Lachman–Chapin, M. *A Self Psychology Approach to Art Therapy*. *Approaches to Art Therapy*. J. Rubin, ed. New York: Brunner Mazel, 1987.

Laing, R.D. *Self and Others*. New York: Pantheon Books, 1969.

Langer, S. *Feeling and Form*. New York: Scribner, 1953.

277

Leepa, A. "The New Art," *Anti-art and Criticism.* New York: E.P. Dutton, 1966.

Lerner, J.W. *Learning Disabilities: Theory Diagnosis and Teaching Strategies.* Boston: Houghton Mifflin, 1981.

Licht, F. "Beyond the Reach of Critics," *Dubuffet and Art Brut.* New York: Guggenheim Museum of Art, 1987.

Lindsay, Z. *Art and the Handicapped Child.* New York: Van Nostrand-Reinhold, 1972.

Lorenz, K. *On Aggression.* New York: Harcourt, Brace, Jovanovich, 1966.

Lorenz, K. *Studies in Animal and Human Behavior.* Cambridge, MA: Harvard University Press, 1971.

Lowenfeld, Berthold. "Psychological Problems in Children with Impaired Vision." *Psychology of Exceptional Children and Youth.* Cruick Shark, ed. New York: Prentice Hall, 1955.

Lowenfeld, Viktor. *Creative and Mental Growth.* Third Edition. New York: Macmillan, 1957.

Lowenfeld, V. *Lowenfeld Lectures.* J.A. Michael, ed. University Park, PA: Pennsylvania State Press, 1982.

MacGregor, J. *The Discovery of the Art of the Insane.* Princeton: Princeton University Press, 1989.

Madeja, S. "Gifted and Talented," *Art Education.* Reston, VA: National Art Education Association, 1983.

Mahler, M. *On Human Symbiosis and the Vicissitudes of Individuation.* NY: International Universities Press, 1968.

Mahler, M. Pine, F., and Bergman, A. *The Psychological Birth of the Human Infant.* New York: Basic Books, 1975.

McNiff, S. and Cook, C. "Video Art Therapy," *Art Psychotherapy.* Vol. 2, 1980.

Meltzoff, A. and Moore, M. "Imitation of Facial and Manual Gestures by Human Neonates," *Science,* 218, 1982.

Moores, P. *Educating the Deaf—Psychology, Principles and Practices.* Boston: Houghton-Mifflin, 1978.

Morris, D. *The Biology of Art.* New York: Alfred A. Knopf, 1962.

Moustakas, C.E. *The Authentic Teacher.* Cambridge, MA: Howard A. Doyle Publishing, 1966.

Myklebust, H. *Psychology of Deafness.* New York: Grune and Stratton, 1960.

Nathan, P. *The Nervous System.* New York: J.B. Lippincott Co., 1969.

Naumberg, M. *An Introduction to Art Therapy.* New York and London: Teachers College Press, 1973.

Neill, A.S. *Summerhill: A Radical Approach to Child Rearing.* New York: Hart Publishing, 1960.

Paine, S. *Six Children Draw.* New York: Academic Press, 1982.

Pariser, D. *A Discussion of Nadia.* Cambridge, MA: Technical Report #9. Harvard Project Zero, 1979.

Patterson, P.F., and Linden, E. *The Education of KoKo.* New York: Holt, Rinehart, and Winston, 1981.

Pine, S. "Fostering Growth Through Art Education, Art Therapy, And Art in Psychology." *Art Therapy in Theory and Practice.* E. Ulman and P. Dachinger, eds. New York: Schocken Books, 1975.

Public Law 94-142. Federal Register, 1977.

Rimland, B. *Infantile Autism: The Syndrome and its Implications for a Neural Theory of Behavior.* New York: Appleton-Century-Crofts, 1964.

Rimland, B. "In the Mind of the Autistic Savant." *Psychology Today,* 12(3), 1978.

Robbins, A. "An Object Relations Approach to Art Therapy." *Approaches to Art Therapy.* J. Rubin, ed. New York: Brunner/Mazel, 1987.

Robertson, S. *Rosegarden and Labyrinth.* London: Routledge and Kegan Paul, 1963.

Rubin, J. *Child Art Therapy.* New York: Van Nostrand–Reinhold, 1978.

Schaefer-Simmern, H. *The Unfolding of Artistic Activity. Its Basis, Processes and Implications.* Berkley, CA: University of California Press, 1948.

Schlesinger, H. and Meadow, K. *Sound and Sign: Childhood Deafness and Mental Health.* Berkley, CA: University of California Press, 1972.

Schwartz, J. *National Art Education Association Newsletter.* Vol. 31, No. 4.

Skinner, B.F. *Science and Human Behavior.* New York: Free Press, 1965.

Seiden, D. Unpublished Manuscript. The School of the Art Institute of Chicago, 1987.

Selfe, L. *Nadia: A Case of Extraordinary Drawing Ability in an Autistic Child.* London: Academic Press, 1977.

Silver, R. *Developing Cognitive and Creative Skills Through Art.* Baltimore: University Park Press, 1978.

Slavin, R.E. *Cooperative Learning: Student Teams.* National Education Association, 1987.

Torrence, E. *Torrence Tests for Creative Thinking.* Princeton: Personnel Press, 1976.

Tinbergan, N. and E. *Autistic Children: New Hope for a Cure.* London: Allen and Unwin, 1983.

Tinbergan, N. *The Study of Instinct.* Oxford: Oxford University Press, 1989.

Uhlin, D. and DeChiara, E. *Art for Exceptional Children.* Dubuque, IA: William C. Brown, 1984.

Varnadoe, K. "Abstract Expressionism." *Primitism in 20th Century Art.* Museum of Modern Art Catalogue. William Rubin, ed. Boston: Little Brown and Company, 1984.

Wilson, B., Hurwitz, A. and Wilson, M. *Teaching Drawing from Art.* Worcester, MA: Davis Publications, 1987.

Wilson, B. "An Assessment Strategy for the Arts," *Education in the Nineties, Arts in the Curriculum.* Illinois Alliance for Arts Education, 1988.

Wilson, B. "Primitivism, the Avant Garde and The Art of Children: A Modernist Discovery and Post-Modernist Disassembly." Paper, The National Society for Education in Art and Design. July, 1989.

Wilson, L. "Theory and Practice of Art Therapy with the Severely Retarded." *American Journal of Art Therapy* Vol. 16 (3); 1977.

Wilson, L. "Introduction" *Childhood and Art Therapy.* Edith Kramer. New York: Schocken, 1979.

Winner, E. *Invented Worlds: Psychology of The Arts.* Cambridge, MA: Harvard University Press, 1982.

Winnicott, D.W., *The Maturational Processes and the Facilitating Environment.* New York: International Universities Press, 1965.

Index